Growing
Bulbs

Alan Titchmarsh
how to garden

Growing
Bulbs

BOOKS

10 9 8 7 6 5 4 3 2 1

Published in 2011 by BBC Books, an imprint of
Ebury Publishing, a Random House Group Company

The Random House Group Limited Reg. No. 954009

Addresses for companies within the Random House
Group can be found at www.randomhouse.co.uk

The Random House Group Limited
supports The Forest Stewardship
Council (FSC), the leading
international forest certification
organisation. All our titles that are
printed on Greenpeace approved
FSC certified paper carry the FSC
logo. Our paper procurement
policy can be found at www.
rbooks.co.uk/environment

FSC
www.fsc.org
MIX
Paper from
responsible sources
FSC™ C004592

A CIP catalogue record for this book is available from
the British Library.

ISBN 978 1 84 607407 3

Produced by OutHouse!
Shalbourne, Marlborough, Wiltshire SN8 3QJ

BBC BOOKS
COMMISSIONING EDITOR: Lorna Russell
PROJECT EDITOR: Caroline McArthur
PRODUCTION: Antony Heller

OUTHOUSE!
COMMISSIONING EDITOR: Sue Gordon
SERIES EDITOR: Polly Boyd
SERIES ART EDITOR: Robin Whitecross
CONTRIBUTING EDITOR: Andi Clevely
EDITOR: Selina Mumford
DESIGNERS: Heather McCarry, Louise Turpin
ILLUSTRATIONS by Julia Cady, Lizzie Harper,
Susan Hillier, Janet Tanner
PHOTOGRAPHS by Jonathan Buckley except where
credited otherwise on page 128
ORIGINAL CONCEPT DEVELOPMENT & SERIES DESIGN:
Elizabeth Mallard-Shaw, Sharon Cluett

Colour origination by Altaimage, London
Printed and bound by Firmengruppe APPL,
Wemding, Germany

Contents

Introduction	7
INTRODUCING BULBS	**8**
What are bulbs?	9
Bulbs and their allies	10
Designing with bulbs	12
Design palette	16
Bulbs in beds and borders	18
Bulbs in grass	23
focus on Bulbs for cutting	26
Woodland bulbs under trees	28
Bulbs in gravel, rockeries and scree	30
Bulbs in containers	34
focus on Collections	38
Bulbs indoors	40
Plants for a purpose	**42**

PLANTING AND GROWING 44

Choosing and buying bulbs	45
Tools and equipment	47
Growing conditions	48
Planting in the ground	50
focus on Invasive bulbs	52
Planting in containers	53
focus on Forcing bulbs	55
Looking after bulbs	56
focus on Bulb frames	61
Lifting and storing bulbs	62
Caring for bulbs indoors	64
Propagation	66
Plant problems and remedies	70

RECOMMENDED BULBS 74

A–Z directory	75

CHALLENGING SITES 104

Shady sites	105
Wet sites	106
Dry sites	108
Windy sites	110
Cold sites	111

SEASON BY SEASON 112

A flower for every day	113
Spring	114
Summer	116
Autumn	118
Winter	120
Index	122

Introduction

Gardening is one of the best and most fulfilling activities on earth, but it can sometimes seem complicated and confusing. The answers to problems can usually be found in books, but big fat gardening books can be rather daunting. Where do you start? How can you find just the information you want without wading through lots of stuff that is not appropriate to your particular problem? Well, a good index is helpful, but sometimes a smaller book devoted to one particular subject fits the bill better – especially if it is reasonably priced and if you have a small garden where you might not be able to fit in everything suggested in a larger volume.

The *How to Garden* books aim to fill that gap – even if sometimes it may be only a small one. They are clearly set out and written, I hope, in a straightforward, easy-to-understand style. I don't see any point in making gardening complicated, when much of it is based on common sense and observation. (All the key techniques are explained and illustrated, and I've included plenty of tips and tricks of the trade.)

There are suggestions on the best plants and the best varieties to grow in particular situations and for a particular effect. I've tried to keep the information crisp and to the point so that you can find what you need quickly and easily and then put your new-found knowledge into practice. Don't worry if you're not familiar with the Latin names of plants. They are there to make sure you can find the plant as it will be labelled in the nursery or garden centre, but where appropriate I have included common names, too. Forgetting a plant's name need not stand in your way when it comes to being able to grow it.

Above all, the *How to Garden* books are designed to fill you with passion and enthusiasm for your garden and all that its creation and care entails, from designing and planting it to maintaining it and enjoying it. For more than fifty years gardening has been my passion, and that initial enthusiasm for watching plants grow, for trying something new and for just being outside pottering has never faded. If anything I am keener on gardening now than I ever was and get more satisfaction from my plants every day. It's not that I am simply a romantic, but rather that I have learned to look for the good in gardens and in plants, and there is lots to be found. Oh, there are times when I fail – when my plants don't grow as well as they should and I need to try harder. But where would I rather be on a sunny day? Nowhere!

The *How to Garden* handbooks will, I hope, allow some of that enthusiasm – childish though it may be – to rub off on you, and the information they contain will, I hope, make you a better gardener, as well as opening your eyes to the magic of plants and flowers.

Introducing bulbs

Bulbs are among the most successful plants in the wild, largely because of their useful strategy of avoiding trouble by hiding underground until it's safe to grow once more. In the garden, they form a dazzling profusion of versatile plants for almost every situation, season and role. Familiar bulbs such as lilies, crocuses, daffodils, irises and tulips have become traditional stars of any flower display, but there's a host of other worthwhile kinds you can explore and try in your garden. All bulbs come ready to grow – just plant and enjoy them.

What are bulbs?

Bulbs don't look particularly exciting. They come wrapped in a rather drab cover, but beneath this exterior is a store of concentrated energy. Once they're buried below ground and exposed to moisture and warmth, bulbs quickly spring into life and go on to fulfil their potential, developing into stunning plants that work brilliantly in so many settings.

'Bulbs' – as used in the title of this book and by bulb suppliers – is in fact a loose term that encompasses true bulbs, corms, tubers and rhizomes (see pages 10–11). They might look slightly different from each other, but these plants are quite rightly grouped together because all share one key feature: a swollen underground food store that will keep the plant safely nourished when times are bad.

Bulbs behave basically like rechargeable batteries, supplying energy when it's called for and then replenishing it and storing it for the next time. It's a remarkably simple but efficient solution to the problem all plants face, that of survival when the going gets tough. From the gardener's point of view, this quality makes them particularly reliable and undemanding plants, equipped as they are to survive the kind of conditions they are likely to encounter in our gardens.

Given the right soil and situation, with enough water and food after flowering is over (the period when the leaves take in nutrients to

Visually very different, drumstick alliums, with their hardy bulbs, and gladioli, which grow from slightly tender corms, share the same efficient growth cycle underground.

replenish the bulb's stores), they should go on to repeat their performance year after year. Some bulbs, such as florists' cyclamen and amaryllis (*Hippeastrum*), fatten with age and produce more blooms as the years pass. Others can spread and self-seed steadily with little encouragement: think bluebell woods, or lawns carpeted with crocuses and wild daffodils. With some very basic care, all should grow well for you.

Plentiful choice

Bulbs are possibly the largest and most versatile group of plants available to gardeners, and the huge range on offer in catalogues incorporates plants from different habitats around the world. With such a wide choice, it should be easy

to find suitable bulbs for your site and soil, and for the season when you want them to flower.

In the wild, bulbs have adapted to grow in an impressive range of locations, which is why they are such an astonishingly diverse and varied group. There are miniature bulbs barely 8cm (3in) high, such as *Narcissus asturiensis* and some crocus species, giants like cardiocrinums that can top 4m (13ft), and even climbers – gloriosa lilies and flame nasturtiums, for example. They offer a huge spectrum of colour, including green, true pure blue and nearly black, as well as outstanding form, texture and often stimulating fragrance that can provide pleasure throughout the year. In the pages that follow you will find a selection of truly stellar performers.

Bulbs and their allies

When you browse a bulb catalogue you'll find dahlias, gladioli, trilliums and possibly lily-of-the-valley, even though none of these are bulbs in the botanical sense of the word. The term 'bulb' often embraces a wide range of bulbous plants, and as well as true bulbs it includes corms, tubers and rhizomes. Although all these plants have fleshy food-storage organs, they do differ in structure. Get to know the different types and their requirements and you'll soon grow all bulbous plants with confidence.

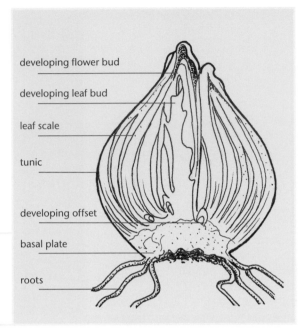

developing flower bud

developing leaf bud

leaf scale

tunic

developing offset

basal plate

roots

This cross-section shows the components of that unique storage organ, the true bulb.

True bulbs

A complete plant in a package, a true bulb is made up of fleshy concentric layers, or scales, joined together at the bottom by a basal plate, from which the roots will grow. At the centre of all these scales is a dormant bud that will form the growing point when the bulb revives. Within it are contained all the essentials: stem, leaves and flowers. The whole of this really remarkable structure is generally enclosed by a tough coat, or tunic, of tissue, which may be papery or netted like a mesh – although some bulbs have no protective outer coat and are naked.

The most familiar true bulbs are alliums, daffodils (*Narcissus*), fritillaries (*Fritillaria*), lilies (*Lilium*), grape hyacinths (*Muscari*) and tulips (*Tulipa*).

Corms

A corm is a solid structure formed from the swollen base of the flower stem. It has no scales, other than one or two papery layers that form the outer tunic, and one or more growing points which, unlike bulbs, are at the top rather than wrapped up in the centre. Whereas bulbs are permanent, producing growth each year and then dying back to the same underground organ, a corm withers away after flowering and is replaced by a new one, which forms on top.

Examples of familiar corms are crocuses, freesias and gladioli.

Tubers

These solid underground organs are modified stems or roots that store energy-rich starch during a plant's resting phase. They do not have a protective covering or a basal plate, and have several growing points, which can appear anywhere on the surface, including the sides. Single tubers, such as anemones, tuberous begonias and cyclamen, increase in size every year as the plant grows. Multiple tubers, such as dahlias and a few ranunculus, disintegrate once the food is used up and are replaced by new ones.

Rhizomes

These swollen stems also serve as storage organs but, unlike tubers, they have the ability to multiply and spread. Some rhizomes travel underground (*Anemone nemorosa*, for example), while others, such as Bearded irises, lie on the surface. They can vary widely in appearance: those of lily-of-the-valley (*Convallaria*) are long and slender, and can extend great distances, whereas trilliums have short, fat rhizomes that tend to crowd into tight clumps. Most rhizomatous perennials expand into big clumps, which should be divided every few years.

Examples of familiar rhizomes are agapanthus, cannas, red-hot pokers (*Kniphofia*) and foxtail lilies (*Eremurus*).

Bulbous plants

What all types of bulbous plant have in common is a capacity to store food. In a bulb, food is stored in scales (in lilies these are separated, with no outer covering). A corm, flatter than a true bulb, stores food in what is an enlarged basal plate. Tubers, single or multiple, and rhizomes are swollen stems or roots acting as storage organs.

TRUE BULB (*Narcissus*)

SCALY BULB (*Lilium*)

CORM (*Crocus*)

SINGLE TUBER (*Cyclamen*)

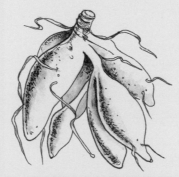

MULTIPLE TUBER (*Dahlia*)

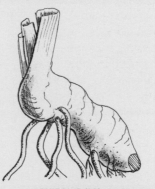

RHIZOME (*Iris*)

Pseudobulbs

Orchids are a huge plant group with their own dedicated suppliers, but you occasionally find one or two listed in bulb catalogues because of their superficial resemblance to bulb-like perennials.

To cope with seasonal droughts in their native habitats, many orchids have short-lived modified stems with swollen storage organs called pseudobulbs. These may be flattened or spherical, and range in size from pinheads in some Australian species to the 3m (10ft) tall cylinders of a few Asian orchids. The species you are most likely to meet in a bulb catalogue are *Bletilla striata,* for sheltered borders or a cold greenhouse, and *Pleione formosana* (*see* right), which can be grown indoors or in a sheltered rock garden.

Bulbs in the vegetable garden

Bulbs are n̶ ̶rely ornamental. Many vegetabl̶ ̶ ̶ ̶ ̶bs too. The best known̶ ̶ ̶ ̶ ̶ ̶ ̶ ̶selected members of th̶ ̶ ̶ ̶ ̶ ̶ ̶ ̶llots, garlic and bulbing̶ ̶ ̶ ̶ ̶ ̶ ̶ ̶to the ornament̶ ̶ ̶ ̶ ̶ ̶n we harvest and eat when̶ ̶ ̶ ̶ ̶ ̶s have finished storing food rea̶ ̶ ̶ ̶their next growing season. We cultivate potatoes, yams and Jerusalem and Chinese artichokes for their nutrient-packed tubers, while mint, rhubarb, asparagus and ginger all grow from perennial rhizomes.

Designing with bulbs

Easy to grow and with an impressive array of flower colour, form and shape, bulbs in borders and containers create eye-catching displays all year round. Add fragrance, sometimes intense or penetrating, and occasionally attractive foliage to these qualities, and you have one of the most versatile and beloved of all plant groups – and the perfect ingredients for enhancing any garden design.

The tiny, golden flowers of *Narcissus* 'Tête-à-tête' are perfect for early-spring ground cover under a camellia, and will spread gently over the years.

Colour and size

Bulbs come in almost every colour imaginable, even blue and green. Tulips are probably the most varied of all bulb types, ranging from subtle pastel shades to outrageous, gaudy splashes of colour.

Explore the infinite range of bulb colours available, experimenting with them to create wonderful effects and conjure up memorable combinations. Simplicity and restraint is often the best policy. A single variety supplies saturated

colour, for example, while similar shades that are closely related produce restful harmonies. On the other hand, a direct contrast, such as yellow daffodils with purple irises or orange hyacinths with intensely blue chionodoxas, adds a dash of excitement to the garden. Hot colours and harlequin mixtures are vibrant and stimulating on a dull day, but may be overpowering in midday sunshine compared with softer yellows or pinks. The scope is so wide that you can easily design the exact effect you desire.

Bulbs vary greatly in height too, from the tiniest crocuses and yellow *Iris danfordiae* or blue *Iris histrioides* only 8cm (3in) high to giant eremurus, lilies and cardiocrinums that can be up to 2.5m (8ft) tall.

Eremurus, great for supplying height at the back of a border, flowers at the same time as many Bearded irises and then takes over as the last tulips fade.

Seasonal bulbs

Most popular bulbs tend to group themselves neatly into distinct flowering seasons. There's an endearing glow and transparency about spring-flowering bulbs such as crocuses, snowdrops (*Galanthus*), bulbous irises and squills (*Scilla*). These smaller species and varieties herald the start of spring, hence their great value for bedding and naturalizing in joyous quantities as an overture to the gardening year.

Their welcome performance is a key component of garden schemes up to early summer, when larger bulbs that love warmth or take a bit of time to get going appear to rival or complement the main garden display. Alliums and summer hyacinths (*Galtonia*), together with tender dahlias, gladioli, begonias and cannas, all command attention now and make an important

Allium × *hollandicum* is a versatile bulb, ideal for highlights in a border or naturalizing under deciduous trees.

Bulbs with attractive foliage

Gardeners often complain about bulb leaves looking tatty as they die down, or getting in the way of other plants, and there's no doubt some kinds may need cunning camouflage. The foliage of some bulbs, however, is a positive asset and part of the reason for growing them. A number of dwarf tulips have strongly mottled or striped leaves, wavy-edged in the case of some Greigii hybrids. Several rhizomatous irises, notably 'Variegata' forms of *Iris ensata*, *Iris japonica*, *Iris pallida* and *Iris pseudacorus*, have cream- or yellow-striped foliage, adding a year-round bonus to their lovely month-long blooms. Above all, the wild European arum, or cuckoo-pint, has relatives, including *Arum* 'Chameleon' and *Arum italicum* subsp. *italicum* 'Marmoratum', with leaves embellished in astonishing patterns, abstract swirls and complex marbling in white, cream and different shades of green.

The evergreen, variegated foliage of *Iris pseudacorus* 'Variegata'

The marbled leaves of *Arum italicum* subsp. *italicum* 'Marmoratum'

contribution to summer bedding and herbaceous border schemes. 0For the summer patio, pots of trumpet-shaped lilies make striking focal points – many of them providing delicious fragrance.

However, the varied bulb community really re-awakens in autumn as days shorten, rain returns and the temperature drops. This is the time when colchicums and autumn crocuses raise their naked stems, dainty wild cyclamen decorate patches of ground with their tiny nodding blooms and marbled leaves, and South African species such as crinums, nerines and *Amaryllis belladonna* revel in the late summer sunshine. Last of all are schizostylis, whose gladiolus-like blooms continue until overwhelmed by frost. (*See also* Season by Season, pages 112–21.)

One of the last tulips to flower, *Tulipa sprengeri* is a good species for gardens. Here, its vibrant blooms glow in early summer sunshine.

Extending the season

Bulbs might have a fleeting moment of glory, but there is often sufficient variety within a genus to spread the display over many weeks, or even months, by carefully blending a sequence of flowering times. Different lilies, for example, can flower between late spring (*Lilium mackliniae*) and early autumn (*Lilium speciosum*), with a peak at midsummer. Tulips span the whole of the spring season, starting with *Tulipa humilis* and the earliest Kaufmanniana hybrids, building up to a climax with Single Late and Darwin hybrids, and finishing in early summer with *Tulipa sprengeri*. Some crocus species flower about a month earlier than large-flowered crocus hybrids, and then you can reprise the display at the end of the year with autumn-flowering *Crocus pulchellus*, *Crocus sativus*, *Crocus speciosus* and *Crocus zonatus*.

Integrating bulbs

Being so easy to plant, bulbs can be used singly to punctuate a community of herbaceous plants, in larger numbers to create loose drifts weaving through later-flowering neighbours, or *en masse* as blocks and phalanxes of colour in a bold bedding scheme. They may be planted formally, in military lines and geometrical patterns, or more informally, such as a few camassias for a speckling of blue in a summer

Here, naturalized colchicums flower at the base of a tree in autumn. The fallen leaves create a perfect backdrop and support the naked flower stems.

border, or a bulk planting of fritillaries among primroses on a lawn and massed anemones under deciduous trees. (*See* pages 18–22, 23–5 and 28–9).

All they need is to be planted in the right place at the right time. Because of their unique life cycle of rest and growth, the right moment in most cases is while they're dormant. This is not as limiting as it might seem, because they can be added to a scheme before or after other plants are in place. You can incorporate bulbs wherever there is space – just one bulb per hole in the smallest available nook will do – and then leave them there to settle down permanently or lift them later after they have died down. On the other hand, they can be in place first, which is often the best way when planting up seasonal containers (*see* page 37), providing you can make sure they're not damaged by subsequent planting.

Scented bulbs

Fragrance is a priority for many gardeners when choosing plants, and some bulbs immediately bring this quality to mind. Freesias are favourites for their scent as well as their glowing colours, and while a bowlful of hyacinths can be breath-taking, just a tiny vase of lily-of-the-valley will perfume a whole room, as can a solitary specimen of a tropical bulb such as polianthes (tuberose), eucharis, chlidanthus or pancratium.

Most daffodils are sweetly scented, although few can compare with renowned Tazetta varieties such as tender *Narcissus* 'Grand Soleil d'Or' and 'Paper White' (now called

The upward-facing, rich crimson flowers of *Lilium* 'Nerone' are fine companions for the coral-orange foliage of *Macleaya cordata* for several weeks in high summer.

Narcissus papyraceus) or hardy Poeticus hybrids like 'Actaea', old pheasant's eye (*Narcissus poeticus* var. *recurvus*) and the double white Poeticus, 'Tamar Double White'.

Grow them close to where you sit in the garden, alongside paths to savour as you pass by, or in containers near a door or window. Save a few, though, to keep in pots indoors or plant some in rows in a piece of spare ground – perhaps at the side of a vegetable bed – to cut and bring indoors (*see* pages 26–7).

An unexpected lack of scent in knock-out flowers such as nerines, amaryllis (*Hippeastrum*) and many gladioli often brings disappointment.

Gladiolus tristis has many soft yellow or creamy-white blooms that produce their strongest scent in the evening.

Plant breeders have recognized this and in some cases they have gone back to wild relatives in search of genes that carry fragrance. Night-scented *Gladiolus tristis* has been used, for example, as a source of heady perfume for hybrid gladioli.

Design palette

These pages will help you choose bulbs for particular colour schemes. The limitless possibilities are narrowed down to a few ideas in each category. *See also* the A–Z directory, pages 74–103.

DEEP MAROON RED

Allium sphaerocephalon
Dahlia 'Nuit d'Eté'
Dierama pulcherrimum 'Merlin'
Hippeastrum 'Benfica'
Hyacinthus orientalis 'Woodstock'
Iris 'Langport Wren'
Lilium 'Ebony'
Rhodohypoxis baurii 'Tetra Red'
Trillium erectum
Tulipa 'Black Parrot' (right)

GREEN

Allium vineale 'Hair'
Eucomis autumnalis
Fritillaria persica 'Ivory Bells' (right)
Galtonia viridiflora
Gladiolus 'Green Star'
Hippeastrum 'Lemon Lime'
Narcissus 'Sinopel'
Nectaroscordum siculum
Ornithogalum nutans
Tulipa 'Spring Green'

BRIGHT RED

Anemone coronaria De Caen Group
Begonia 'Memory Scarlet'
Bessera elegans
Canna 'Assaut'
Dahlia 'Witteman's Superba' (right)
Hippeastrum 'Red Lion'
Iris foetidissima
Tulipa 'Madame Lefeber'
Tulipa 'Shakespeare'
Tulipa sprengeri

PALE YELLOW

Allium obliquum
Crocus chrysanthus 'Dorothy'
Dahlia 'Promise'
Erythronium 'Pagoda' (right)
Gladiolus 'Green Woodpecker'
Hemerocallis lilioasphodelus
Iris 'Apollo'
Lilium 'Luxor'
Narcissus 'Trevithian'
Tulipa tarda

ORANGE

Begonia 'Orange Cascade'
Crocosmia 'Orange Devil'
Fritillaria imperialis
Gladiolus 'Ovation'
Hyacinthus orientalis 'Gipsy Queen'
Lilium 'Fire King' (right)
Narcissus 'Orangery'
Physalis alkekengi
Tulipa 'Ballerina'
Tulipa 'Orange Emperor'

GOLDEN YELLOW

Allium flavum
Anemone ranunculoides
Crocus × *luteus* 'Golden Yellow'
Eremurus stenophyllus (right)
Fritillaria imperialis 'Lutea'
Iris danfordiae
Lilium 'Golden Stargazer'
Narcissus 'Dutch Master'
Sternbergia lutea
Tulipa 'West Point'

MULTI-COLOURED – VIVID

Crocosmia × *crocosmiiflora* 'Harlequin'
Dahlia 'Kenora Sunset' (right)
Gladiolus 'Jester'
Hemerocallis 'Frans Hals'
Lilium pardalinum
Oxalis versicolor
Sparaxis
Tigridia pavonia
Tulipa 'Cape Cod'
Tulipa 'Little Princess'

CREAMY WHITE

Camassia leichtlinii 'Semiplena'
Crocus chrysanthus 'Cream Beauty'
Dahlia 'Swan Lake'
Erythronium californicum 'White Beauty'
Lilium 'Vivendum' (right)
Narcissus 'Dove Wings'
Polygonatum × *hybridum*
Sisyrinchium striatum
Triteleia 'Starlight'
Tulipa turkestanica

PALE BLUE

Camassia cusickii
Crocus chrysanthus 'Blue Bird'
Hyacinthus orientalis 'Sky Jacket'
Ipheion uniflorum 'Wisley Blue' (right)
Iris 'Jane Phillips'
Leucocoryne ixioides
Muscari armeniacum 'Valerie Finnis'
Puschkinia scilloides
Scilla mischtschenkoana
Sisyrinchium 'Californian Skies'

MID- TO DEEP BLUE

Agapanthus 'Blue Giant'
Allium azureum
Anemone blanda blue-flowered
Chionodoxa sardensis
Commelina coelestis
Hyacinthoides non-scripta
Iris reticulata 'Harmony' (right)
Muscari armeniacum
Scilla peruviana
Scilla siberica 'Spring Beauty'

DEEP PURPLE

Allium 'Mars'
Crocus vernus 'Flower Record' (right)
Dracunculus vulgaris
Fritillaria persica 'Adiyaman'
Gladiolus 'Purple Flora'
Hippeastrum 'Black Pearl'
Hyacinthus orientalis 'Purple Sensation'
Iris germanica 'Titan's Glory'
Iris reticulata 'Purple Gem'
Iris sibirica 'Shirley Pope'

LILAC

Allium 'Globemaster' (right)
Chionodoxa forbesii 'Pink Giant'
Corydalis solida
Crocus banaticus
Crocus 'Ruby Giant'
Erythronium dens-canis 'Lilac Wonder'
Hyacinthus orientalis 'Anna Lisa'
Muscari plumosum
Notholirion bulbuliferum
Tulbaghia violacea

PURE WHITE

Anemone nemorosa
Colchicum speciosum 'Album'
Galanthus nivalis
Galtonia candicans
Gladiolus 'The Bride'
Hyacinthus orientalis 'White Pearl'
Hymenocallis × festalis (right)
Lilium candidum
Muscari botryoides 'Album'
Trillium grandiflorum

CORAL PINK

Begonia sutherlandii
Dahlia 'Peach Delight'
Hippeastrum 'Darling'
Hyacinthus orientalis 'Gipsy Queen'
Lilium 'Saboneta'
Nerine 'Maria'
Schizostylis coccinea 'Salome' (right)
Tulipa 'Palestrina'
Veltheimia bracteata
Watsonia pillansii

DEEP PINK

Colchicum 'Waterlily'
Dahlia 'Radiance'
Gladiolus communis subsp. byzantinus
Gladiolus 'Silvana' (right)
Hippeastrum 'Bolero'
Hyacinthus orientalis 'Pink Pearl'
Lilium Pink Perfection Group
Nerine bowdenii
Tulipa 'China Pink'
Tulipa 'Peach Blossom'

MULTI-COLOURED – CALM

Allium bulgaricum
Arisaema griffithii
Calochortus venustus
Fritillaria michailovskyi
Hermodactylus tuberosus
Lachenalia aloides var. quadricolor
Lilium 'Lady Alice'
Muscari 'Golden Fragrance'
Tulipa 'Green Wave' (right)
Tulipa 'Prinses Irene'

Bulbs in beds and borders

Growing bulbs in beds and borders is the time-honoured way of using them, and there's no other class of plant that works quite so successfully. Daffodils or tulips pushing their way up among a sea of wallflowers mean spring to many gardeners, while cannas and dahlias in formal bedding schemes or lilies in a cottage-garden border are traditional summer highlights. Choice generally revolves around a few familiar kinds, but there are many more bulbs worth trying in this kind of arrangement.

Bulbs for seasonal bedding schemes

Although less fashionable now than a few decades ago and considered by some as the height of artifice, temporary seasonal bedding schemes are still a triumphant way to decorate the garden and celebrate the beauty of bulbs. Bulbs are often arranged in patterns or rows, but you can be as simple or complex as you like with your designs. Classic combinations include pink Darwin tulips above pale yellow dwarf wallflowers (*Erysimum*) and a frothy cloud of forget-me-nots (*Myosotis*), or deep-purple hyacinths planted with white arabis around the base; alternatively, you might decide to go for a minimalist composition, using tulip varieties of different heights in serried ranks, or even a solid bank of tigridias in summer.

Short-growing chionodoxas can mingle happily with mat-forming *Arabis caucasica* without competing.

Spring bedding

Only a few bulb types are used for spring bedding because the timing of their flowers is usually critical and they need to withstand lifting afterwards. Bulb size is important too, as digging up anything tiny, like crocuses, is not practical. Bulbs to try include: tulips (Single or Double Early, Triumph, Darwin and Lily-flowered varieties are old favourites) combined with wallflowers, forget-me-nots or polyanthus; hyacinths (medium-size bedding bulbs) with pansies, bellis daisies (*Bellis perennis*) or Cowichan primulas; and daffodils, especially Trumpet and Large-cupped varieties, with chionodoxas or grape hyacinths (*Muscari*), forget-me-nots or a dark hyacinth such as *Hyacinthus* 'Blue Pearl'.

Bear relative heights in mind (shorter tulips or daffodils will be lost among tall varieties of wallflower, for example) as well as flowering times. However, a deliberate sequence of bloom can be more effective than simultaneous flowering and could ensure almost three months of colour throughout the spring, until the beds are cleared for the summer.

Prepare the ground by digging the empty bed in autumn, cleaning out any weeds and forking in plenty of garden compost. Alternatively, just

Orange *Tulipa* 'Ballerina' and red 'Doll's Minuet' team with wallflowers and honesty in a carpet of spring colour.

Don't forget

True blue can be decidedly rare in spring. Most 'blue' bulb and forget-me-not varieties contain at least a hint of pink or mauve. Yet a good blue is the ideal partner for most yellow-flowered bulbs. Try the Siberian squill (*Scilla siberica*), especially such rich blue forms as 'Spring Beauty' and subsp. *armena*.

lightly fork through the bed to loosen the surface and then leave the compost spread on the surface as a mulch; some of this will be stirred in as you plant. Wait a week or two while the soil settles before planting spring bedding (either bought in or raised in trays or a nursery bed), starting with the bedding and then adding bulbs in between. The soil should still be warm enough for the bedding to become established. Add a dressing of blood, fish and bonemeal after planting or in spring.

Summer bedding

Spring bulbs are unlikely to have finished their post-flowering phase by the time summer bedding is ready for planting out, and their leaves will still be green and active. For this reason, larger kinds such as daffodils, hyacinths and tulips are dug up carefully with a fork, and transplanted close together in a spare piece of ground to finish recharging and die down naturally (crocuses are tiny and usually left where they are). Weed the bed and lightly fork it over. Replenish the compost mulch or sprinkle with general fertilizer, if you wish. The bed will then be ready for replanting.

In formal summer bedding, bulbs are usually used as 'dot' plants, tall centrepieces within a groundwork of medium-size plants surrounded by dwarf edging. For this purpose they are planted first, followed by the edging and finally the groundwork plants, which usually produce buds or flowers before their neighbours, having been given a head start under glass in late winter or early

Variegated cannas – 'Striata' (green and yellow) and 'Durban' (red, green and yellow) – complement a sumptuous summer display of dahlias and *Lobelia cardinalis*.

spring. Unlike spring bedding, summer bulbs will need watering regularly in dry weather.

The most popular choices for dot plants are brightly coloured canna and dahlia varieties, because they flower continuously from planting time until the bedding is cleared in early autumn. Tuberous begonias, notably upright Multiflora varieties, make excellent groundwork plants. Other kinds have shorter

flowering periods but could still be used as part of a summer bedding scheme, including groups of *Lilium regale* within a groundwork of salpiglossis and purple heliotrope; galtonias with purple petunias, tall blue ageratums or crimson snapdragons (*Antirrhinum*); tigridias in masses of blue lobelia; or multi-coloured Butterfly gladioli over a drift of *Phlox drummondii* or eschscholzias. The possibilities are endless.

In a vibrant border *Hedychium densiflorum* 'Assam Orange' expands into large clumps, perfect partners in late summer for the arching stems of crocosmias.

This yellow-themed planting uses *Tulipa* 'West Point', *Thermopsis lanceolata* and variegated *Hosta* 'Spinners'.

Bulbs in mixed borders

A mixed border is by definition a bed of variable depth along the side of the garden or house containing a mixture of shrubs and herbaceous plants, perhaps with a tree or two. Bulbs are as useful here as they are in seasonal bedding, but there is a wider choice of types, which means greater scope for adventurous combinations of plants. Almost any weatherproof kind is worth trying.

The planting style is usually less formal than in a bedding scheme, especially in cottage-style borders.

Depending on the sorts used, bulbs may be temporary, for filling gaps or heralding spring before the main display starts: you might have a cluster of early tulips amid young geranium foliage, for example; or groups of gladioli to punctuate a thicket of artemisias; or just a patch of hyacinths in front of a bare-branched deciduous shrub. Or they may be permanently integrated into the design. This is a huge advantage from a maintenance point of view, because they do not need annual planting and lifting and can be left to fatten up and spread out into respectable clumps.

Creative combinations

As well as being star soloists, bulbs are inexhaustible team-players that can be used in innumerable combinations and contrasts. Here are just a few.

■ Tall purple *Allium* 'Globemaster' with late-flowering tulips, columbines (*Aquilegia*) and silver foliage in a well-drained border or gravel garden; also try contrasting them with cool white flowers or yellow foliage.

■ A carpet of lavender-blue *Anemone blanda* or *Anemone apennina* to hide bare Bearded iris rhizomes (especially effective with the gold-striped leaves of *Iris pallida* 'Variegata'); or for underplanting hostas, bush roses and euphorbias.

■ Orange turkscap lilies (*Lilium martagon*) in groups with fiery red crocosmias, apricot or peach daylilies (*Hemerocallis*), purple or bronze foliage plants such as fennel or physocarpus, or with other warm or intense flowers, to make a tropical composition in a hot border or deep container.

■ Dainty dwarf daffodils naturalized with lavender-blue chionodoxas, purple crocuses, blue mertensias, pulmonarias, scillas and violas; left in place to develop into a spring woodland composition, perhaps followed by cowslips (*Primula veris*), forget-me-nots (*Myosotis*) and old pheasant's eye narcissi.

■ Arum lilies (*Zantedeschia*) in moist soil under deciduous shrubs and trees in partial shade; the flowers teamed with astilbes, filipendula, *Iris sibirica* and rodgersia, and the foliage later complementing hedychiums and hostas.

■ Statuesque white galtonias combined with rich red dahlias, green nicotianas, agapanthus and late lilies, or to follow nearby oriental poppies as they die down in late summer.

■ White-eyed blue chionodoxas around the emerging purple foliage of herbaceous peonies, or blended with dark bugle (*Ajuga reptans*), white heathers (*Erica*), and blue-green grasses such as *Festuca glauca*.

Don't forget

The flowers of some bulbs, including daffodils and anemones, look only one way, so they don't have as much impact in beds where they can be seen from all sides. Plant them against a background of taller plants or a wall, and concentrate on tulips or hyacinths for places with all-round viewing.

Different varieties of the same plant often make the most effective combinations: here, orange *Fritillaria imperialis* with a yellow cultivar, 'Lutea'.

Temporary plantings

Always arrange the bulbs in bold groups or informal drifts, to match the style of the border. Temporary plantings will need to be accessible when the time comes to lift them, and you may need some other plants in reserve to plug the gap they leave. One way is to plant the bulbs in large pots, either sinking them to their rims in the soil or using them as a focal point. Most tulip varieties are ideal candidates for this and, as they will have to be dried off over the summer, growing them in pots will make it easy to move them under cover. Then infill with a similar pot planted up with summer bulbs, tender bedding or a few hardy annuals sown several weeks earlier.

Permanent plantings

Choose positions carefully for permanent plantings. The border might be warm and sunny enough to offer a home for frost-shy bulbs such as crinums, belladonna lilies, nerines and some of the dwarf tulips, which can be left there if covered with a winter mulch.

Bulbs within an established border need to complement rather than compete with neighbouring plants in terms of height, colour and form. For instance, try teaming lilies with tall delphiniums, spiky irises with billowing fennel or hardy geraniums; or put crown imperials (*Fritillaria imperialis*) next to low shrubs such as Japanese maples, dwarf philadelphus or a peach-coloured chaenomeles.

Above all, explore the host of less obvious bulbs available, like eucomis, sternbergias or triteleias. Eremurus,

A bright blue glazed pot of tulips and wallflowers is an eye-catching highlight in an orange-and-yellow scheme.

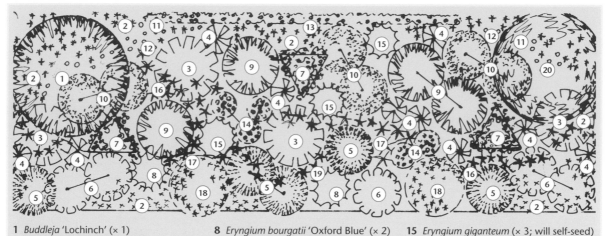

1 *Buddleja* 'Lochinch' (× 1)
2 *Chionodoxa sardensis* (× 100)
3 *Geranium* 'Patricia' (× 4)
4 *Lilium regale* (× 10)
5 *Nepeta racemosa* 'Walker's Low' (× 5)
6 *Sedum* 'Herbstfreude' (× 5)
7 *Clematis* 'Venosa Violacea' (× 3; trained on willow wigwams or obelisks)
8 *Eryngium bourgatii* 'Oxford Blue' (× 2)
9 *Penstemon* 'Stapleford Gem' (× 4)
10 *Alchemilla mollis* (× 6)
11 *Galanthus* 'Atkinsii' (× 30)
12 *Cyclamen coum* (× 20)
13 *Rosa* 'Madame Alfred Carrière' (× 1; trained on wall)
14 *Verbena bonariensis* (× 5)
15 *Eryngium giganteum* (× 3; will self-seed)
16 *Tulipa* 'China Pink' (× 50)
17 *Gladiolus communis* subsp. *byzantinus* (× 10)
18 *Anthemis* 'Tetworth' (× 2)
19 *Tulipa* 'Marilyn' (× 25)
20 *Sambucus nigra* f. *porphyrophylla* 'Eva' (× 1)

erythroniums, blue camassias, tall late daffodils and native snakeshead fritillaries (*Fritillaria meleagris*) can all find a permanent home in different parts of a border; dwarf and species daffodils could be left to naturalize at the front under mats of pinks (*Dianthus*); and some of the outrageously large alliums could be used as bold accents above clumps of euphorbias or sea hollies (*Eryngium maritimum*). Lilies vary so widely in height and flowering time that a variety could be found for almost any purpose or position in the border, and they are not choosy about their companions, whether these are hostas or hydrangeas.

The pink *Lilium speciosum* is safe left in the ground year after year, whereas in frost-prone gardens *Eucomis pallidiflora* needs overwintering indoors.

BULBS IN A MIXED COTTAGE-STYLE BORDER (7.5M/25FT × 2.5M/8FT)

Backed by a rose-clad wall, this all-year border should provide continuous colour and interest, from earliest spring bulbs through to late-autumn flowers and seedheads. Summer-flowering perennials fill out to cover the ground as the spring bulbs fade, while tall lilies and traditional willow wigwams, each supporting a classic clematis, add height. Some plants may self-seed, filling gaps and helping to create a natural, harmonious effect. Lilies and the climbing rose provide summer fragrance, and there are many plants here to attract bees and butterflies.

Lift or leave?

Whether you dig up bulbs after flowering or leave them to establish and repeat their performance next year depends on the type of planting scheme and what you intend doing later in the area where the bulbs are buried. It is usual to lift and transplant bedding bulbs to finish their growth cycle elsewhere – watch out for small offsets, as these may drop off unnoticed or be left behind, and they are always useful for propagation (see pages 66–7). In borders the dying bulb foliage may be an eyesore, but neighbouring plants often conceal this as they expand, or you can oversow the bulbs while in bloom with a fast-growing annual such as cornflower or clarkia. If you leave them in place, make sure they are clearly marked or lie deep enough to avoid injury as you tend the border.

Bulbs in grass

With the exception of showy, highly bred varieties, most bulbs look their best when growing in generous swathes and informal drifts, very much as they would in their natural surroundings. Visualize, for example, fields carpeted with wild daffodils, a streamside meadow stippled with snakeshead fritillaries, or wild lilies clothing a sun-baked Crimean hillside. This is the picture that naturalizing bulbs in areas of grass or in a wildflower meadow aims to create.

Dainty and highly fragrant, the poet's daffodil (*Narcissus poeticus*) is perfectly at home naturalized in taller grass.

Natural effects

The scale is vastly reduced in a garden, of course, but the impact can be just as breathtaking, whether the bulbs are planted in a corner of a small lawn or as an ingredient of a wildflower patch. Ironically, making a garden look uncontrived and natural can take a disproportionate amount of conscious planning and effort, but growing bulbs as nature intended is one of the simplest and most immediately effective steps towards achieving this effect. After three or four years, the bulbs will look as though they have always lived there.

The bulbs you choose for naturalizing and how they look in your garden depends on their surroundings. Remember all bulbs originally came from specialized habitats such as grazed alpine pastures, lush water meadows or the wildflower margins of deciduous woodland. Artificial versions of all these habitats exist in gardens, and there are particular bulbs that are suitable for each one.

Bulbs in lawns

The favourite part of a garden for naturalizing bulbs is the lawn, which in plant terms represents short, regularly grazed and usually well-drained grassland. A surprisingly large number of different species enjoy this type of habitat, where competing grasses are kept short while the bulbs themselves survive because most grazing animals carefully avoid them. Lawns, however, need mowing, and dodging bulbs is impractical unless they are confined to a specific patch for just part of the year. For this reason, the choice is usually restricted to early- and mid-spring bulbs, or occasionally autumn-flowering kinds.

Both crocus species and larger Dutch crocus (*Crocus vernus* subsp. *albiflorus*) are easily managed in lawns, the foliage dying back in time for the first mowing.

Too tall and late in flower for lawns, *Camassia quamash* is an excellent choice for a wildflower meadow that is not mown until late summer.

disturbed, and they will usually readjust their depth if they're unhappy: plant daffodils no more than 8cm (3in) deep and crocuses 2.5cm (1in) or so below the surface. And don't plant too densely: two to three times the width of the bulb is close enough, or you may have to divide them after only a few years.

Wildflower meadows

Many more bulbs can be grown in taller grass and wildflower areas that are mown just once or twice a year, usually in mid- or late summer. They will look even more impressive if they're combined with other flowers: perhaps daffodils with herbaceous geraniums, astrantias and trollius, or fritillaries among drifts of cowslips and anemones. Some lilies, especially *Lilium martagon* and *Lilium pardalinum*, romp happily through

Planting for success

You can create a wonderful picture with just a few handfuls of crocuses in a small corner of the lawn. Concentrate on large-flowered kinds as these show up best, especially very early and vigorous *Crocus vernus* subsp. *albiflorus* varieties such as purple 'Grand Maître' or striped 'Pickwick'. Add groups of short-stemmed daffodils such as *Narcissus* 'Carlton', dainty double 'Telamonius Plenus' (syn. 'Van Sion') or the native Tenby daffodil *Narcissus obvallaris* for

a spring display that will be finished and cleared in time for you to restore a smooth green sward by midsummer. *Narcissus bulbocodium*, the charming hoop-petticoat daffodil, loves very damp turf, and there are several other bulbs you could try in lawns (see page 42).

Keep your design as simple as possible for maximum impact. Mixtures of varieties or colours look unnatural and visually confusing – keep yellow and white daffodils well apart, for example. If you want two varieties or colours of crocus, grow them separately in irregular patches. Make sure several kinds flower within the same space of time, if not simultaneously, as this simplifies the mowing regime. There's no need to plant very deeply because they are unlikely to dry out too much or be

see page 42

Don't forget

The essence of any naturalistic planting scheme is informality, which means restraining the temptation to space bulbs evenly. Aim for a random group or drift (see page 51), with a few scattered outliers to suggest the bulbs are beginning to spread here and there. Always leave room for natural increase.

see page 51

Mowing regimes

The key to success with bulbs planted in grass is to refrain from mowing over them until their leaves have died down or, if you want them to spread, after they have self-seeded. This often means waiting for about six weeks after flowering is finished, which would be late spring for most crocuses or even midsummer in the case of daffodils. The later the bulbs bloom, the longer you need to wait; if you plant colchicums and autumn crocuses in the lawn, you will have to stop mowing the area where they are growing in late summer.

Cut the lawn fairly short in late autumn to allow spring bulbs a clear area in which to emerge. When you first mow after flowering, set the blades fairly high and gradually lower them over the next two to three cuts; the brown patch first revealed will quickly green up and match the rest of the lawn. Cut taller grass and wildflower meadows after all the plants have seeded themselves, leaving the loose clippings on the surface for a week or so to dry while seeds filter through to the soil, and then clear for composting.

wild grassland, as will more robust camassias such as *Camassia cusickii* and *Camassia quamash*, embroidering flowering grasses with their steely blue or white stars in damp ground.

Native bulbs

Snakeshead fritillaries (*Fritillaria meleagris*) in spring and *Colchicum autumnale* in autumn are typical native grassland bulbs, but it's worth experimenting with other less obvious choices. Smaller gladioli, for instance magenta *Gladiolus communis* subsp. *byzantinus,* flourish among taller wild grasses and cow parsley, together with *Tulipa sylvestris,* happiest in a meadow where their slightly straggly habit is concealed.

Many daffodil varieties fit well in these surroundings, not the showy large-headed kinds but vigorous, wilder sorts such as native Lent lilies (*Narcissus pseudonarcissus*), twin-flowered *Narcissus × medioluteus* or the white-and-yellow poet's daffodil *Narcissus poeticus* and its varieties. (*See also* page 94 for more daffodils.)

Consult a wildflower gardening book or a native flora while researching the kinds of bulbs likely to do well and look after themselves in wild grass. Don't ignore the rest of the world, though, because almost any temperate grassland could supply further options, depending on the climate and soil prevailing in your garden. If in doubt, buy just a few bulbs and grow them in a container or a corner of their potential site to assess their appearance and performance. If they pass the test, try a wholesale bulb merchant to see if you can buy the bulbs in bulk; most generally give a generous discount.

As might be expected of a native species, the Lent lily spreads more freely than most *Narcissus* varieties and is ideal for naturalizing.

Snakeshead fritillaries grow best in the conditions found in damp meadows, where they self-seed to form large, permanent colonies.

Bulbs for cutting

Bulbs are popular cut flowers, especially in spring, when little else is available. Choosing and gathering your own brings extra value as well as freshness (they will often last longer than bought flowers) and can even benefit some bulbs. Far from harming them, as some gardeners fear, cutting the flowers can save bulbs from investing a huge amount of effort in completing the fairly exhausting natural cycle of flowering and seed production.

Types to grow

There is a wide range of garden bulbs suitable for cutting (*see* page 43), and you can expand this either by growing tender kinds, like freesias or polianthes under glass, or forcing some into early flower in pots (*see* page 55), in a greenhouse border or in a bulb frame (where they could flower two to four weeks earlier than outdoors, *see* page 61). Cutting for vases is also a good way to rescue collapsed or damaged flowers, such as double tulips and daffodils after rain and wind, or potted hyacinths if the stems have bent under the weight of the heavy heads.

Many bulbs will be specifically recommended in catalogues as good for cutting, but you need to choose varieties carefully and consider practicalities. Foxtail lilies last well in water, but popular kinds, including *Eremurus himalaicus* and *Eremurus robustus*, are far too tall for most vases, whereas *Eremurus bungei* is more manageable and just as impressive. Larger alliums, for example *Allium cristophii* and *Allium tuberosum*, are

Both familiar and less common bulbs can be used for cutting.

① *Narcissus* 'Hawera' and whole hyacinth heads make good vase partners.

② *Eremurus bungei* stems can be effective for weeks in a taller vase.

③ *Allium cristophii* provides dramatic colour without a hint of onion fragrance.

better value than dwarf kinds; the bunched flowers of multi-headed daffodils such as *Narcissus* 'Hawera' or *Narcissus jonquilla* have greater impact than those that bear solitary blooms; and plain tulips are more robust than fancy kinds such as the showy but weak-stemmed Parrot varieties.

Don't forget

Lilies are among the best bulbs for cutting and can remain in good condition for many weeks, but some produce lavish amounts of indelible pollen that can stain your skin and clothing. Either pull off the anthers as florists do – which seems sacrilege – or position vases well clear of curtains and furniture. If you do pick up pollen on any material, don't rub it but carefully press a strip of adhesive tape over the area, and repeat until you have lifted it all off. Note too that lilies are poisonous to cats.

Harvesting bulb flowers

All bulb flowers are best gathered early in the morning, just as buds begin to show a hint of colour. Cut them with a good length of stem, right to the base if it carries no leaves; otherwise, aim to remove no more than a quarter of the leaves or you could jeopardize the bulb's chances of flowering again (daffodils look better in vases with a few leaves – a 'spiked bunch'). In the case of lilies, leave a good length of stem and leaves on the plant, to avoid having to wait several years for them to rebuild their strength and flower again.

Remove the lowest leaves where there are any on cut stems (submerged leaves promote the growth of bacteria). As soon as you have trimmed the

For long vase life, cut gladioli spikes when the two lowest flowers have opened.

stems, plunge them into a bucket part-filled with water. Keep daffodils separate at first, as their stems ooze a type of latex popularly known as 'daffodil slime', which is toxic to tulips and can shorten the vase life of other flowers if they are mixed together in the first 24 hours after cutting. Tulips also need special treatment, as they tend to continue growing and bend and conform to the shape of any vase. The answer is to wrap them all together fairly tightly in paper and stand the package upright in cold water for a day or two, after which they can be displayed normally.

Don't forget

You can extend the cutting season of some of your favourite bulbs by planting varieties that flower at different times. For example, Single Early through to Single Late tulips can spread the supply over three months. Alternatively, stagger the bulbs that take a fixed number of weeks to bloom by planting a few at a time at regular intervals. This works particularly well for gladioli and *Anemone coronaria*.

Keeping the show going

Maintaining your cut flowers in top form and prolonging their life is easy as long as you follow just a few simple precautions. Use a vase that is about one-half to two-thirds the height of the flowers, and stand this in a cool position away from direct sunlight, draughts and heat sources such as a radiator. Also, keep it away from ripe fruit as these produce ethylene gas, which hastens maturity and can shorten the life of the flowers. Remove yellowing leaves and fading blooms promptly; check and top up water every day, and change it at least once a week, at the same time cutting a centimetre or two off the stems.

A cutting bed

While cutting a few daffodils here and there will hardly spoil a border display, you may prefer to establish a special bed for larger quantities, or a steady year-round supply, of cut flowers. Any spare piece of ground may be used, with some plants left in permanently and others replanted annually – but all arranged in rows for easy maintenance, cutting and, where needed, support. Grow popular subjects such as daffodils, dahlias, gladioli and tulips alongside herbaceous perennials like achilleas, chrysanthemums, peonies and verbascums, annuals such as cornflowers or stocks, and even roses and shrubs for foliage.

Bulbs left over from being divided, those lifted when bedding is cleared, and hyacinths after forcing can all find a new life here. Care is simple: all can be fed and watered at the same time, hardy perennials can be left in to gain in strength, and only tender kinds need lifting and replanting each year.

Woodland bulbs under trees

Forests, woods and woodland glades are all habitats in which wild bulbs are found, and these have their counterparts in gardens where the same bulb species will feel at home naturalized under a lilac or an apple tree. There is something particularly delightful about a carpet of spring bulbs dancing in the dappled light under a group of trees.

Establishing bulbs

Many bulbs that are suitable for lawns and taller grass (*see* pages 23–5) are equally appealing in a grassed-down orchard or under garden trees, where grass often grows sparsely or not at all. And without the need for any mowing, the scope for planting bulbs is even wider – depending only on the amount of shade cast by the tree and whether the soil under it is too dry or moist. For example, you

Cyclamen coum and snowdrops will finish flowering and seeding before this birch starts to spread shade.

could plant groups of different varieties of snowdrop to flower throughout their full season – from, say, *Galanthus reginae-olgae* in early winter to *Galanthus plicatus*, which blooms in mid-spring.

Some of the commonest bulbs, for example aconites (*Eranthis*), daffodils, lilies and trilliums, are associated with wooded areas, where they will naturalize and

Shady characters both, *Galanthus* 'Atkinsii' and marbled arum help to relieve gloom with flowers and foliage.

Don't forget

If you dig up spring-bedding bulbs after flowering or grow them in pots for forcing or in seasonal containers, you may have a lot of perfectly sound bulbs looking for a new home. These are ideal for naturalizing elsewhere in the garden, where they can recover, establish, and hopefully multiply over future years.

Tree types

Before planting under trees, assess how much shade they cast and whether this can be reduced. While a few obliging bulbs, such as bluebells or crocuses, survive quite dense shade provided they have enough sunlight during their crucial weeks of growth and flowering, others can be more particular. Colchicums, for example, are woodland margin plants, adapted to the partial sunlight at the edge of open glades, whereas lilies such as *Lilium ciliatum* and *L. rubellum* are happiest in the year-round shade of conifers. Shade under trees varies according to species. Flowering cherries, rowans and oaks come into leaf late enough for most early-spring bulbs to complete their life cycle, whereas beeches and some conifers cast shade that's too deep for most kinds. The soil condition under trees varies too, so needs to be checked. For example, the acid leaf mould formed by fir trees is ideal for a lot of woodland bulbs, whereas birches, while only casting light shade, dry out the ground with their shallow roots.

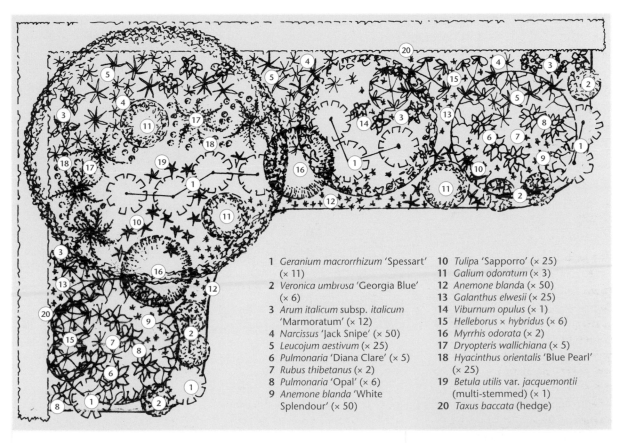

1 *Geranium macrorrhizum* 'Spessart' (× 11)
2 *Veronica umbrosa* 'Georgia Blue' (× 6)
3 *Arum italicum* subsp. *italicum* 'Marmoratum' (× 12)
4 *Narcissus* 'Jack Snipe' (× 50)
5 *Leucojum aestivum* (× 25)
6 *Pulmonaria* 'Diana Clare' (× 5)
7 *Rubus thibetanus* (× 2)
8 *Pulmonaria* 'Opal' (× 6)
9 *Anemone blanda* 'White Splendour' (× 50)
10 *Tulipa* 'Sapporro' (× 25)
11 *Galium odoratum* (× 3)
12 *Anemone blanda* (× 50)
13 *Galanthus elwesii* (× 25)
14 *Viburnum opulus* (× 1)
15 *Helleborus* × *hybridus* (× 6)
16 *Myrrhis odorata* (× 2)
17 *Dryopteris wallichiana* (× 5)
18 *Hyacinthus orientalis* 'Blue Pearl' (× 25)
19 *Betula utilis* var. *jacquemontii* (multi-stemmed) (× 1)
20 *Taxus baccata* (hedge)

BULBS IN A SPRING WOODLAND CORNER (7.5M/25FT × 5M/16FT)
Designed to recreate something of the magic of a bluebell wood, the spring-like quality of this corner planting scheme is emphasized by its dark backdrop of clipped yew hedging. The white bark of a multi-stemmed birch and ornamental brambles give structure in winter, echoed in early spring by white bulbs such as snowdrops, snowflakes and anemones, and all building into a more varied tapestry of blue, green and white, starring hyacinths and tulips, as the season progresses.

multiply freely if they get just a few hours of sunlight daily. Also, this is the natural element of bulbs such as *Crocus tommasinianus* and golden *Crocus flavus* subsp. *flavus* (formerly known as *Crocus aureus*), *Lilium superbum* and *Lilium canadense*, and the majestic *Cardiocrinum giganteum*. Bulbs with attractive foliage, especially arums and cyclamen, prolong the ground-cover effect far beyond their flowering season. Just give all these bulbs an autumn top-dressing of leaf mould and they could be self-seeding and spreading for many years. For more bulbs for planting under trees, *see* page 42.

The Lent lily (*Narcissus pseudonarcissus*) and *Anemone blanda* are two of the loveliest native woodland flowers.

Bulbs in gravel, rockeries and scree

It's not often appreciated that stones are the perfect surfacing material for mulching soil and keeping the earth beneath cool and moist in hot, dry weather. Gravel, loose scree and the large boulders of a rock garden all help to improve drainage and also encourage bulb growth with the extra warmth reflected from their surfaces. Bulbs can add colour and vitality to these austere settings, especially early or late in the year, when stone absorbs and retains more of the sun's heat than does bare soil.

If watered in really dry weather, *Camassia leichtlinii* subsp. *suksdorfii* will be happy growing in gravel.

Growing in gravel

Although more often used to top off drives and paths, gravel is an effective finish for growing areas too. Planting in a well-made gravel bed is an excellent low-maintenance strategy, with the added benefit of providing the kind of specialized hot, well-drained sites that are demanded by many Mediterranean and Californian bulbs. Many of these can also be grown at the edges of an existing gravel drive or path.

Practicalities

Before laying gravel, you might want to spread landscape fabric over the area to stop weeds from coming through and, where desired, prevent

Nectaroscordum, irises and even fussy little *Gladiolus communis* subsp. *byzantinus* will thrive in the enhanced drainage that gravel provides.

plants from self-seeding. Otherwise, thoroughly weed the site and fork in some garden compost, leaf mould or, if the soil is clay-based, grit (light, sandy soil should not need any improvement) and rely on the gravel to suppress weeds.

There are various types of gravel, pebbles and chippings available. Avoid limestone if you want to grow acid-loving species. Fine grades, about 10mm (½in) or less, look attractive in small patches, whereas a coarser type is suitable for paths and larger areas. If you aim for a minimum depth of 5cm (2in), reckon that a cubic-metre bagful will cover about 20 square metres (18 square yards). Arrange larger cobbles in natural groups to relieve wide, unbroken expanses of gravel while also providing a little shade and shelter for those bulbs that need it.

To plant bulbs, scrape aside the gravel to expose the soil; if there

Despite sounding harsh and unsympathetic, a gravel garden is a congenial habitat for all kinds of shrubs, perennials and bulbs such as these alliums and irises.

Alpine troughs

If space is at a premium, you could create a mini gravel garden in a deep trough or sink, planting it with the smaller bulbs that like the conditions of a gravel or scree bed. This is a favourite way to display alpine and rock garden plants, while also ensuring efficient drainage.

These troughs are available in stone (real or imitation), terracotta or concrete. You can make your own by coating an old, glazed sink or similar container with hypertufa, a mixture of equal parts peat substitute, coarse sand and cement, blended with water to make a paste.

Raise the trough on sturdy supports so it will shed excess water freely. The soil needed depends on the type of plants: for rock garden species, fill with soil-based potting compost (use lime-free or ericaceous compost for acid-loving plants) mixed with one third grit by volume; for true alpine species, follow the same procedure as when building a scree bed (see page 32).

is a weed-suppressant membrane, cut a cross in this large enough for you to insert a trowel or bulb planter. Then simply bury the bulbs at their recommended depth, and replace the membrane and gravel. Lifting the bulbs at the end of the season is difficult, so this method is suitable only for permanent plants.

Bulbs for gravel gardens

Almost all bulbs recommended for dry or sunny sites (see pages 108–9) will succeed in gravel, especially larger kinds that prefer exceptionally good drainage, such as agapanthus, alliums, hardy gladioli, crocosmias, sisyrinchiums and irises. Smaller, lower-growing bulbs that will thrive

here include chionodoxas, crocuses, cyclamen, winter aconites (Eranthis hyemalis), ipheions, Spanish irises (Iris xiphium), scillas and sternbergias. When choosing bulbs for gravel, find out where they normally grow in the wild. If they come from rocky hillsides, stony soils or even cliff tops, they should feel perfectly at home, especially when combined with their natural companions, whether grasses, herbaceous perennials or shrubs.

Creating a whole garden under gravel is feasible. Only those bulbs that come from woodland (see pages 28–9) or prefer damp, leafy habitats might feel uncomfortable, because their native surroundings would be

1 *Hebe* 'Mrs Winder' (× 4)
2 *Eremurus himalaicus* (× 10)
3 *Stipa tenuissima* (× 10)
4 *Perovskia atriplicifolia* 'Blue Spire' (× 5)
5 *Geranium tuberosum* (× 10)

6 *Allium cristophii* (× 25)
7 *Iris pallida* 'Argentea Variegata' (× 8)
8 *Limonium platyphyllum* (× 4)
9 *Triteleia laxa* 'Königin Fabiola' (× 50)
10 *Heuchera* 'Obsidian' (× 7)

11 *Tulipa turkestanica* (× 50)
12 *Thymus serpyllum* 'Pink Chintz' (× 5)
13 *Salvia nemorosa* 'Caradonna' (× 10)
14 *Sedum* 'Bertram Anderson' (× 5)
15 *Scilla peruviana* (× 20)

Tender types

If you want to grow tender species – such as *Ixia*, *Moraea* and dwarf gladioli – in gravel or scree, plant them in pots (the lattice kind or normal ones with plenty of drainage holes), then sink these to their rims in the soil and cover with gravel. The pots can be lifted before the first frosts.

BULBS IN A SUNNY, SHELTERED GRAVEL BED (7.5M/25FT × 2.5M/8FT)

Designed to span the width of a small garden and to be seen from both sides, this bed has dense, low planting to divide two areas without interrupting views. Drifts of bulbs (scillas, triteleias, tulips and alliums) create splashes of dramatic colour as they flower, while the ornamental seedheads of the tulips and alliums add more lasting interest. The low, evergreen shrubs and perennials contribute not only seasonal flowers but also longer-term structure and foliage interest.

emphatically organic rather than mineral. It is worth experimenting with some of these species, though, if you are prepared to give them extra water during dry weather. Start by trying wild anemones or lily species from Greece and Turkey.

A scree garden

Scree is the scientific term for the banks and drifts of broken and weathered stone fragments that accumulate at the foot of mountain slopes, producing a home for some exquisite alpine plants. Recreating this unique habitat is not difficult and provides an authentic setting for the smallest rock garden bulbs, and some of the rarer true alpine species;

it is an alternative to a rock garden if the site is level rather than sloping, or it could be part of a larger rock garden, or – perhaps best of all – a freestanding raised bed with walls and plenty of drainage holes.

Visually, the scree will need to blend with the rest of the garden. Otherwise, only two site conditions are crucial for plants in scree: good light and good drainage. Avoid overhanging trees, which will cast shade and drip water on plants below, and any position exposed to very cold or drying winds. Many scree plants start growing very early in the year, so avoid planting them in a frost pocket, where young growing-tips could be damaged (in the wild they're protected by snow).

Scree garden practicalities

To make a scree bed, hollow out an area about 30–45cm (12–18in) deep and half-fill it with stony material, such as shingle, broken bricks or builders' rubble. Lay porous landscape fabric over it, to prevent the planting mixture percolating through the base layer, then add a layer of scree mix, 15–20cm (6–8in) deep, made of three parts coarse grit or chippings; one part garden soil or loam-based potting compost; and one part shredded bark or peat

Don't forget

Alpine sections in garden centres often include plants that have untidy foliage or are prolific self-seeders and will crowd out more modest neighbours (see page 52).

Miniature and species tulips such as *Tulipa* 'Little Beauty' and orange *Tulipa* 'Little Princess' look effective growing in a scree bed.

substitute. Tread firm and water well. Once the bed has settled, top with a 2–3cm (¾–1¼in) layer of gravel or chippings, and any larger rocks and boulders to complete the landscape.

Scree-loving plants

Before introducing bulbs, choose and plant other alpines that might grow in scree, for example dianthus, aethionemas, raoulia, androsaces, saxifrages and sempervivums. Add bulbs in natural arrangements between the other plants, beginning with good, reliable miniatures such as *Fritillaria michailovskyi, Narcissus* 'Canaliculatus' and *Crocus ancyrensis* before trying some truly alpine kinds, for instance spring-flowering *Colchicum luteum*, tiny *Scilla verna* or the almost legendary Chilean blue crocus *Tecophilaea cyanocrocus*. Make sure they are all buried at their appropriate depths, then securely cover with the stone mulch, topping up annually wherever it thins out.

A rock garden

A small collection of unwanted rocks and stones, planted with clumps of aubrieta and arabis, or an impressive imitation of a mountain outcrop with boulders, rock strata and crevices for alpine plants from high altitudes: a rock garden can mean many things to many people. No two rock gardens are alike, but all share features that offer the perfect home for a wide range of bulbs.

The best rock gardens look like a natural outcrop, and it is the sloping profile and the raised level, together with a gritty porous soil mixture, that help to eliminate all risk of waterlogging. A well-made rockery is mulched with grit or fine gravel, a further aid to free drainage and also a source of radiated warmth. In addition, exposed rocks offer the sun or shade that can give extra protection to more sensitive species. They also help to create an authentic background: a solitary cluster of snowdrops or dwarf irises can look stunning tucked against a weathered

boulder. The stony setting and raised level of most rock gardens will bring the tiniest bulb into greater prominence, and just a few plants can make a huge impact.

Suitable bulbs

Rock garden plants tend to be dwarf and compact, mimicking the true alpine species found in rocky and mountain landscapes. Naturally small bulbs, such as crocuses, snowdrops, winter aconites, wild cyclamen and sternbergias are more in keeping with these surroundings. Look for simple dwarf varieties and unimproved wild species among larger genera, for example daffodils like *Narcissus* 'Minnow', bulbous iris varieties such as 'Joyce', and low-growing *Tulipa humilis*. Smaller alliums as well as fritillaries and sisyrinchiums will also work well. (*See* page 42 for more suggestions.)

Little *Narcissus* 'Jack Snipe', *Anemone blanda* and *Tulipa* 'Scarlet Baby' are comfortable in a rock garden setting.

Bulbs in containers

Bulbs work very well in containers and can add a unique extra dimension to planting schemes, whether you have a large garden, a tiny courtyard or a high-rise balcony. Some kinds are intended to provide a spectacular few weeks of seasonal colour, others as permanent features, but all will revel in the spotlight and, with careful planning, provide a changing display from winter's end until the last days of autumn.

There are certain commitments, of course, because container plants are less able to fend for themselves than their garden cousins – you need to keep a more frequent eye on watering, feeding and their health, for example – but the rewards are many. You can move them around to avoid frost or hot sun, and displays are easy to stage-manage and rearrange, enabling you to bring bulbs in flower to the fore.

Container size

Almost anything that holds soil, retains moisture and drains efficiently, even improvised or recycled utensils, can make an acceptable container for bulbs. What is important is size, so always choose the largest. Garden centres might sell a few daffodils or a dozen crocuses planted in a small pot, and these will usually flower well, but they are subsisting on the bulbs'

Vigorous *Muscari armeniacum* 'Valerie Finnis' is ideal for pots, as it looks best in large, crowded groups.

stored energy. They are unlikely to perform well the following year unless given more rooting space immediately after flowering so they can recharge. Small pots and other shallow containers, such as window boxes, need to be watered more frequently, may be less stable in windy positions, and are really suitable only for the smallest bulbs, such as crocuses and cyclamen.

However, small and slow-growing bulbs can resent 'overpotting' in an overwhelming amount of compost that could remain very wet for long periods, especially over winter. The solution with these is to mass generous numbers of bulbs in a large container, or use it to hold smaller pots plunged up to their rims until flowering finishes. They can then be lifted out to make way

Don't be shy of mixing varieties in pots to flower in sequence or together, as in this blend of 'Burgundy', 'Generaal de Wet' and 'Uncle Tom' tulips.

for replacement pots of later plants. Either plant the exhausted bulbs in the garden or re-bury the pots in a bulb frame.

Choreography

One of the great joys of growing in pots is that their mobility allows you to organize a revolving display. You can shield spring bulbs from the worst weather until they come into flower and then position them in the foreground until flowering finishes. After this, they can be moved off-stage to finish their growth cycle unobtrusively, while summer bulbs such as ixias, sparaxis and tigridias take their place. Combining pots of lilies with indoor bulbs, such as caladiums and gloriosas, can add hints of tropical luxuriance to the midsummer garden.

Being able to move containers around makes it easier to experiment with bulbs in a part of your garden that has a more challenging microclimate, and to meet any fussy cultural requirements of a particular variety. Some heat-loving bulbs might need one or several moves to follow the sun or avoid cold winds; tall kinds can be tucked in among supporting neighbours; and you can gather smaller pots together for easy maintenance, such as watering during droughts and holiday periods, or to provide protection from cold weather.

Slow-growing *Gladiolus murielae* started in pots under glass will then bloom earlier outdoors.

Balconies and roofs

On a city balcony or roof garden you can display all kinds of spring bulbs in the shelter of windbreak plants such as amelanchier, choisya, elaeagnus and cotoneaster. Follow these with lilies and zantedeschias mixed with other summer plants, and then end the year with pots of nerines, colchicums and cyclamen.

Weight is a crucial factor on a balcony or roof garden, so position heavy pots over load-bearing walls and on steps. To reduce weight, use light, loamless compost mixtures and chunks of polystyrene instead of crocks for drainage.

If you don't have a sunny border next to a warm wall, grow nerines in large pots, which are easily moved into the summer sunshine.

Don't forget

Always take care when moving large pots; a 1.2m (4ft) wide half-barrel full of moist compost can weigh up to 200kg (over 30 stone). Position the pot in a permanent site or, if you have to move it, use castors or a trolley.

Bulbs on their own

For maximum impact, try growing a single variety or, at the most, two per container. Bulbs are made for solo stardom and merit singling out from the crowd. Their flowering period is often shorter and more concentrated than that of many other plant types, so a few bulbs here and there may be overlooked if there is an abundance of other plants in flower at the same time. Limiting the selection also helps avoid mismatches, with one variety flowering before or after another (ideal if you want a sequence, but dead flowerheads and extra foliage can dilute the display).

Any crocus variety *en masse* makes a vibrant pool of colour, while trailing begonias are sufficient unto themselves in a hanging basket. Creamy-white and primrose *Narcissus* 'Ice Follies' is cheerful and uplifting on its own, with seven to nine bulbs planted evenly in a 30cm (12in) diameter pot. For fragrance, try the lovely Tazetta variety *Narcissus* 'Martinette', with pale yellow petals and a small orange cup. A few dainty multi-headed *Narcissus* 'Hawera', or a white or soft-yellow Multiflora hyacinth make good companion plants but anything more could be too much.

Narcissus triandrus varieties, such as the pure white 'Petrel', are among the prettiest and most graceful, and deserve star prominence.

Aristocratic agapanthus is a classic partner for a weathered terracotta or wooden tub; it flowers better when it is overcrowded.

Some bulbs are always best grown on their own in pots. Agapanthus, for example, gradually bulks up into a vast clump, the bulbs and rhizomes of nerines, Bearded irises and Solomon's seal (*Polygonatum*) need room to spread and cover the surface, while bushy, multi-stemmed kinds such as dahlias and begonias leave little space for other plants.

Most tulips are also best grown alone, because they rarely survive a typical summer without being lifted and dried off after flowering (*see* pages 62–3).

Don't forget

If you tailor the drainage and compost mix carefully, you can use a large container such as a trough or tub to create a specialized environment that particular bulbs enjoy but your garden doesn't offer. For example, acid, alkaline, scree and bog habitats can all become feasible options.

Lilies are superb bulbs for containers and among the select few that are best left there undisturbed from one year to the next. Provided they are top-dressed annually (*see* page 56), almost all kinds will be happy for at least four to five years before needing repotting. It is an excellent way to appreciate new lilies or very fragrant varieties such as *Lilium regale* or 'Royal Gold' (*see* below) at close quarters.

If you keep their containers under cover from autumn until spring, you can grow slightly frost-sensitive kinds such as *Lilium formosanum*, *L. longiflorum*, *L. parryi* and *L. sulphureum* with more certain success than in the open garden. Only lilies like *L. pardalinum* and *L. superbum*, which spread by rhizomes or stolons, dislike the confined space in a container.

Combining plants

Despite the advantages of growing bulbs on their own, many gardeners like to use them as components of planting schemes, especially as the presence of other plants can often camouflage the bulbs' uninteresting pre- and post-flowering stages.

Dwarf daffodils or tulips combine perfectly with aubrietas and dicentras in spring, for example, or you can team alliums with heucheras and hostas in a summer container. A simple spring recipe might include

Tulipa 'Queen of Night' looks particularly sumptuous teamed with variegated dwarf ribbon grass.

Tulipa 'Spring Green', 'Yellow Spring Green' and 'Blue Diamond' combine beautifully with white hyacinths.

blue muscari and white *Fritillaria meleagris* with arisaema or a dryopteris fern for a cool woodland effect, especially if you add some hardy geraniums and *Alchemilla mollis* after the bulbs die down.

A few *Narcissus* 'Tête-à-tête' or blue *Anemone blanda* bulbs can add a contrasting splash of colour to a leafy arrangement of daphne, heuchera and sarcococca, or try blending *Helleborus foetidus* and a dwarf grass as foliage plants with *Narcissus* 'Jetfire', a yellow mid-season tulip and cowslips. Leave the daffodils *in situ* but transplant the tulips and cowslips after flowering and replace with summer bedding.

Narcissus 'Tête-à-tête' makes a fine partnership with young willow stems, combining harmonies of colour with contrasting forms and textures.

Growing bulbs is addictive. Sooner or later you could discover a particular bulb genus or group that captures your fancy, compelling you to grow more of the same type. Familiar or mainstream varieties are likely to be early candidates, but you might not be able to resist moving on to more exotic kinds, even some challenging rarities as you accumulate experience. Almost before you know it, a collection is born.

Which bulbs to choose?

Any special part of the bulb world could be the subject of a collection, depending on the available resources. For example, the type of soil or climate, whether you have a greenhouse or intend growing the plants indoors, and how much specialized care is needed.

Some enthusiasts concentrate on a particular garden category, such as Lily-flowered tulips with their unbelievably perfect blooms, which makes them ideal for containers or a dedicated bed. In a rockery, or a scree or gravel area (see pages 30–3), you can build a charming collection of dwarf or species daffodils, from tiny

The various grape hyacinth (*Muscari*) species and varieties make an excellent subject for collecting and displaying in containers, where any inclination to sprawl or spread is easily controlled.

Don't forget

To some people, unfortunately, 'collecting bulbs' means hunting for them in the wild and possibly endangering their existence. Natural communities of the lovely white *Fritillaria liliacea*, for example, survive in only three tiny locations in California. Always buy from responsible sources that offer bulbs from cultivated, not wild-collected, stock.

There are hundreds of varieties of snowdrop; here are just a few that are available.

① *Galanthus* 'Modern Art'
② *Galanthus nivalis* Sandersii Group
③ *Galanthus* 'Ophelia'
④ *Galanthus gracilis*
⑤ *Galanthus plicatus* 'Trym'

More bulbs for collecting

Allium	*Haemanthus*
Begonia (rhizomatous; fancy-leaved)	*Iris*
	Lachenalia
Crocus (wild)	*Lilium* (turkscap)
Cyclamen	*Nerine*
Dahlia	*Sisyrinchium*
Fritillaria	*Trillium*
Gladiolus (butterfly)	*Tulipa* (Parrot or Viridiflora)

Narcissus minor, just 10cm (4in) tall, to the numerous varieties of *Narcissus cyclamineus* such as 'February Gold', 'Jack Snipe' and 'Peeping Tom'. There are dozens of dierama hybrids and more than 150 alliums to explore.

Collections under glass – in a greenhouse or bulb frame, or on a windowsill – could focus on bulbs from warmer climates. New and ever-more extravagant amaryllis (*Hippeastrum*) are being introduced, including many with double, striped or spidery blooms. They all make excellent pot plants for winter and spring colour, and may lead you on to wanting to try growing other members of the family (Amaryllidaceae) with similar requirements, such as scadoxus, Jacobean lily (*Sprekelia*) and Scarborough lily (*Cyrtanthus*).

Establishing a collection

The detective work involved once the collecting bug gets hold of you can be very satisfying, and you'll almost certainly find yourself exploring the background to your favourite bulbs. There are many lovely and easily acquired achimenes varieties, for example, but hundreds of other forms bred from Victorian times onwards would also be worth tracking down, especially the rare yellow ones. Then there's a score or more of wild species that deserve growing from seed. A collection will thrive quite happily in a cool greenhouse, with flowers in a huge range of colours all summer and autumn, and there is a good chance of producing new hybrids from cross-pollinated seeds.

Keep the bulbs in their favourite surroundings, ideally together to make it easier for you to maintain (and admire) them. Grouping together species that share behaviour patterns or cultural requirements greatly simplifies tending a collection in a greenhouse or bulb frame (*see* page 61).

Ventilation and water management are more straightforward if you can give the whole house or a section of a frame the same treatment. Always propagate more plants from your collection, both as insurance against losing a solitary specimen, and as a potential source for other enthusiasts.

An unheated greenhouse is ideal for assembling a collection of spring bulbs that need protection from cold or damp weather.

Bulbs indoors

Almost every conceivable variety of bulb can be grown indoors, with obvious benefits in some cases. Hardy kinds produce their flowers safe from the elements and where they can be appreciated at close quarters before being returned outside; frost-tender varieties can be given the temporary protection they need; and tropical species can take up permanent residence in a heated greenhouse or in the home, where they will be treated as house plants.

The tropical bulb *Gloriosa superba* 'Rothschildiana' spends the summer climbing up to the greenhouse roof.

Polianthes tuberosa will repay heat and humidity under glass with weeks of intense fragrance in midsummer.

Easter lilies brought into bloom in deep pots under glass are now ready to go into the house or out in the garden.

Greenhouse and conservatory bulbs

Just a small amount of heat, for example a minimum of 5°C (41°F), makes a huge difference to the bulbs you can grow, and considerably extends your range of choice to include some of the magnificent species from South Africa, South America, California and Australia. The extra protection advances flowering by several weeks (this is known as forcing, *see* page 55), shelters immaculate, delicate blooms of bulbs like nomocharis or the Easter lily (*Lilium longiflorum*) from the elements, and ensures a dry resting period for plants such as nerines and hymenocallis. With space in the home limited to flowering displays and a few permanent house plants, most of this specialized care takes place in a greenhouse or conservatory.

The favourite method is to grow bulbs in pots, which allows you to give each plant the type of compost and attention it needs. Some kinds, such as cannas or eucomis, are started under glass and then transferred outdoors to flower after the last frosts, either in beds or in their containers. Those like gloriosa lilies or polianthes, accustomed to humidity and warmth in their native habitats, usually stay indoors all their lives. A few can be shuttled between a cold or bulb frame while dormant or in leaf and the greenhouse as they come into flower or when winter is approaching.

Greenhouse beds

An extra facility well worth considering is a greenhouse bed as a display and growing area. This can be organized as a complete garden with tender and heat-loving species like clivias, eucharis and pancratiums for a natural mixed-bulb community, together with other compatible plants such as anthuriums, coleus and New Guinea impatiens. Planted direct into the bed, these will all grow and flower more vigorously with less attention than they demand in pots, but you need to make sure that all need similar amounts of water, rest, humidity and ventilation.

An alternative method is to use the bed for plunging pots as they start or finish flowering. If you grow similar kinds together, they can share particular treatments, such as summer dormancy, or you can water

Clivia miniata will grow and flower equally well in greenhouse pots and borders or as a house plant.

Unhappy outdoors in British winters, *Cyclamen graecum* makes a handsome and easily grown house plant.

Traditional house plants

Apart from spring bulbs grown naturally or traditionally forced in bowls for early colour indoors (*see* page 55), there are a few that have been grown and cherished as house plants for generations and still deserve special affection.

One that has become almost legendary is *Aspidistra elatior*, popularly known as the cast-iron plant because of the extraordinary ease with which it shrugs off deep shade, fluctuating heat and cold, and general neglect (it seems impossible to over- or under-water these plants). The ultimately large, spreading plants have long, glossy leaves, usually rich green but speckled or striped with white or cream in some varieties; these individually last for years, with a few more added annually as its meandering rhizomes creep across the surface. In early summer it bears broad, solitary, cream-and-maroon flowers at compost level, often going unnoticed – in the wild these are fertilized by slugs and snails.

Another rhizomatous plant from yesteryear still popular with florists and indoor gardeners is the asparagus fern (*Asparagus setaceus*), a twining climber that can reach far into the roof of a greenhouse or conservatory, although indoors it generally tends to be trained around a moss stick or encouraged to weep gracefully.

each plant individually as required and move it elsewhere as it comes into flower or goes to rest. This approach might not be as glamorous as a planted-up greenhouse 'garden', but it does allow you to grow or force bulbs like *Anemone coronaria*, lily-of-the-valley (*Convallaria*) or freesias in the same bed in batches and rows for cut flowers.

Bulbs in the home

Bulbs that are grown within the home fall into two distinct groups. The first is made up of bulbs like hyacinths, dwarf daffodils or large-flowered cyclamen, which are housed for as long as they are in flower and then moved back to the greenhouse or outdoors, and the second is the relatively few kinds that spend their whole lives as house plants, such as caladiums and clivias.

The range of plants that can be kept indoors as true house plants is unfortunately limited by the home

environment. Few are happy for long where they're exposed to draughts, central heating or a dry atmosphere. But, just as permanent indoor bulbs welcome occasionally being moved outdoors into better light or gentle rain, so the much larger range kept mainly in a greenhouse or bulb frame could be selectively brought inside for you to enjoy them while they are in flower.

Although used in tropical regions for bedding, caladiums are eye-catching foliage house plants in cooler areas.

Plants for a purpose

The range of bulbs now available is huge, and gardeners are definitely spoilt for choice. Use these lists to help you find the right bulb for the job, bearing in mind the particular conditions of your garden and the effect you want to achieve.

Bees love the spectacular foxtail lily
Eremurus × isabellinus 'Cleopatra'.

Best for bees

Allium (all)
Anemone (species)
Colchicum (all)
Convallaria majalis
Crocus (all)
Eremurus (all)
Galanthus nivalis
Hyacinthoides non-scripta
Leucojum (all)
Narcissus (species)

Best in lawns

Anemone blanda
Anemone nemorosa
Colchicum autumnale
Crocus (large-flowered)
Fritillaria meleagris
Galanthus elwesii
Galanthus nivalis
Leucojum aestivum
Narcissus bulbocodium
Narcissus pseudonarcissus
Scilla bifolia
Scilla siberica

Best in taller grass

Camassia leichtlinii subsp. *suksdorfii*
Fritillaria meleagris
Gladiolus communis subsp. *byzantinus*
Hyacinthoides non-scripta
Iris latifolia
Lilium martagon
Lilium pyrenaicum
Ornithogalum narbonense
Scilla bifolia
Tulipa sylvestris

Best under trees

Anemone nemorosa
Arisaema candidissimum
Chionodoxa luciliae
Colchicum speciosum
Convallaria majalis
Cyclamen coum
Cyclamen hederifolium
Erythronium dens-canis
Galanthus (all)
Hyacinthoides non-scripta
Lilium martagon
Muscari armeniacum
Scilla siberica 'Alba' and 'Spring Beauty'
Trillium grandiflorum
Tulipa sprengeri

Best low bulbs for gravel, rock or scree gardens

Allium cyaneum
Allium insubricum
Bellevalia romana
Crocus ancyrensis 'Golden Bunch'
Crocus chrysanthus 'Cream Beauty'
Cyclamen hederifolium
Cyclamen purpurascens
Eranthis hyemalis Cilicica Group
Fritillaria meleagris 'Alba'
Fritillaria michailovskyi
Galanthus 'Atkinsii'
Ipheion uniflorum
Iris histrioides 'Major'
Narcissus cyclamineus
Narcissus 'Minnow'
Ornithogalum nutans
Oxalis adenophylla
Oxalis laciniata
Rhodohypoxis baurii 'Harlequin'
Sisyrinchium 'Californian Skies'
Sisyrinchium idahoense
Sternbergia sicula
Tulipa humilis
Tulipa kaufmanniana
Tulipa tarda
Zephyranthes candida

Best for alkaline soil

Anemone blanda
Crocus (all)
Fritillaria imperialis
Fritillaria persica
Habranthus tubispathus
Hermodactylus tuberosus
Lilium candidum
Lilium henryi
Lilium pardalinum
Lilium pyrenaicum
Narcissus hybrids (most)
Narcissus jonquilla
Narcissus tazetta
Sisyrinchium (all)
Sternbergia lutea
Sternbergia sicula

Best for acid soil

Anthericum liliago
Cardiocrinum giganteum
Iris (Bearded)
Iris ensata
Iris sibirica
Lilium (all except L. candidum, L. henryi)
Narcissus asturiensis
Narcissus bulbocodium
Narcissus cyclamineus
Narcissus triandrus
Nomocharis saluenensis
Notholirion macrophyllum
Roscoea cautleyoides
Tricyrtis (all)
Trillium cuneatum
Trillium grandiflorum
Trillium luteum

Best in the greenhouse

Brodiaea californica
Canna (hybrids)
Eucomis bicolor
Eucomis comosa
Freesia (all)
Gladiolus (small-flowered hybrids)
Gladiolus murielae
Gloriosa superba 'Rothschildiana'
Habranthus robustus
Hymenocallis × festalis
Ipheion 'Rolf Fiedler'
Ixia (hybrids)
Lilium formosanum
Lilium longiflorum
Nerine sarniensis
Nerine undulata
Ornithogalum thyrsoides
Pancratium maritimum
Polianthes tuberosa
Tritonia crocata
Tritonia crocata 'Princess Beatrix'
Veltheimia bracteata
Veltheimia capensis
Zantedeschia elliottiana
Zantedeschia rehmannii
Zephyranthes citrina
Zephyranthes grandiflora

Best for cutting

Agapanthus campanulatus
Allium caeruleum
Allium giganteum
Allium 'Globemaster'
Anemone coronaria
Clivia miniata
Convallaria majalis
Dahlia (hybrids)
Freesia (all)
Galanthus (all)
Galtonia candicans 'Moonbeam'
Gladiolus communis subsp. byzantinus
Iris (Bearded)
Iris unguicularis
Ixia (species)
Leucojum aestivum 'Gravetye Giant'
Lilium (all)
Narcissus (most)
Nerine bowdenii
Polianthes tuberosa 'The Pearl'
Ranunculus asiaticus
Tulipa (most)
Zantedeschia aethiopica

Best flowering pot plants to bring indoors

Achimenes (all hybrids)
Begonia × tuberhybrida
Convallaria majalis
Crocus (large-flowered)
Eranthis hyemalis
Galanthus (all)
Hippeastrum (large-flowered hybrids)
Hyacinthus orientalis (prepared bulbs)
Iris histrioides
Iris reticulata
Lachenalia aloides
Lilium pumilum
Muscari comosum
Muscari macrocarpum
Narcissus jonquilla
Narcissus papyraceus
Narcissus tazetta
Narcissus triandrus and their hybrids
Tulipa greigii and their hybrids
Tulipa kaufmanniana

Best permanent house plants

Agapanthus africanus
Agapanthus praecox subsp. orientalis
Begonia rex (hybrids)
Begonia sutherlandii
Caladium bicolor
Clivia miniata
Crinum × powellii
Cyclamen (large-flowered hybrids)
Cyrtanthus elatus
Eucharis amazonica
Haemanthus albiflos
Haemanthus coccineus
Haemanthus sanguineus
Lycoris aurea
Lycoris radiata
Lycoris squamigera
Sprekelia formosissima

Best scented bulbs

Anthericum liliago 'Major'
Asphodeline lutea
Cardiocrinum giganteum
Chlidanthus fragrans
Convallaria majalis
Crinum × powellii
Eucharis amazonica
Freesia
Galanthus 'S. Arnott'
Hyacinthoides non-scripta
Hyacinthus (all)
Iris unguicularis
Lilium auratum
Lilium 'Casa Blanca'
Lilium longiflorum
Lilium regale
Narcissus 'Actaea'
Narcissus 'Grand Soleil d'Or'
Narcissus jonquilla
Narcissus × odorus
Narcissus papyraceus
Pancratium maritimum
Paradisea liliastrum 'Major'
Polianthes tuberosa 'The Pearl'
Trillium luteum

Planting and growing

Compared with other plants, bulbs are almost self-sufficient, with their growth and flower buds safely prepackaged in embryonic form and primed to go. With a few exceptions, their later care is relatively undemanding, too, especially as they spend much of the year resting below ground with no need for regular attention. For best results you need to start with top-quality stock, prepare the ground well and plant them correctly. Your bulbs will then do the rest.

Choosing and buying bulbs

Starting with the best bulbs is half the secret of success. What's on offer varies widely in quality and availability, so you need to have a clear idea of the kinds appropriate to your planting site and how many to buy, together with when and where to buy them. Knowing a good bulb when you see it is important, too.

Where to buy

With so many kinds of bulbs on sale, it's hardly surprising that in addition to general retailers, who tend to concentrate on popular and familiar varieties, there are specialist suppliers of more unusual kinds. Mail-order catalogues and the internet have made specialist bulbs accessible to a much wider public.

Garden centres These usually have a dedicated section displaying a selection of popular bulbs, both prepacked and loose. The range will depend on the garden centre's size, larger places frequently offering a selection of less common kinds, plus expert advice. Beware of impulse buying, though!

Wild bulbs

All bulbs originally came from the wild, and some were plundered so greedily that natural populations dwindled or died out altogether. Strict international regulations are now in force to prevent collection from the wild, although in many cases this has been limited to seeds rather than mature bulbs, but the practice continues. Make sure any you buy, especially rare and unusual species, come from cultivated stocks.

Many bulbs that are not available in the shops can be bought by mail order from specialist nurseries. Plant the bulbs as soon as possible after receiving them.

Bulb catalogues In addition to the usual familiar, popular kinds, bulb catalogues tend to sell many new plants that are not yet widely available; try specialist firms for less common species and rare varieties. Separate lists may be issued for autumn and spring planting.

Specialist societies These supply bulbs, both dormant and in growth, at their regular shows, and generally include rare or challenging genera and species; their annual seed lists may offer even more enticing or elusive kinds.

Other outlets Seed catalogues and high-street shops usually have a very limited selection, often at higher prices than elsewhere – you pay for the convenience of buying bulbs while purchasing other goods. Avoid discount stocks at the end of the season, as these may have dried out or died while trying to grow.

When to buy

Bulbs are available at various times of the year, according to their flowering time and their period of dormancy. For information on when to plant different types of bulbs, *see* the planting calendar on page 121.

Dry bulbs Most bulbs are supplied in a dry state in their dormant period. Buy and plant these as early as possible before they start into growth. Until then, keep them safe from damp, heat and light.

Moist bulbs A few bulbs, usually the shade-loving woodland types, are generally supplied packed in moist material such as bark, wood shavings or shredded paper when dormant. This applies to cyclamen, lilies, erythroniums, trilliums, and some anemones and fritillaries. It's important to ensure these are planted before they get the chance to dry out.

Pot-grown bulbs You can buy pots of bulbs in active growth, often in flower, at garden centres and nurseries. They can either be planted immediately, or kept in pots until they've flowered and planted out in the garden, usually at a greater depth than they are in the pot.

How to buy
Bulbs are available as mixtures or collections, or as single species or varieties (either loose or prepacked), which is often the best choice for group planting or as an ingredient of a carefully planned colour scheme.

Loose bulbs The most popular bulbs are often sold loose in bins or sacks. The advantage of these is you can select the exact quantity you need, it can be an economical way to buy large numbers of bulbs, and you can check their condition.

Prepacked bulbs Available in small quantities, these are ideal for containers or small beds, or if you just want to try something new. Make sure the bag has ventilation holes to prevent the contents from

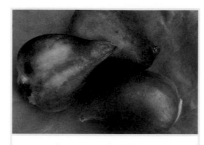
Tulip bulbs should be firm and plump, with no signs of growth.

rotting, and check the condition of the bulbs through the bag if possible. For very large quantities of bulbs – multiples of 100 perhaps, or if you're buying daffodils for naturalizing – it's cheaper to buy large sacks from a bulb wholesaler.

Mixtures Perfect for naturalizing, mixtures are a random, usually anonymous blend of varieties, colours or species.

Don't forget
Warn small children not to eat flower bulbs. Some can be harmful and others lethal, even in very small quantities. Colchicums, gloriosa tubers and lily-of-the-valley rhizomes are highly toxic, while daffodils, snowdrops, irises and scillas can cause stomach upsets if consumed.

Collections These contain several different types of bulbs that the supplier considers compatible in some way; each type is packaged and labelled separately.

What to look for
Check the quality of your bulbs when you buy them or accept delivery; damaged or unhealthy specimens are unlikely to recover and could spread trouble to others.

Healthy bulbs A sound bulb should be plump and solid, with a firm neck and no sign of growth other than a very short, thick shoot. Make sure it's clean, with a firm base and no new root growth, although 'root initials', which appear as tiny, white pimples, are acceptable. There should be no diseased tissues, splits or damaged scales in the outer tunic.

Poor bulbs Reject bulbs that are soft and spongy or light, dry and shrivelled. A soft neck or base plate, pale, spindly leaf growth and long, active roots are all tell-tale signs that the bulb has started active growth. In addition, avoid those that are showing obvious symptoms of pests or diseases (*see* pages 70–3).

Buying and planting bulbs 'in the green'

Snowdrops are notoriously difficult to grow from dry bulbs, and many don't revive after planting. For this reason they're often bought packed in moist material or, better still, 'in the green', as a potful of growing plants still in leaf. They should be planted immediately at the same depth, either as an intact group or carefully separated into single bulbs (*see* left). You can tell how deep to plant them by the change in colour of their stems, from green above ground to bleached yellow or white below. Some other small bulbs, especially wild cyclamen and the daintier alliums, are supplied and treated in the same way.

Bulb sizes
Bulbs are often available in a number of sizes. Generally, the largest bulbs tend to be more reliable than smaller ones, particularly in the first season, and will produce the best blooms. However, in the case of hyacinths the top-size bulbs (16–18cm/6½–7in upwards) are specially prepared for forcing indoors in bowls (*see* page 55) and produce heads that are too top-heavy for planting outdoors. For the latter, you should use smaller, untreated bulbs.

Tools and equipment

The tools needed for planting and looking after bulbs are very few and, with the exception of a traditional bulb planter, you are likely to own them already. If you're buying new tools, always buy the best-quality implements you can afford and make sure they're comfortable to use. If they're right for you, they can make tasks much more manageable and enjoyable.

A good trowel is useful for planting and moving bulbs. Some gardeners prefer the slimline type for planting.

Tools for soil preparation

To prepare the planting site you'll need a spade and a fork. These are also useful when naturalizing bulbs or planting in larger groups and drifts. Choose sturdy, well-balanced types that you can use comfortably, preferably with stainless-steel blades if you have to work sticky clay. A hoe is useful for removing annual weeds

Don't forget

Some bulbs can cause skin irritation in some people, so to be safe it's worth wearing gardening gloves when handling the following bulbs: alstroemerias, arums, hyacinths, irises, daffodils, ornithogalums, scillas and tulips.

before planting; use it only when the soil is dry. A garden rake (see below right) can also be a valuable levelling tool before and after planting.

Planting tools

The basic tool for planting bulbs in the ground and in containers is a trowel, ideally stainless steel (see left). You can buy special kinds with narrow blades annotated in inches or centimetres, which can be a great help for getting the planting depth right, but an ordinary trowel is just as effective. If you have to buy one, test whether you prefer a straight or cranked neck, check the handle fits your palm easily, and make sure the blade is securely attached to the handle with a metal ferrule.

Bulb planters

Some gardeners like to use a bulb planter, which is basically a metal tube with a serrated cutting edge at one end and a handle at the other. There are small hand-held planters (see above right), which you use by twisting the blade into the ground to remove a core of soil or turf, and long-handled versions, which you push into the ground with your foot. Sophisticated models are engraved with depths on the outside of the tube, which in some cases is split to open like jaws when squeezed to instantly release the plug of soil.

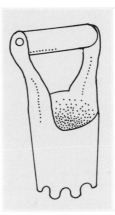

A hand-held bulb planter is pushed into the soil, removing a core of earth and leaving a planting hole for bulbs. It is a useful tool, but by no means vital.

Other equipment

In addition to digging and planting tools, you'll need some other items of equipment. You may want to pot up outdoor or indoor bulbs, including those for forcing, in which case you'll need some containers. Other items that are useful are stakes and wires for supporting weak-stemmed plants; secateurs or a garden knife for dead-heading; seed trays and small pots for propagation; and, for the true bulb enthusiast, possibly a bulb frame (see page 61).

A rake with a flat head is useful for levelling and firming the soil before and after planting.

Growing conditions

As ever in gardening, the rule of thumb is to put the right plant in the right place. The majority of bulbs hail from warm, dry climes, where soils are free-draining; some are from cool, moist woodland, with rich, peaty soil. Whatever their origins, it's important to give them similar conditions in your garden.

Aspect and climate

There are bulbs to suit all aspects and climates; it's really just a case of understanding the conditions in your garden and the needs of individual bulbs that you'd like to grow. When you're exploring bulbs outside the usual popular range, it's vital to check the plant's wild origins and pedigree, as this will give you some indication of its cultivation needs – whether it requires sun or prefers shade, for example. Narrowing your shortlist according to what you can provide will prevent a lot of disappointment. The A–Z directory (see pages 74–103) will help you to identify the cultivation needs of many bulbs.

Microclimates

The conditions are never the same in any two gardens, and even within one garden there will be several different microclimates – for example, areas where sunshine never penetrates or frost lingers longest, or perhaps where rain seldom gets through. Certain microclimates can be beneficial for some bulbs and harmful for others.

Don't forget

Most bulbs will usually flower well the first year after planting because they're supplied in peak condition, but don't expect a repeat performance every year. The conditions in your garden and regional weather patterns will affect performance and quality.

For example, early-morning sunshine after a frosty night can prove lethal to some species but will stimulate others to start growing. A fence or hedge can provide much-needed protection or unwelcome shade, while exposure to prevailing winds can supply either vital ventilation or deadly draughts. You may not be able to do much to change these conditions, but once identified they can be taken into account when you're planning which bulbs to buy and where to plant them.

Soil texture and pH

Type of soil is important, too. All bulbs need reasonably good drainage, even those from wet climates and streamside habitats, because constantly waterlogged soil is dangerous while they're dormant. Larger, taller bulbs like to root deeply and tend to suffer in shallow soils over hard bedrock.

The level of soil acidity can also be a key influence on a plant's ability to

Identifying your soil type

Before planting bulbs, your first step should be to find out what type of soil you have, as it will affect how well different plants grow. The five main types are shown here, but yours might not be clearly one or another. It's possible to have a mixture of soils, say peaty loam or chalky clay, or different types in one garden.

① Sandy soil feels gritty, like sand at the beach. Take a handful and it will feel light and pour out between your fingers rather than forming a ball, because it's loose-textured and usually dry.

② Clay soil feels heavy and sticky, and can be rolled into a smooth ball. It forms lumps when wet, and is hard and solid when dry.

③ Chalky soil is usually full of pale lumps of chalk, which crumble if you rub them together. The soil has a loose texture, making it easy to dig.

④ Loam is even-textured, feels soft and is a mid- to dark brown. It can be squeezed into a ball, but if it is rubbed it easily breaks into crumbs again.

⑤ Peat is very dark and open-textured, almost like a sponge. It holds on to water well, but can be rather crumbly and difficult to re-wet when it does dry out.

thrive: while many species of bulb are happy almost anywhere, others have a strong preference for acid or alkaline soil. For example, some varieties of lily and iris are acid-lovers, while *Anemone blanda* and fritillaries like chalky, alkaline soil. The best way to assess the soil pH is to buy a simple soil-testing kit from the garden centre.

There are some influences that can be amended – trees casting dense overhead shade can be thinned, for example, and drainage can be improved by installing a drainage system (*see* below), but unless the situation is really bad it's

rarely worthwhile trying to make major changes to the nature of your soil. A far more practical approach is to appreciate that your garden offers opportunities rather than problems, and only select bulbs that match its prevailing character and conditions. (*See also* Challenging sites, pages 104–11.)

Improving the soil

Unless you intend to plant in an existing, well-managed border or bed, the soil is likely to need some initial preparation to render it suitable for bulbs. The first priority is good drainage, in order to prevent any risk of the bulbs rotting during the winter months.

Light soils
Light or sandy soils are naturally porous, so there are rarely problems with drainage. However, they can lack nutrients. Dig in lots of well-rotted garden compost or leaf mould two or three weeks before planting. Even if the soil is fairly well drained, rockery and scree bulbs will appreciate additional coarse grit forked into the top 23–30cm (9–12in) of their planting sites.

Heavy soils
Heavy ground needs more improvement as the drainage will be poor. Dig or fork over the site two to three weeks before planting, and work in plenty of coarse grit or coarse sand (at least a bucketful per square metre/yard) plus some well-rotted garden compost.

Shady sites
Shade-loving bulbs that originate from woodland habitats like a rich, moist soil. Before planting, add plenty of leaf mould or well-rotted garden compost or manure. Acid-loving woodlanders particularly benefit from large quantities of leaf mould and peat substitute.

Improving drainage

If you have very poor drainage in your garden, or if there's an area where waterlogging is evident, you may have to install a simple soakaway system in order to grow some bulbs successfully. Excavate the poorly drained area to a depth of 35cm (14in) and spread a layer of rubble 15cm (6in) deep. On top of this add a layer of gravel or coarse sand 5cm (2in) deep, then replace the topsoil so that it is about 15cm (6in) deep all over.

Don't forget
If you want to grow a certain type of bulb but don't have the right conditions in your garden, don't despair – you can grow them in containers, or you may be able to create the ideal habitat in a greenhouse (see pages 64–5) or bulb frame (see page 61).

Adding good garden compost to the soil before planting will give your bulbs the best possible start.

Planting in the ground

There is something almost sacramental about burying these little packages of promise out of sight in the ground, confident that they're all set to grow and will almost certainly reward your simple efforts with glorious colour and form. And if you get the simple techniques right, planting them will be more than just an act of faith.

Preparing for planting

How you plant your bulbs will depend on whether you're planting single bulbs or groups of bulbs in a border, or are naturalizing bulbs in an area of grass.

Whichever method you use, always arrange the bulbs on the surface first, to check they're the right distance apart. When you're planting in groups and larger drifts, try to avoid obvious geometry, unless you're aiming for a strictly formal layout. A symmetrical pattern or a regimented outline is likely to completely ruin the impact, especially if gaps appear later on.

Planting depths

The standard advice when planting bulbs is to make sure they sit at the bottom of a hole that is two to three times as deep as the bulb's height, measured from basal plate to tip. Choose the deeper extreme when you're planting in well-drained, light soils, and the shallower depth for heavy ground.

There are always exceptions (some are mentioned in the A–Z directory, pages 74–103). Cyclamen and rhizomatous irises, for example, like to be near the surface. A few lilies, such as the Madonna lily (*Lilium candidum*), need burying no

more than 2.5cm (1in) deep, whereas most other lilies are stem-rooting and prefer to be at least 20cm (8in) deep. Sometimes shallowly planted bulbs, for instance crocuses and chionodoxas, adjust their depth by developing thick, contractile roots called 'droppers', which shrink and pull the bulb down to its correct position. On the other hand, if crocuses are planted too deep they may fail to flower.

Planting in soil

Just before planting, rake in a handful of blood, fish and bonemeal. Use a spade or, in the case of single bulbs, a trowel or bulb planter (never

Don't forget

There is plenty of scope to experiment with planting depths, especially in borders, where planting deeper than normal may well save you the misfortune of spearing bulbs with a fork as you dig over the ground.

Planting bulbs

There are different ways to plant bulbs depending on whether they're planted in groups or individually. Once you've dug the hole, test the depth is two to three times the height of the bulb. Remember to add fertilizer and grit if necessary.

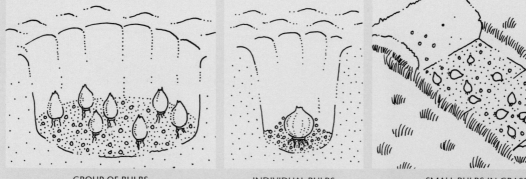

GROUP OF BULBS

Loosen the soil at the bottom of the hole. Arrange the bulbs evenly but informally, making sure they're the right distance apart.

INDIVIDUAL BULBS

Ensure the sides of the hole are vertical and the base flat. Push the bulb to the bottom.

SMALL BULBS IN GRASS

Fold back the turf flaps, loosen the exposed soil, excavating to the right depth, and arrange the bulbs randomly on the bottom.

a dibber) to dig out holes that are the right depth for the type of bulb and a few centimetres wider than the bulbs. You can take out a larger hole and plant in bigger groups if need be. On heavy ground, add a thin layer of grit or coarse sand.

Plant the bulbs as shown opposite. In heavy soil, trickle some more grit or sand around them. Break up any lumps in the excavated soil (adding grit or leaf mould if it is heavy), then trickle it carefully around the bulbs to prevent any movement. Refill the cavity, level the surface and tamp it lightly with a rake head.

Planting in grass

Before planting bulbs in grass (*see also* pages 23–5), cut the turf short to make the work easier, then scatter the bulbs randomly over the area to produce an irregular effect; adjust them only if they fall too closely together, but otherwise resist any impulse to organize them!

Plant large bulbs individually (*see* opposite, centre). Separate the turf from the plug of earth, and use this to cap the crumbled, replaced soil.

For smaller bulbs, use a spade to cut a large H-shape in the grass right through to the soil beneath. Open

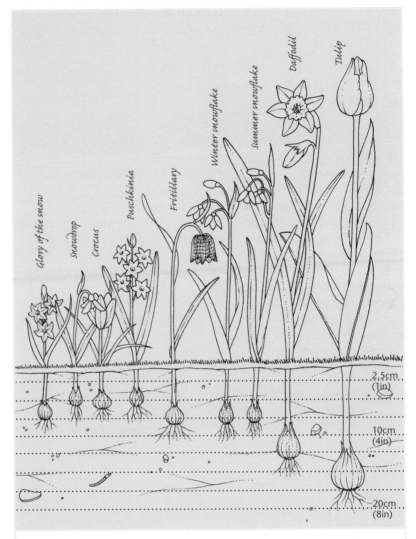

Bulbs are planted at different depths. The rule of thumb is to plant at a depth equal to two or, in light soils, three times the bulb's height. However, some bulbs do not follow this rule. Where relevant, this is noted in the A to Z Directory, pages 75–103.

Plant bulbs the right way up!

This might seem obvious with a tulip or hyacinth, but it can be hard to tell the top from the bottom of some corms and tubers. Some anemones look shrivelled and shapeless, for example, and you need to inspect cyclamen closely to spot their buds. Many bulbs still grow if planted upside down, but if in doubt compromise and plant them on their sides. Planting lilies on their side prevents water getting between their scales and causing rot.

the two turf flaps by slicing underneath with the spade and fold them back (*see* opposite, right). Plant the bulbs. Loosen the soil on the underside of the turf flaps, replace and tread firm. Alternatively, if you're planting very small bulbs such as

crocuses or fritillaries in grass and want a speckled effect, use a narrow-bladed trowel to make a hole for each one. On poor soils you can trickle compost and fertilizer into each hole before planting a bulb at the bottom and then refilling.

Although energetic growth and spread of bulbs may be acceptable or even desirable in a wild garden or when naturalized, bulbs that multiply or sprawl freely could compete for space in small gardens and formal planting schemes. Whether this becomes a problem usually depends on the context in which they're growing and how closely you supervise the plants.

The main culprits

Bulbs vary considerably in their territorial ambitions. There are some, such as *Crocus tommasinianus*, which soon begin to pop up cheekily all over the garden, but any unwelcome proliferation is easily controlled by weeding or cutting back. However, there are a few notorious bulbs that can become positively invasive. Possibly the worst culprits belong to the genera *Allium*, *Muscari*, *Oxalis* and *Ornithogalum*, although usually only a few varieties are misbehaved (*see* box, below right), while others can safely be planted anywhere in the garden. Both types of bluebell (the Spanish and the English kinds) seed themselves freely, but the robust Spanish bluebell (*Hyacinthoides hispanica*) can be a real thug, overwhelming its more demure English relative *Hyacinthoides non-scripta* (*see* left), and even crossing with it to produce unappealing hybrids.

Precautions

Be wary of potentially antisocial bulbs if they don't fit the style and structure of your garden, or at least site them carefully where they're not likely to cause problems in future years. Settle bulbs with creeping roots among strong neighbours or an impenetrable boundary, such as edging tiles, to restrain their spread. Never plant invasive bulbs such as grape hyacinths (*Muscari*) and ornithogalums near your lawn: the foliage could survive mowing for years, and you wouldn't be able to control them with herbicide. Divide mat-forming plants such as lily-of-the-valley (*Convallaria*) and montbretia (*Crocosmia*) every three or four years, or their tangled roots could become

Several lovely plants can spread too much for the tidy gardener.
① Lily-of-the-valley will spread to become a dense mat.
② The foliage of *Muscari* can become untidy and smother other plants.

too extensive and impenetrable to manage easily. Fork up seedlings of bulbs like bluebells and sisyrinchiums while still small.

Native bulbs such as bluebells (*Hyacinthoides non-scripta*) and ramsons (*Allium ursinum*) seed themselves lavishly.

Antisocial bulbs

Allium oleraceum	*Ornithogalum nutans*
Allium triquetrum	*Ornithogalum umbellatum*
Allium ursinum	
Allium vineale	*Oxalis acetosella*
Convallaria majalis 'Bordeaux'	*Oxalis oregana*
	Oxalis violacea
Crocosmia	*Schizostylis coccinea*
Hyacinthoides	
Muscari armeniacum	*Scilla bifolia*
Muscari botryoides	*Sisyrinchium graminoides*
Muscari neglectum	*Sisyrinchium striatum*

Don't forget

The most effective way to reduce the chances of invasion is to dead-head flowers after they have faded (see page 60). Never put unwanted bulbs on the compost heap – some bulbs can actually multiply in compost bins!

Planting in containers

A perfect example of the versatility of a bulb is the way most of them tolerate life in pots and other containers, at least for part of the year. As they flower so well, they are some of the most popular container subjects. Growing them in such confined spaces, away from conditions they're used to, may mean adjusting their soil type and their planting depth and distance.

Composts and additives

The big advantage of growing bulbs in containers is that you can tailor the compost mixture to suit any likes and dislikes. The type of compost you use depends on the type of bulb and, occasionally, the container. Mix in slow-release fertilizer at planting.

Loam-based compost Most bulbs, including those grown indoors, prefer a free-draining, loam-based compost (also called soil-based), such as John Innes No. 3. For even better drainage, blend this with one-quarter to one-third its volume of grit or coarse sand.

Loamless compost Bulbs from moist and woodland habitats, such as cyclamen and anemones, prefer a leafier, more organic medium such as loamless (soilless) compost, whether they're grown outdoors or indoors. However, the compost still needs to be well drained, so add extra grit for drainage, plus an equal amount of leaf mould or composted bark. To prevent the compost from drying out in dry weather, you can add water-absorbent crystals to the compost at planting time.

Bulb fibre For traditional indoor bulb bowls without drainage holes, you'll need special bulb fibre, which is a blend of organic materials with added charcoal to prevent sourness and waterlogging. Alternatively, you can mix your own from eight parts universal loamless potting compost and one part crushed charcoal.

Planting depths and distances

Ensure pots are sufficiently large to contain the bulbs at the correct planting depths and distances. After planting, top-dress the pot with horticultural grit.

Permanent displays Bulbs for permanent outdoor displays, such as lilies, need to be planted at the same depths and distances apart as they would need in the ground (*see* pages 50–1).

Seasonal displays Still aim for the correct depth, but the spacing can be reduced to a minimum of one bulb's width apart. After flowering, lift and plant the bulbs out in the ground.

When planting a mixture of bulbs (here, *Iris reticulata* and crocuses), plant the taller varieties in the centre or at the back of the pot.

Bulbs for forcing Bulbs for forcing indoors (*see* page 55) need at least 2.5cm (1in) of compost below the basal plate and a spacing of one bulb's width; their tips can be at surface level.

When planting a winter container, plant some spring bulbs first (here, tulips) to emerge through the compost and prolong the display.

Don't forget

Make sure all containers have adequate drainage holes at the base, unless you're using traditional bulb bowls planted with bulb fibre.

Planting spring bulbs

There is a huge range of bulbs suitable for eye-catching displays in spring. For maximum flower power you can choose at least three different types of bulb and plant them together in layers (*see* box, right). Either choose varieties that bloom simultaneously or, to provide several weeks of colour, select those that flower in succession for a long-lasting display.

It's vital to use a sufficiently large container to accommodate the different layers. A pot 30cm (12in) deep and wide (the minimum practical size) will hold seven to eight daffodils, the same number of tulips, and 15 to 18 crocuses.

When the display is over, separate the bulbs and plant in the garden.

Planting bulbs in layers

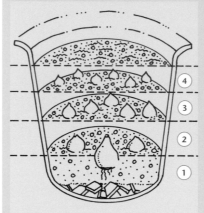

① Lay a piece of fine mesh or old tights over the drainage hole to deter vine weevils, then add crocks (broken flowerpots) or bits of polystyrene to aid drainage.

② Add an 8cm (3in) layer of moist, loam-based compost, then arrange the largest bulbs (tulips, for example) on this, without allowing them to touch each other or the sides of the container.

③ Cover the bulbs with more compost and add the next-largest bulbs (muscari or dwarf narcissi perhaps) between the lower bulbs. Repeat this process and plant the final layer of small bulbs (such as crocuses).

④ Cover these with compost so their tips are 5cm (2in) below the surface. Water well and keep in a frost-free place until buds show.

Pots of tulips can be plunged into gappy borders to provide a splash of colour in spring. Lift them after they've flowered so their leaves can die down somewhere out of sight.

Planting summer-flowering lilies

The secret of success when planting lilies is to use deeper-than-average containers, at least 30cm (12in) deep, with plenty of drainage material in the bottom topped with loam-based compost. Allow a minimum of 2.5cm (1in) space between each bulb and calculate how many to use per pot. A pot 23cm (9in) wide, for example, will comfortably take three turkscap lily bulbs, but the same number of larger, trumpet-shaped lilies will need a pot at least 30cm (12in) in diameter and depth. Like all soft-stemmed bulbs, lilies in pots benefit from staking at planting (*see* page 59). Keep the pot in a sheltered spot and, if planting in autumn, protect from excessive winter wet.

Don't forget

Spring-flowering bulbs left outside in containers are more vulnerable to frost than those buried in the ground. Always check hardiness, which can vary within a genus.

A bowl of hyacinth bulbs ready to bloom at the turn of the new year makes a lovely Christmas present, and there are many other bulbs that can also be coaxed into flowering early. Here's how to do it.

Bulbs are creatures of habit and if we want them to bloom at Christmas rather than spring we have to trick them into thinking their normal resting period is over, even though the natural cycle is being artificially speeded up. This is done by manipulating temperature so as to condense summer, winter and spring (warm–cold–warm) into a matter of weeks. Bulbs sold as specially 'treated' or 'prepared' will have been given that first warm period by the supplier, so for many bulbs – including crocuses, hyacinths, tulips and most daffodils – forcing starts with the cold period (an artificial winter), followed by a warm one, then an even warmer one.

Plan your forcing programme ahead: allow a total of 18–20 weeks before blooming for crocuses, 15–20 weeks for daffodils, 11–16 weeks for hyacinths and 17–23 weeks for tulips.

Hyacinths are understandably a favourite bulb for forcing.

Forcing timetable

Below is a chart showing the requirements needed for a forcing regime for crocuses, hyacinths, tulips and those varieties of daffodil that need cold treatment.

TIMING	WHAT TO DO	IDEAL TEMPERATURES
COLD PERIOD Crocus: 15 weeks Daffodils: 12–15 weeks Hyacinths: 8–11 weeks Tulips: 14–18 weeks	Store bulbs in dark conditions in a cold cupboard or in a black plastic bag in a shed, or plunge them in a cold frame or outdoors in the soil under a 10cm (4in) mulch to keep out light. Check occasionally that the compost is still moist.	2–9°C (35–48°F)
WARM PERIOD When shoots are 2.5–5cm (1–2in) high with flower buds just emerging All bulbs: 2–3 weeks	Bring them indoors for light and warmth. Keep them cool in a lightly shaded place while leaves green up and flower buds develop. Turn pots regularly to keep stems upright.	10–13°C (50–55°F)
WARMER PERIOD When flower buds first show colour All bulbs: 1–2 weeks, then throughout the flowering period	Move bulbs into a warmer, well-lit place to bloom.	Maximum 16–18°C (60–65°F); in higher temperatures their flowering time will be reduced
AFTER FLOWERING All bulbs	Strip off dead blooms but leave stalks intact and harden off for 1–2 weeks. Plant outside if conditions allow. Or, water and feed pots regularly until growth dies down naturally. Then clean and dry bulbs and store in a cool, dry place (see pages 62–3). Plant outdoors the following autumn.	5–10°C (40–50°F)

Don't mix varieties in the same pot as they will vary in forcing times. Start by planting top-size bulbs in pots or bowls (see page 53), then follow the instructions given in the chart (see left).

Other bulbs

Not all bulbs need cold treatment. Most daffodils need a cool period before forcing, but there are some that don't: *Narcissus papyraceus* ('Paper White'), 'Cheerfulness', 'Grand Soleil d'Or' and other Tazetta daffodils. Late spring- and summer-flowering bulbs, such as anemones, amaryllis (*Hippeastrum*), freesias and lily-of-the-valley (*Convallaria*), don't need a cool period either, and can be forced to flower early just by giving them heat.

Don't forget

Forcing is an exhausting process for plants, so don't use the same bulbs two years running. They can be planted out in the garden the following year, but the flowers will be smaller.

Looking after bulbs

Tending your bulbs is neither onerous nor time-consuming. Many of them can look after themselves completely, while a few might require special treatment at crucial stages in their life cycle. Provided the soil and situation suit their character, the majority need only basic attention to perform well, in most cases year after year.

To encourage daffodils to flower more freely next year, use blood, fish and bonemeal or a high-potash fertilizer as the flowers start to fade.

Once they have been safely planted below ground, bulbs are almost self-sufficient. With their storage tissues packed with food and their buds fully primed, all they have to do is to wait for the right conditions to send the signal to start growing. There's nobody to look after them in the wild, after all. However, many of the bulbs we like to grow come from climates that are often quite different from those prevailing in our gardens, and that's why we have to intervene occasionally – by watering, feeding, protecting from inclement weather, providing support and dividing overcrowded clumps.

Feeding

This is particularly important after flowering, when bulbs are working hard to recharge their food stores. Unless you're growing them for exhibition, bulbs planted outdoors need little or no feeding beyond a handful of fertilizer at planting time. It also pays to give them another sprinkling of blood, fish and bonemeal as the flowers go over, or to feed them with a high-potash

(potassium) liquid fertilizer. Organic mulch will add further nutrients as it decomposes. Never give nitrogen-rich feed to bulbs that are growing in grass, as it will stimulate stronger grass growth.

Feeding bulbs in containers

Even if you added a slow-release fertilizer at the planting stage (see pages 53–4), bulbs in containers need extra feeding, whether they're temporary or permanent residents. The nutrients in most standard composts last for about six weeks, after which you should give them a high-potash liquid feed every 10

Top-dressing containers

The structure of potting compost gradually deteriorates with use, so bulbs in containers will need repotting in fresh compost at the usual planting time – small pots annually and larger containers every second or third year. In non-repotting years, just scrape off the old surface compost down to the bulb-tips and replace with a fresh covering. Don't waste the discarded compost, because provided the bulbs were completely healthy it can be used for topping up a bulb frame, leavening heavy soil in preparation for planting, or for backfilling holes afterwards.

to 14 days until the growth dies down. Top-dressing (see box, below left) provides a fresh but limited supply of food in spring, which should be supplemented with regular liquid feeding after six weeks.

Watering

Rain that has been absorbed and stored in the soil over winter should be enough to satisfy spring bulbs growing outdoors in the ground, at least until they finish flowering. If drought sets in afterwards while they're recharging for next year, water them every 10 to 14 days, because their roots can take up nutrients only in solution.

Don't forget

There's no need to water bulbs that are dormant. Tulips in particular must have a dry rest after flowering, so don't leave them buried in containers of bedding likely to be regularly watered all summer; instead, lift and dry them after they die down, and store safely until late autumn (see pages 62–3).

Summer- and autumn-flowering bulbs should be watered in dry weather in the same way as other garden plants, making sure they have a really good soak every time rather than a superficial sprinkle.

Watering bulbs in containers

Bulbs in containers need more regular watering than those in the ground, so check every day or two in dry weather, testing to see if the compost is still moist about 5cm (2in) below the surface. Pay particular attention to bulbs in loamless (soilless) compost, which can be difficult to re-wet if allowed to dry out too much. You can reduce the need for frequent watering by adding water-absorbent crystals to the compost at potting time, or by plunging containers to their rims in a bulb frame (*see* page 61) or into the garden soil (*see* page 54).

Protecting from the elements

Since many bulbs in the garden are growing far from their home environment, they can't be expected to have natural tolerance of extreme conditions, and this is where a helping hand may be beneficial. For example, shade-loving species will have little resilience in a heatwave, the soft, lush foliage produced by plants stimulated by rich garden soil will be unable to withstand high winds, and alpine bulbs used to

being tucked up snugly under snow may succumb to a sudden hard frost or a cold, soggy spring. For bulbs outside the usual garden range, it's important to find out a plant's origin and the type of conditions it would experience in the wild. (*See also* Challenging sites, pages 104–11.)

Summer protection

Timely watering, shading and health checks should protect plants from the most obvious summer dangers, together with good, strong support in windy gardens (*see* page 110). Try arranging suitable companion plants to supply shade, shelter and support at critical times of the year, and perhaps to take over as the bulbs die down. Keep an eye on containers, monitoring them daily in extreme

conditions and, if necessary, changing their position.

Manage the bulb frame according to the contents – some plants will require shade and ventilation, while others need covering to ensure a hot, dry rest. Inspect all bulbs regularly for early pest and disease symptoms (*see* pages 70–3).

Unusually hot, sunny weather may cause some flowers to go over very quickly (tulips, for example, in a matter of days) and drain the colour from others – orange daffodils, such as *Narcissus* 'Professor Einstein', can bleach in a few hours. Take simple precautions in hot gardens: plant susceptible bulbs where they are shielded from midday sunshine, and move containers into shade at the hottest times of the day.

In hot weather, it's a good idea to group pots of bulbs, as larger ones can provide shade. Move vulnerable kinds out of midday sun if necessary.

A greenhouse provides excellent protection for plants in winter. You can stick bubble wrap on the glass for extra insulation in very cold weather.

Providing support

When growing in surroundings similar to their native habitat, bulbs are almost always self-supporting. However, in windy gardens weak-stemmed kinds, such as freesias, schizostylis and tricyrtis, can be dashed down, jeopardizing their appearance if not their welfare. In really wild weather, even more robust bulbs like lilies (*see* opposite) and camassias may be vulnerable to wind damage, while top-heavy varieties such as double tulips, dahlias and gladioli (*see* opposite) can collapse in wind or rain.

Don't forget

Strong wind doesn't just cause structural injury, it also dries soil and compost rapidly and dehydrates foliage faster than roots can absorb moisture. In exposed gardens, guard against water loss by permanently mulching bulbs, as well as shielding them with a windbreak or a screen of wind-resistant plants.

Winter protection

Frost and damp are the two main winter hazards, as bulbs can die in waterlogged or frozen soil. Mulching (*see* box, below) can protect hardy bulbs from both risks; make sure tender bulbs, such as begonias, dahlias and gladioli, are lifted, dried off or potted up, and tucked away in frost-free surroundings (*see* pages 62–3). Containers need extra care against the same twin threats, and moving them under cover to a greenhouse or into a bulb frame will protect against both; otherwise, make sure containers have immaculate drainage (or lay them on their sides in a wet season) and insulate them from frost by wrapping them in bubble wrap.

Mulching bulbs

Gravel mulch

Leaf-mould mulch

Slugs may feel safe under organic mulch and foraging blackbirds scatter the material everywhere. But, those minor disadvantages apart, mulching bulbs is wholly beneficial and can even save life. The winter foliage of *Amaryllis belladonna*, the tips of early crinum shoots and the surface bulbs of nerines are all vulnerable to frost unless covered with thick mulch until the weather warms up. Erythroniums, on the other hand, have contractile roots that pull them down safe from frost, but they welcome the cool, moist conditions created by a permanent mulch.

Suitable materials to use for mulch depend on its purpose and what you have to hand. Alpine bulbs and those needing immaculate drainage can be covered with a 5cm (2in) layer of grit or 6mm (¼in) gravel, while those preferring moist conditions are best covered with at least 8cm (3in) of garden compost, leaf mould, chipped or composted bark, bracken, straw or conifer prunings – the last two are ideal for protecting forced bulbs during their cold period outdoors. All mulches must be loose and porous to allow air and rain to penetrate.

A winter mulch should be carefully scraped off after the last hard frosts to allow the soil to warm up; permanent, organic mulches decompose (providing bulbs with a gentle supply of nutrients) and need topping up annually.

In most instances, the least conspicuous protection is supplied by appropriate neighbours. Shrubs can be used to screen and filter wind, and nearby herbaceous plants (even grass) can provide physical support for stems with their foliage. This is the most satisfying solution for climbing bulbs such as sandersonia and tropaeolums.

Where this is not possible, use wire plant hoops or canes and string; support groups with one or two canes in the centre and tie stems to these with figure-of-eight loops. Dahlias and gladioli grown for cut flowers usually need tying individually to strong canes or stakes while still small (*see* right). Double-flowered bulbs, for instance tulips, and daffodils are best grown in containers sheltered from wind. (*See also* page 110.)

Care after flowering

Although the whole point of planting bulbs is to encourage and enjoy their remarkable flower displays, it is important not to forget them once the drama is over. Giving you pleasure is of less concern to them than ensuring their own survival and the production of offspring, and these vital matters occupy their attention between flowering and (in most cases) winding down to their seasonal rest. You can help them and also increase the chances of more flowers next year by giving them some basic care during these crucial weeks.

The leaves

The first priority is always to protect bulb foliage until it dies down of its own accord, when its work is finished. Until then, leaves are still busy manufacturing energy and food materials that will be stored in the bulb to fuel next season's cycle. Feed and water as necessary to keep the process going strong, and never knot, shorten or cut off the leaves just because they're slightly dishevelled and uninteresting. If they look too untidy, plant obliging neighbours whose growth will conceal the leaves, or over-sow the bulbs before they flower with fast-growing annuals, such as cornflowers (*Centaurea*) or love-in-a-mist (*Nigella*, *see* right), to follow on. Don't mow naturalized bulbs in lawns until the leaves have withered.

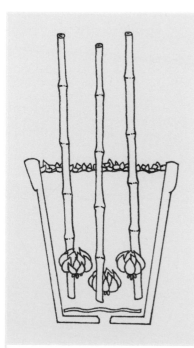

Tall, soft-stemmed plants, such as lilies, benefit from staking at planting, particularly in windy gardens.

A system of stakes and runner bean netting supports the flower spikes of *Gladiolus* 'Green Star'. Insert stakes when plants are about 15cm (6in) tall.

Love-in-a-mist, feverfew and sedum surround *Tulip linifolia* Batalinii Group; after the tulip has flowered, the other plants will hide its dying leaves.

Allium cristophii is one of several alliums to produce very attractive seedheads after flowering.

The flowers

Up to three-quarters of a plant's vigour can go into forming and ripening its seeds, so preventing these from developing is a valuable way to conserve and redirect its energy into replenishing its food store. Dead-heading immediately after flowering prevents unwelcome

When dead-heading daffodils, simply pull or cut off the faded flowers. The food produced by the stalk will be transported back into the bulb.

self-seeding (obviously you should leave seeds to mature if you want plants to spread more); it can also improve appearances by making the plants less conspicuous.

Large heads, such as those of tulips and daffodils (*see* below left), can be cut or pinched off, but leave the stalks intact. Dead-head galtonias, hyacinths and puschkinias by stripping the flowers from their spikes between your fingers.

A few bulbs, notably some of the larger alliums (*see* left), have decorative seedheads even after these have ripened and died. If you want to save seeds or retain seedheads (*see* page 63), select a few for this purpose and dead-head the others to prevent over-enthusiastic seeding in the garden.

The plants

Permanent bulbs in the ground should be left to die down naturally, and containers can be moved out of sight, if required, while this is in progress. Bulbs used for spring bedding, however, are often still green when follow-on batches of plants are ready to take their place. You can usually work around small bulbs like crocuses, but daffodils, hyacinths and tulips are likely to be in the way. Lift them carefully with a fork while the ground is moist (or water them first), and replant them at the same depth in a spare corner elsewhere in the garden. You can pack them fairly closely together in rows, but remember to label them and continue watering until their foliage finally dies down. Then lift, clean and dry them for storage (*see* pages 62–3).

Dividing plants

When grown in conditions where they're really happy, some plants multiply rapidly into congested clumps of bulbs or mats of rhizomes and need dividing regularly, on average about every three or four years. You can tell when the time is right: plants tend to produce a lot of leaves but fewer flowers, their vigour starts to decline and they overflow their allotted space. Any of these symptoms could be the cue to lift and divide them for replanting in fresh soil (*see* pages 66–7).

Bulbs that may need dividing

Albuca	Fritillaria
Allium	Hyacinthoides
Alstroemeria	Ipheion
Asphodelus	Iris
Belamcanda	Muscari
Camassia	Narcissus
Convallaria	Nerine
Crocosmia	Ornithogalum
Crocus	Schizostylis
Eranthis	Scilla

Uncommon bulbs

Always check to see if an unfamiliar species has any unusual requirements. This applies particularly to bulbs from specialized habitats such as more temperate parts of tropical regions. For example, haemanthus can be evergreen in mild gardens and should not then be denied water at any time; crinums like moist rooting conditions all year round (despite their South African origins); and the flower stems of some dietes are perennial and should not be cut off. In the wild, some less common irises rest after flowering, start growth with the autumn rains, rest again when there would normally be snow, and then revive in spring – so in cultivation they are kept under supervision in a bulb frame and given two dry periods, after flowering and in winter.

A bulb frame is an inexpensive and easily managed alternative to an alpine house or unheated greenhouse, for somewhere to protect bulbs while they are dormant or being forced. It also offers a sanctuary for more delicate or capricious kinds unlikely to do well in the garden. It's also a good place for propagating and growing on bulbs to flowering size.

What is a bulb frame?

Basically, it is a raised bed, devoted solely to bulbs. It has a glass-paned lid that can be opened or closed according to the weather. An ordinary cold frame on the ground can provide sufficient protection for some bulbs, but a covered raised bed is better, because bulbs are happier and less trouble to look after if they're planted or plunged in pots in a good depth of special free-draining soil mixture.

How to make a bulb frame

Either adapt an existing solid-sided cold frame or build your own with walls of brick, concrete blocks or stout, treated timber; it should be at least 60cm (2ft) deep with a clear, sloping glass lid (ideally in several independent panes or 'lights') that can be opened or removed easily.

How to use a bulb frame

Bulbs can be planted direct into the compost/grit mix – just for flowering or permanently – or you can temporarily plunge them in pots, up to their rims, while their flowers develop or during their resting period.

The important thing is to keep bulbs with similar requirements together so that they can all be ventilated or kept dry during growth or dormancy. With this kind of protection you can push on spring bulbs, such as crocuses and dwarf irises or narcissi, until they're ready to transfer indoors for flowering, and then cover them again from early summer until early autumn to ripen the bulbs fully. Frost-tender, summer-flowering bulbs that originate from warm, dry regions, on the other hand, need protecting against unwelcome wetness from autumn until spring.

A bulb frame is useful for plants that are fussy about their growing conditions.

① The early growth of the Chilean blue crocus (*Tecophilaea cyanocrocus*) needs protection from frost.

② The summer-flowering *Rhodohypoxis baurii* 'Douglas' dislikes winter wet.

Bulbs for a bulb frame

Almost all kinds of bulbs could benefit from frame protection, but avoid the more spreading varieties (*see* page 52). The most obvious candidates for a bulb frame are tender bulbs, those that are borderline hardy and any described in catalogues as 'difficult', which usually refers to a sensitivity to wet conditions at some stage in their annual cycle. Examples include anomathecas, brodiaeas and habranthus. Also try growing some of the smaller, less common bulb varieties.

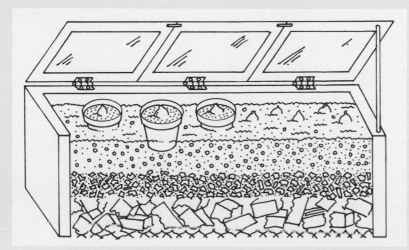

Spread chicken-wire over the base inside to keep out mice, then cover with a 15–23cm (6–9in) thick bed of broken bricks, stones or gravel, topped with 10–15cm (4–6in) of leaf mould or garden compost. Finish off with a 15–20cm (6–8in) layer of loam-based potting compost mixed with an extra 25 per cent by volume of coarse grit or 6mm (¼in) gravel.

Lifting and storing bulbs

There are several reasons for lifting and storing bulbs after flowering. Many varieties need to be stored in a dry, cool place over winter rather than being left in the cold, damp soil. Also, you may want to remove flowered bedding bulbs so that you can make room for other plants. Not all bulbs need lifting; many are happy left where they are – particularly bulbs that are naturalized in grass – and some indoor bulbs are best left in their pots without water when dormant.

Pack cleaned dahlia tubers in boxes of dry compost and vermiculite. Store in a dry, cool, frost-free place.

The procedure for storing bulbs varies according to the species. Many of the common bulbs are relatively straightforward to deal with (*see* opposite), but it's helpful to understand what's happening to the bulbs while they're resting, particularly if you're planning to store more unusual kinds.

Bulbs at rest

Bulbs are still functioning while at rest, gently consuming their food stocks, which is why they can't be stored indefinitely, unlike truly dormant seeds. Kept much past its normal planting time, a tulip or triteleia will go soft as it starts using up food in its outer layers, while corms and naked bulbs such as fritillaries shrivel and dry out. In the right conditions, many common kinds withstand storage over a single resting period – hyacinths all summer, for example, or gladioli over winter. But if they're left any longer they deplete their reserves, to the point of jeopardizing flowering and then ultimately life itself. For this reason, bulbs should be planted soon after buying, as they've already been stored for several weeks.

Lifting and storing

Whether you're digging up bulbs for storing over the summer or keeping them dry over winter, the procedure is the same.

When to lift outdoor bulbs

Wait until growth has turned yellow and died down, because leaves that are green are alive and functioning. Bedding bulbs that have flowered and are now in the way can be lifted and replanted elsewhere to finish their post-flowering phase before being stored.

In the case of begonias and dahlias, wait until the growth is first touched by frost in autumn, then trim back the stems to about 15cm (6in) before lifting.

When dahlia foliage has been blackened by the first frosts, trim back the stems and lift the tubers using a garden fork.

How to store outdoor bulbs

Once you've lifted the bulbs, you need to clean and dry them for storage (*see* right). Throw away any that show signs of disease (*see* pages 70–3), and as a precaution dust them with a sulphur-based fungicide before packing them away.

Use paper bags for storing bulbs, not plastic, as these won't provide ventilation and the bulbs will rot. Alternatively, you could layer them without touching each other in plastic boxes filled with vermiculite or a compost and vermiculite mix. Store the bulbs in a dry, cool place until the next planting season.

How to store bulbs in pots

Many bulbs grown in containers can be left in the compost until the usual planting time if they are kept completely dry during the dormant

HOW TO dry and store bulbs

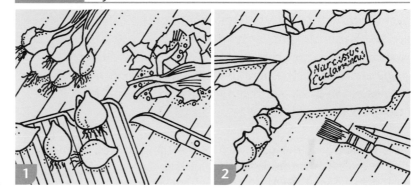

1 Discard any bulbs that are damaged or diseased, and then clean the soil, dead foliage and any loose, flaking skin from the sound bulbs. Spread them out on a wire-mesh or cake-cooling rack so they don't touch each other, and keep in a dry, airy place for a few days to finish drying.

2 Dust the bulbs with fungicide as a precaution against disease, and pack them in clean, labelled paper bags. Store them in a cool, dry, well-ventilated place, ideally at 5°C (40°F), for the rest of the season until it is time to plant them out in the garden again.

period. This group includes *Achimenes*, amaryllis (*Hippeastrum*), *Begonia sutherlandii*, *Dichelostemma* and tulips (*Tulipa*). A frost-free greenhouse is an ideal place to keep them (many gardeners keep them

under the greenhouse staging, laid on their sides). Alternatively, put them into a cold frame or plunge the pots to their rims in a bulb frame (*see* page 61), where they're protected from rain and frost.

More bulbs to store dry and well-ventilated

MUST LIFT FOR OVERWINTERING	CAN LIFT AFTER USE AS BEDDING
Eucomis	Allium
Freesia	Anemone
Gladiolus	Brodiaea
Haemanthus	Crocus
Ixia	Hyacinthus
Lachenalia	Iris (most)
Lycoris	Ixiolirion
Polianthes	Leucojum
Scadoxus	Muscari
Sparaxis	Narcissus
Triteleia	Scilla
Zephyranthes	Tulipa

Storing bulb seeds

Bulb seeds can be collected, stored and sown in the same way as seeds from any other plants. Wait until seedpods are fully ripe – they should dry out and turn brown or yellow; in the case of lily capsules, which hold vast numbers of flake-like seeds, this may take many weeks. Store the seedpods in a paper bag and hang it up in a dry, airy place until the seeds fall out. Discard the stalks and seedhead debris. Pack the seeds in labelled envelopes, film canisters or dark jars or bottles, and keep them cool and dry until you're ready to sow.

How long you can keep them depends on the type of bulb. Many ripened seeds stay in good condition for three to four years in a dry, dark place, or up to ten times that in a freezer. However, many members of the Amaryllidaceae family, including daffodils, amaryllis (*Hippeastrum*) and snowdrops, don't remain viable for long, and some gardeners prefer to sow all bulb seeds as soon as they're harvested and cleaned.

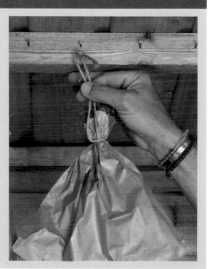

Don't forget

If you're storing a variety of bulbs, keep the bulbs separate and label them well to avoid confusing different species.

Caring for bulbs indoors

Hardy bulbs that grow outside and are brought indoors to flower have a very different care routine from tender species that live indoors as house plants all year round. The two types are planted in the same way (*see* pages 53–4), but vary in their planting times, their need for light, and their watering and feeding requirements. A greenhouse is useful for growing more tender bulbs, but is not essential.

Hardy bulbs

Some bulbs are encouraged to bloom early by a process known as forcing. Such bulbs have their own planting and care routine (*see* page 55).

For unforced bulbs, which will flower indoors at the same time as they would outdoors, plant bulbs in containers at the normal time, placing them close together and with their tips just below the surface. Leave the pots out in the garden in a sheltered place until the flower buds are almost ready to open, then bring them indoors to bloom. The indoor site should not be too warm and

should be bright but not in full sun. During their period of short but intense stardom, these bulbs need little more than regular watering and feeding (*see* pages 56–7). After flowering, treat the bulbs in the same way as you would forced bulbs.

Half-hardy and tropical species

Bulbs that have to be kept indoors permanently because they will not grow happily in the garden need more well-defined climate control all year round, which means getting to know the temperature, humidity and

The dwarf *Narcissus* 'Tête-à-tête' looks wonderful in the garden, but it can also be potted up and brought indoors for a lovely spring display.

The importance of light

Light – or, at certain times, its absence – is a vital influence on all plants because leaves use it to manufacture energy, while changes in the length of day and night trigger key stages in their growth cycles.

Plants grow irresistibly towards a light source, which is why flowering bulbs indoors need turning every day or so to prevent their stems bending towards the nearest window. Light intensity varies from room to room depending on which way a window faces, and bulbs need to be matched with their preferred amount of sunlight and shade.

Light levels within a room are always lower than they are outdoors (and often less than you might expect), and this can affect growth rate and health. As a rule of thumb, the amount of light reaching a plant diminishes by the square of its distance from the source – this means, for example, that doubling its distance away from a window reduces the light it receives to a quarter of what it was before.

Amaryllis (*Hippeastrum*) is one of the most popular indoor bulbs and flowers in spring. It needs a warm greenhouse or conservatory and a bright spot.

When bulbs are dormant, they can be transferred to a bulb frame or greenhouse, depending on the time of year.

Watering and feeding

The routine maintenance required for indoor bulbs is very similar to that of other house plants, but it's a little more complicated because you need to take into account the bulb's life cycle.

While actively growing, bulbs need watering whenever dry, but some plants have individual quirks which should be checked. For example, begonias are best allowed to dry almost completely before being placed in water to soak the rootball, and you need to ration water for evergreen clivias when their flower buds appear or these may not develop properly. Evergreen bulbs often welcome a refreshing break outdoors during a mild, showery summer's day, and usually need reduced watering in winter.

Unless they've just been repotted or top-dressed, feed bulbs regularly while in growth, using a high-potash, low-nitrogen fertilizer. And watch out for signs of house-plant pests and diseases (*see* page 73); they can strike at any time of year.

rainfall they would experience in their home territory. As always, get to know your plants.

Bear in mind that you may be growing bulbs from a range of diverse regions: caladiums, for example, are used to Mexican heat and humidity with lots of water in summer; Mediterranean species, such as *Cyclamen graecum* (*see* page 41), grow in spring and rest through the hot, dry summers; and South African lachenalias grow all winter and need to be kept cool in summer.

Many enthusiasts prefer to keep their house plants in a greenhouse or conservatory, with better light and higher humidity than in the home, and just bring the plants into the house as they come into bloom. If you choose this option, make sure that you can supply the right amount of heat for the different bulbs (*see* right). Alternatively, disperse the plants in particular rooms round the home according to their required temperature.

Temperature requirements for indoor bulbs

Greenhouses are usually described as being unheated, cool, warm or hot, and below is a chart showing the bulbs that benefit from their protection. Note: this is an approximate guide only, and not all the bulbs in the genus listed are tender. For further information on individual species, refer to the A–Z directory (*see* pages 74–103).

GREENHOUSE/CONSERVATORY TEMPERATURES REQUIRED	TYPE OF BULB
Unheated greenhouse or conservatory or a bulb frame	All hardy spring bulbs, those that overwinter outdoors in mild and/or dry areas, e.g. *Brodiaea, Cardiocrinum, Dracunculus, Homeria, Ipheion, Ixia, Ixiolirion, Lilium, Romulea, Roscoea, Tecophilaea, Tigridia* and *Tulipa*. Also, those that need to be kept dry during their summer dormant period, especially species from the Mediterranean, California and central Asia
Cool greenhouse – minimum 7°C/45°F during growing season	*Albuca, Amaryllis, Anomatheca, Bessera, Calochortus, Chlidanthus, Cyclamen, Dahlia, Dichelostemma, Dietes, Freesia, Gladiolus, Habranthus, Lachenalia, Leucocoryne, Lycoris, Nerine, Pancratium, Scilla, Sparaxis, Tritonia, Tropaeolum, Tulbaghia, Veltheimia, Watsonia, Zephyranthes*
Warm greenhouse – minimum 13°C/55°F during growing season	*Achimenes, Babiana, Canna, Clivia, Commelina, Crinum, Cypella, Cyrtanthus, Eucomis, Gloriosa, Haemanthus, Hippeastrum, Hymenocallis, Moraea, Ornithogalum, Polianthes, Sandersonia, Scadoxus, Sprekelia, Zantedeschia*
Hot greenhouse (stove greenhouse) or heated conservatory – minimum 18°C/65°F	*Caladium, Eucharis, Hedychium, Sinningia* and many rhizomatous, fancy-leaved begonias, as well as *Arum* and *Arisaema* species from tropical regions provided the atmosphere is sufficiently humid

Propagation

With so many bulbs available to buy, propagating your own might seem unnecessary, but most methods are really quite simple – and it's great fun to experiment. Dividing clumps that have spread underground and split into new bulbs (offsets) rapidly increases your stock, while sowing the seeds that some bulbs readily produce is the cheapest way of acquiring rarities. Some tubers, including dahlias and begonias, can be propagated by taking cuttings.

The time factor

Propagating is cheap and easy, but it does require patience. Many bulbs need a season or two to settle down after being disturbed, and it can sometimes be as much as four years before the offsets flower. Bulb seeds can take at least a year or more to germinate, plus a few more years to reach flowering size.

Division

Division is the usual, and the simplest, method of multiplying established clumps for rapid increase. It is also the regular treatment for overcrowding (*see* page 60). This occurs when the parent bulbs produce so many offsets underground that they lose vigour, producing prolific foliage but very few blooms (*see* Blindness, page 73).

The best time to split a large clump is just after growth dies down

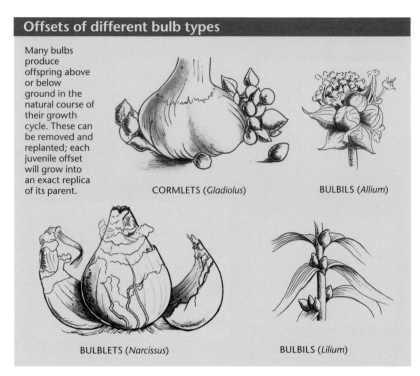

Offsets of different bulb types

Many bulbs produce offspring above or below ground in the natural course of their growth cycle. These can be removed and replanted; each juvenile offset will grow into an exact replica of its parent.

CORMLETS (*Gladiolus*)

BULBILS (*Allium*)

BULBLETS (*Narcissus*)

BULBILS (*Lilium*)

and the roots become inactive. Use a garden fork to lift the whole clump. You might need to delve deeply with some species, so take care not to damage the outer bulbs. Divide the bulbs into several smaller clumps by carefully teasing the roots apart with your hands (*see* page 114) or two hand forks; separate some of these into individual bulbs if you want plenty to replant. To make sure you catch any loose offsets, rest the clump on a ground sheet.

Pull off any dead leaves and roots, loose outer skin and shrivelled or

Bulbs to multiply by offsets

Allium	Iris
Alstroemeria	Leucojum
Arum	Lilium
Crinum	Muscari
Crocus	Narcissus
Fritillaria	Nerine
Galanthus	Ornithogalum
Gladiolus	Tulipa

Don't forget

Not all bulbs need (or tolerate) routine division. Many lilies will flower well for years from a single bulb (*Lilium pyrenaicum* and many American hybrids are notable exceptions), while *Amaryllis belladonna*, anthericums and cyclamen detest disturbance.

diseased bulbs. Then replant the new clumps at the appropriate depths and distances apart in a different site or in the same positions after refreshing the soil with a handful of blood, fish and bone.

You can position individual and immature bulbs between the replanted clumps, or grow them on elsewhere. Large offsets should flower the next year. Collect any very small ones for potting up.

Always replant divided bulbs immediately to prevent them drying out, adding fertilizer to the soil before you do so.

Taking offsets

Separating immature offsets and growing them on in pots or trays until they reach flowering size is a common method of propagating such bulbous plants as 'multi-nosed' daffodils, with a central parent bulb that has one or more offsets or 'bulblets' attached, and gladioli, with numerous 'cormlets' studding the root plate of the corm. A few bulbs, notably some calochortus and lily species, form aerial 'bulbils' at the base of their leaves, while in some alliums and lilies, bulbils replace flowers in the flowerhead.

All these immature bulbs are treated in the same way (*see* above), and usually reach flowering size in two to four years.

Speeding up the process

Various methods can be used to accelerate the production rate of bulblets and cormlets, which you then grow on like normal offsets. It is vital that you sterilize containers and tools, and dress all bulb wounds with a fungicide such as sulphur.

SCALING

Pull off individual scales of fritillaries or lilies (*see* right) and put them in a plastic bag with compost or vermiculite. Place them in a warm, shaded place or a propagator at 20–25°C (68–77°F). Within a few weeks they will form bulblets at their base.

CHIPPING

Cut bulbs from top to bottom into sections; each must include a bit of the basal plate. Soak in liquid fungicide before keeping in a thin plastic bag, with twice their volume of moist vermiculite, in a warm, dark place, ideally at 20°C (68°F). Bulblets should form after two to three months.

SCOOPING

Removing the inner part of the basal plate of bulbs that are reluctant to multiply, notably hyacinths, induces bulblets to form on the plate's outer ring. Using a teaspoon, scoop a hollow out of the base. Set bulbs upside down in a dish of sand in a warm, dry place while the cuts callus over. Then keep moist. Bulblets usually form after 12–14 weeks at 25°C (77°F).

FOR CHIPPING	FOR SCOOPING
Begonia (pre-sprouted)	Albuca
	Galanthus
Erythronium	Haemanthus
Fritillaria	Hippeastrum
Galanthus	Hyacinthus
Hippeastrum	Lachenalia
Hyacinthus	Leucojum
Iris	Muscari
Narcissus	Narcissus
Nerine	Nerine
Scilla	Scilla
Sternbergia	Sprekelia

HOW TO propagate from offsets

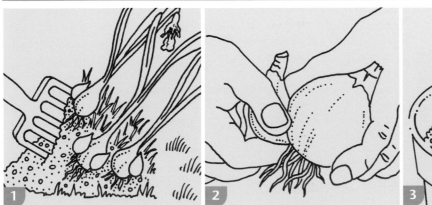
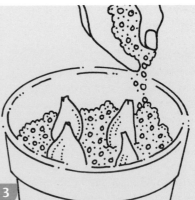

1 Dig up the parent bulbs with a fork while they are dormant or (in the case of gladioli) when the foliage is dying back. Gently shake or brush off any excess soil onto a sheet or tray.

2 Carefully pull offsets from the parent bulb, which can then be replanted (*see* Step 3) or dried for storage (*see* pages 62–3). Check the loose excess soil for any offsets you may have overlooked.

3 Plant offsets in pots or trays of moist, gritty potting compost immediately or in spring, about 2.5cm (1in) apart and deep. Grow on in an unheated greenhouse or bulb frame for 1–2 years before planting out.

Wait until tulip seedpods dry out and turn yellow before breaking them open to extract the seeds.

Sowing bulb seed

Growing from seed is the best way to introduce new bulbs to your collection. It is also the safest way to propagate new stock free from most diseases (other methods pass on the health status of the parent bulb).

Named varieties come true to type only if you multiply them by division (*see* pages 66–7) or by taking cuttings (*see* opposite), but it's worth having a go at sowing the seeds of any species or natural variant, usually listed as subsp. (subspecies) or f. (forma). Dwarf and miniature chionodoxas, crocuses, cyclamen, daffodils, snowdrops, sisyrinchiums and tulips are particularly easy.

Collecting seed

Keep an eye on the seedpods that form after the flowers die back. When these dry out and turn yellow or brown, break them open to extract the seeds or put them in a paper bag until the seeds fall out (*see* page 63). Sow seeds straight-away or store in paper bags in a cool, dark, dry place and sow the following spring.

How to sow seed

Fill a pan or a half-pot at least 9cm (3½in) across with fresh, loam-based (soil-based) seed compost mixed with half its volume of grit, perlite or very coarse sand. Level the surface and firm with a tamper. Sow the seeds evenly and thinly, aiming to space them 6–10mm (¼–½in) apart (do not overcrowd the seeds). Sift a fine covering of seed compost over the seeds, just enough to hide them from sight, and then top this with a layer of grit about 1cm (½in) deep. Water, and label the pot.

Keep the pot outside over winter, in a cold frame or a bulb frame (plunged to its rim), or in a shady place. Protect from mice by fitting a panel of wire mesh over the pot.

Bulbs to propagate by seed

Chionodoxa (dwarf and miniature)	Galanthus
	Narcissus
Crocus	Iris reticulata
Cyclamen	Sisyrinchium
Eranthis	Tulipa

Many modern bulb varieties are sterile, so a ripe crop of fertile tulip seeds is a treasure worth harvesting for sowing.

Cold treatment

Most seeds from hardy bulbs, especially spring-flowering kinds like daffodils and fritillaries, are programmed to wait until the kind of winter experienced in their native habitat has safely past. They use various stratagems to delay germination, such as a hard outer coat that needs freezing, soaking or bacterial action before water can penetrate it, while in some cases the dormant embryo isn't mature enough to grow until the spring. This is why bulb seeds are usually kept outdoors or in a cold frame after sowing. Those sown in spring or summer often don't emerge until after the first winter; if this is mild, it may take another year or two before seedlings appear.

Care of seedlings

Seedlings may take one, two or three years to appear, either because the seeds need more time to break their natural dormancy or (as happens with many lilies) because they're busy underground forming a tiny bulb. For this reason, never discard a pan of ungerminated bulb seeds before three years have past.

Once seedlings appear, move the pan into good light in a cold frame or greenhouse, and water and feed

Don't forget

Seeds of tender bulbs, such as sprekelia and amaryllis (*Hippeastrum*), are sown in the same way as hardy bulbs, but need to be kept indoors after sowing, usually at about 21°C (70°F). Once they've germinated, they can be moved to cooler (but frost-free) conditions.

them regularly until their top-growth dies down naturally; leave them alone from this point until growth reappears. Don't prick out the seedlings yet – it is usually better to transfer the whole contents into a larger pot after one year; plant this out in the garden, still intact, after a further year or two.

Taking cuttings from tubers and rhizomes

True bulbs and corms do not produce the kind of stems or leaves that can be used for cuttings, but many broad-leaved tubers and rhizomes, notably dahlias and begonias, can be propagated by taking soft-tip cuttings. You can also use the technique on several other plants, including *Achimenes*, *Commelina* and *Lachenalia*.

Although the method is not always foolproof, several cuttings can often be taken at once to bulk up stocks quickly. They will be exact replicas of their parents, and if taken early enough in the year will form their own good-size tubers for storing by the first autumn.

Start in spring or early summer by selecting strong, healthy shoots that are still green. Prepare the cuttings and pot them up as below; roots should appear in a few weeks, indicated by new growth from the growing-tip. You can then admit air and move the pot into good light. After a further two to four weeks, carefully empty out and separate the cuttings, and transfer them individually to 10cm (4in) pots.

Other ways to propagate dahlias and begonias

Another way to propagate begonias and dahlias is to take basal cuttings very early in the season, giving them more time to make flowering plants the same year. In late winter, tuck the tubers into a tray of potting compost; keep warm and moist by spraying regularly with water. Shoots will soon develop. When they are about 8cm (3in) long, slice them off with a sharp knife, complete with a small portion of the parent tuber (which can be potted up and planted at the usual time). Pot the shoots up in cutting compost and grow on in the same way as for soft-tip cuttings (*see* below).

Alternatively, dahlia tubers can be cut into sections and potted up in early spring (each section must have a bud). Similarly, begonia tubers can be cut into several pieces just as growth revives in spring (*see* Chipping, page 67).

HOW TO take soft-tip cuttings

1 In spring or early summer, remove strong, healthy, non-flowering shoots that are still soft and green from the plant that you wish to propagate. The cuttings should be up to about 10cm (4in) long.

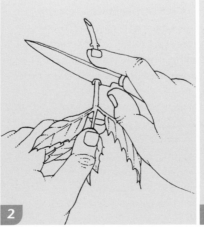

2 Cut off the lower leaves and cut the stem cleanly, with a sharp knife, just below a leaf joint, to leave a neat cutting about 5–8cm (2–3in) long. Insert cuttings round the edge of a pot of compost.

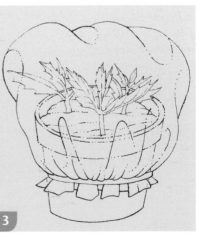

3 Water the pot and cover with a plastic bag to keep humidity high; alternatively, put it in a propagator. Check regularly and pot on when new growth indicates that the cuttings have rooted.

Plant problems and remedies

Bulbs are fortunately subject to fewer pests – and even fewer diseases – than the majority of garden plants. With one or two notable exceptions, problems tend to be specific to a particular genus rather than affecting all kinds alike, and sensible precautions can help to reduce the impact of some of these; a few are serious but uncommon. You can avoid a lot of trouble simply by making your plants comfortable, because happy bulbs are generally healthy bulbs.

Precautionary measures

Prevention is usually much easier than the cure and will avoid disappointing results.

■ Start by buying good-quality bulbs from a reputable supplier (make sure they're not collected from the wild, *see* page 45). They might cost more, but the extra pennies will buy you peace of mind.
■ Make sure the kind you choose matches the site and soil, as the wrong sort in the wrong place is a recipe for trouble (*see* pages 48–9).
■ Discard any soft or damaged bulbs, particularly when you come to replant after winter storage.
■ Make sure you plant bulbs correctly (*see* pages 50–4).
■ Take steps to deter obvious pests, for instance slugs and snails (*see* opposite), and mammals such as mice and squirrels (*see* pages 73 and 120). Also, protect bulbs against fungal rots by dusting dried bulbs with fungicide and storing them completely dry (*see* pages 62–3).
■ Protect borderline-hardy bulbs against frost – if injured by cold, they can be more vulnerable to other troubles.
■ Inspect growing bulbs regularly, as trouble is easier to resolve if spotted early and will be less likely to spread to other plants.

■ Encourage beneficial insects, for example ladybirds, hoverflies and lacewings, to your garden. They will feed on insect pests and keep populations down. Grow plants such as marigolds and sedums, which attract them, postpone the autumn tidy-up, so they can overwinter in your garden, and avoid using chemicals, which could harm them.

Using treatments

Even the most diligent gardeners will experience problems with bulbs and may need to resort to using a treatment. First, it's vital to identify the cause of the problem – whether it's a pest, disease or cultivation disorder – and ensure that you use the right course of treatment, otherwise it won't work and may do more harm than good. Always read and follow the manufacturer's instructions and precautions.

There are many organic treatments available, based on natural ingredients. The safest for the environment are thought to be insecticidal soap and similar fatty-acid sprays against most pests, and copper- or sulphur-based fungicides. Many gardeners find home-made remedies effective – garlic or rhubarb leaf sprays as pesticides, or bicarbonate of soda as a fungicide.

Common bulb pests

Aphids

These small, green or black, sap-sucking insects attack a range of bulbs. Colonies can live under the outer skins of crocus, gladiolus, lily and tulip bulbs, and later multiply rapidly on stems and buds, producing distorted growth. Their sugary secretions encourage sooty mould. As aphids are the main agents that spread virus diseases (*see* pages 72–3), especially on lilies, deal with them promptly.
Prevention and control Rub off light infestations with your thumb; grow plants that attract natural predators such as lacewings and hoverflies; as a last resort, spray serious outbreaks with insecticide.

Capsid bugs

Common green capsids will often congregate on the leaves, buds and flowers of dahlias, sucking the sap and producing ragged holes and distortion. There may be two generations per year, in early summer and again in early autumn.
Prevention and control The bugs are elusive and drop to the ground when they're disturbed, so they're hard to spot and hand-pick. As a last resort, spray plants with insecticide in spring and early summer, and again if symptoms reoccur.

Caterpillars

These are the familiar larvae of butterflies and moths, a few species of which can attack bulbs. The swift moth's caterpillar burrows into various bulbs,  corms and rhizomes, for example, while the Solomon's seal sawfly grub can completely defoliate plants.

Prevention and control Caterpillars on aerial parts are usually obvious, often betraying themselves by holes in the leaves, and can be squashed with finger and thumb. Soil-dwelling caterpillars are less easily dealt with, but keeping the soil clear and cultivated in borders deters moths from laying eggs. Forking over will expose them to birds.

Eelworms

These microscopic nematodes multiply and spread fast, and may attack bluebells, hyacinths, irises, daffodils, tulips 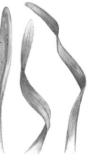 and snowdrops, causing twisted or streaked leaves. When the bulbs are dug up and cut open, the scales bear distinctive brown patches or rings.

Prevention and control Dig up and burn any infested or suspiciously soft bulbs, plus any bulbs growing within 1m (40in) of casualties. Don't plant any bulbs on affected ground for at least three years.

Lily beetles

These handsome, scarlet beetles and their reddish-yellow, hump-backed grubs, covered in slime and resembling bird droppings, can rapidly  defoliate lilies, fritillaries and sometimes Solomon's seal and lily-of-the-valley. Adults overwinter in the soil and emerge to lay their eggs in early spring.

Prevention and control Check plants regularly between mid-spring and early autumn, and remove and destroy any adults, larvae or eggs. As a last resort, spray plants with a contact insecticide when beetles or larvae are first seen in spring, and repeat if they reappear.

Mites

Bulb mites and bulb scale mites look like tiny, yellowish-white spiders, and cause yellowish-brown or red spots on the  scales and neck of dormant bulbs, especially in winter, followed by blotched leaves and rudimentary flower stems.

Prevention and control Badly affected bulbs should be destroyed; others can be cleaned up by immersing them in water at a constant temperature of 44°C (110°F) for an hour. Mites often target damaged tissue, so plant only intact bulbs and cultivate carefully round plants.

Narcissus bulb fly

Fat, white maggots burrow into the bulbs of amaryllis (*Hippeastrum*), daffodils, hyacinths, irises, scillas and snowdrops; the bulbs become 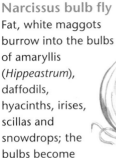 soft and spongy, and eventually rot from the base upwards.

Prevention and control Destroy any soft bulbs found at planting time. Use horticultural fleece to protect bulbs after flowering, during late spring and early summer when the fly is laying eggs. Plant bulbs in shady spots, since the flies prefer sunshine. The hot-water treatment (*see* Mites, left) can be effective.

Slugs and snails

These are perhaps the most destructive and universal pests, attacking bulbs below  ground, young shoots and even ageing leaves after flowering. They are particularly fond of dahlias, gladioli, lilies, daffodils and tulips.

Prevention and control You need to adopt a range of strategies. Protect bulbs at their most vulnerable stages – as seedlings and emerging shoots – with barriers of grit, copper or aluminium-based pellets. Hunt and hand-pick slugs and snails in the evening; catch them with traps and decoys; water only in the morning, so that the soil surface is dry by night-time; encourage natural predators such as frogs, hedgehogs and thrushes.

Thrips

Better known as 'thunder bugs' or 'harvest beetles', these insects can appear in huge numbers in a hot summer, and then feed on leaves and petals, leaving a tell-tale silvery mottling or streaking on susceptible plants such as cyclamen, gladioli and amaryllis (*Hippeastrum*).

Prevention and control Soapy water sprays are useful; as a last resort, spray plants with insecticide when their presence is first seen.

Vine weevils

The hard-shelled adults gnaw holes in leaves, while their grubs (creamy white with brown heads) feed underground on roots from late summer until spring. They are particularly troublesome on plants in containers, especially cyclamen.

Prevention and control Encourage predators such as birds, frogs and hedgehogs. Hunt adults at night and crush those you find. Check soil or compost for grubs when a bulb collapses or is lifted for drying off, and tubers before planting. Squash those you find, or water pots (as a precaution and as a treatment) with the biological control *Heterorhabditis*, outdoors in late spring and again in late summer, indoors any time when the compost is above 12°C (54°F).

Common bulb diseases
Grey mould (botrytis)

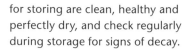

Perhaps the commonest and least discriminating bulb disease, this fungus can be very prevalent in a wet, humid season on anemones, snowdrops, lilies and tulips. First, brown speckles appear on the leaves, stems and flowers, followed by a fluffy mould.

Prevention and control Improving air circulation round plants can reduce attacks. Pick off and destroy affected leaves, buds and flowers. Fungicides may help to prevent infection, but they are usually ineffective once the fungus has entered the plant and become visible. Feed bulbs once growth resumes.

Rots

A number of rots affect bulbs, causing them to soften and decay, both during storage and while growing in wet conditions. Some, including narcissus smoulder or core rot of gladiolus corms, target specific genera; others, such as dry rot and basal rot, affect a range of bulbs.

Prevention and control In all cases prevention is better than control (which almost always involves destruction). Provide efficient drainage for growing plants, and never plant soft, mouldy or discoloured bulbs. Make sure bulbs for storing are clean, healthy and perfectly dry, and check regularly during storage for signs of decay.

Tulip fire

This serious fungal disease causes brownish lesions just under the bulb tunic which soon spread through the tissues, followed by black growths on the outside. Growing bulbs produce distorted leaves and withered shoots covered in grey mould in damp weather. Narcissus fire and hyacinth fire are similar diseases.

Prevention and control Take the same precautions as for Rots (*see left*). There is no effective remedy, so once tulips show signs of infection they must be dug up and destroyed. Soil-borne transmission is possible, so do not grow tulips in the same place for at least three years or problems may reoccur. Rotating bulb bedding round the garden helps ward off infection, as does delaying planting until late autumn.

Viruses

Bulb viruses account for some of the most serious plant diseases. There are many strains of virus, some very specific, for example iris mosaic, narcissus white streak and tulip necrosis. Exact identification is difficult, but most strains produce visual symptoms such as mottling, curling or streaking on leaves and flower stalks, distorted flowers and general unthriftiness. One virus causes colour breaks – darker or lighter streaks on petals – in the flowers of tulips (and occasionally lilies), but it is relatively harmless and may even be attractive.

Prevention and control Almost all viruses are incurable by any means other than removing and destroying the victim, as there are no viricidal sprays to treat infection. However, there are ways to try to prevent a virus from infecting a plant. Always buy healthy bulbs and watch out for symptoms. Most strains of virus are spread by aphids, so it's vital to keep them under control (*see* page 70).

Indoor bulb problems

When grown indoors, bulbs may become vulnerable to some pests and cultural disorders typical of indoor plants. Here are some of the commonest problems.

■ **Draughts** Cold draughts that sneak through cracks in window frames and doors can cause leaves to turn yellow, curl or fall off.

■ **Erratic watering** Over- and under-watering can turn leaves yellow or brown; flowers may fail to open or die in the bud. Bulbs rot in waterlogged compost.

■ **Poor light** Inadequate light (*see* page 64) causes yellow leaves and erratic flowering (or no flowers), long spindly stems or slow growth.

■ **Deformed flowers** If forced bulbs, such as hyacinths, are kept too warm during their cold period (*see* page 55) the flowers may be deformed.

■ **Mealy bugs** Waxy, white fluff hides colonies of tiny, sap-sucking insects at the base of leaves and around the necks of bulbs. Wipe off a small infestation with damp cotton-wool buds and use a biological control if necessary.

■ **Red spider mite** A common, minute pest where conditions are hot and dry, this produces yellow-speckled leaves and fine, white cobwebs between leaves and stems. Spray the undersides of leaves frequently with water and maintain high humidity in the greenhouse.

■ **Scale insects** These feed under small, white, yellow or brown discs stuck to stems and the underside of leaves, and can make plants sticky with honeydew, which encourages black sooty mould. Check leaves and wipe off small infestations with damp cotton-wool buds. Use a biological control in summer.

■ **Sciarid flies** (also known as fungus gnats or mushroom flies). Adult midges hop about on the surface of loamless composts while their larvae feed underground. They can be a particular problem in damp conditions, so avoid over-watering.

Mammals

At first sight, they might seem less sinister than microscopic mites or invisible viruses, but some larger creatures have a distinct taste for bulbs in some areas and can be a real threat. Mice and voles, for example, can decimate a collection of crocuses, rabbits love lily shoots, and squirrels take huge delight in freshly planted tulips. If you garden in country areas, badgers and deer may be additional local hazards. Unfortunately, trapping or exclusion is the only long-term remedy, although growing bulbs in containers securely topped with panels of wire mesh should defeat smaller rodents (*see* page 120).

Birds

Although calling them pests is unfair, there are various common garden birds that will selectively attack the flowers of garden bulbs, such as crocuses (*see* above), and will nibble and sometimes comprehensively shred their petals.

There is no effective treatment other than the acquisition of a cat. Black cotton strung from short sticks to 'net' crocuses simply gets entangled with the birds' legs and may injure them.

Blindness

True blindness in bulbs is non-flowering due to physical injury to the buds or flower stems from a pest, disease or extreme weather conditions. In these cases, the damage is usually visible and you can expect normal flowering to resume the following season. The term is also used, however, to describe a reluctance to flower because of overcrowding, and this tends to get worse year on year.

As bulbs spread into congested clumps, their roots exhaust the local food supply and are then unable to replenish the underground food store with enough nutrients to fuel future flowering. The remedy for this is to dig up and divide overcrowded bulbs, either when the signs of distress appear or routinely after three to four years, for replanting in fresh ground, after which they will bloom as normal (*see* pages 60 and 66–7).

Recommended bulbs

Bulbs and their allies – corms, tubers and rhizomes – form the most wonderful and varied group of plants on earth, and gardeners have always eagerly ransacked the huge natural treasure chest of wild species and countless varieties for their unique qualities. The pages that follow offer a mere sample of those available in bulb and seed catalogues. Some of them are well-known favourites, while others are possibly less familiar. All deserve to be widely grown. In most cases they are representative of much larger families and genera that will reward exploration.

A–Z directory

Bulbs listed here are a representative sample of this huge plant group, and you'll find a good choice for any position, purpose or season. Most are available from garden centres or bulb suppliers; some rhizomatous kinds also appear in catalogues of perennials.

Choosing bulbs

Weigh up the credentials of potential candidates (especially the drainage, aspect and temperature that they prefer) to ensure they're compatible with your chosen spot. Once you find a genus that suits your garden, expand your collection with closely related species and varieties. To explore other options, *see* Plants for a purpose, pages 42–3.

KEY to symbols

In this chapter the following symbols are used to indicate a plant's preferred growing conditions. A rough idea is also given as to what each plant's height (H) and spread (S) might be at maturity. *Unless otherwise specified, plants are fully hardy.*

- ○ Prefers/tolerates an open, sunny site
- ◐ Prefers/tolerates some shade
- ● Prefers/tolerates full shade
- ❄ Will survive winter in a sheltered site
- ❄ Always needs protection from frost
- 💧 Prefers/tolerates moist soil
- ◊ Prefers/tolerates dry soil
- ⇊ Needs well-drained soil
- pH↓ Needs/prefers acidic soil
- pH↑ Needs/prefers alkaline soil
- pH→ Needs/prefers neutral soil
- 🍂 Needs humus-rich soil
- ❖ Season of main interest (e.g. flowers, foliage, stems, berries)

Achimenes Hot water plant

◐ ❄ 💧 ❖ SUMMER to AUTUMN

H 25cm (10in) S 40cm (16in)

These classic Victorian house plants have velvety leaves and striking trumpets. Keep dry all winter, then repot rhizomes from late winter to late spring for a floral sequence. Good varieties: 'Ambroise Verschaffelt' (pale lavender, yellow throat, purple veins; shown above); 'Stan's Delight' (double vermilion).

Agapanthus African blue lily

○ ◊ ⇊ 🍂 ❖ MID- to LATE SUMMER

H 60–90cm (2–3ft) S 45cm (18in)

These striking plants form bold clumps of strap-like leaves (some evergreen) and showy trumpets in rich shades of blue or white. Mulch where winters fall below -5°C (23°F). Good varieties: *A. campanulatus* var. *albidus* (white); subsp. *patens* (pale blue; smaller, late flowering); *A.* Headbourne hybrids (white, light or dark blue; shown above).

Albuca

○ ❄ ⇊ pH→ ❖ LATE SPRING, EARLY SUMMER

H 10–60cm (4–24in) S 5–10cm (2–4in)

Albucas are charming bulbs for rockeries or scree in sheltered sunshine, or in loam-based compost under glass. Mulch outdoor bulbs over the winter; keep pots dry from late summer to early spring. Good varieties: *A. canadensis* (slim leaves; dainty, nodding, light yellow flowers); *A. humilis* (similar to *A. canadensis* but with cup-shaped, white flowers); *A. shawii* (tall, mid-yellow, fragrant flowers; shown above).

Allium caeruleum

○ ◊ ⇊ ❖ EARLY SUMMER

H 50cm (20in) S 2.5cm (1in)

Heads of densely packed stars appear in stunning, deep sky-blue, with a darker central stripe. Make sure it has a hot, dryish spot in a sunny rock garden or well-drained border, where the flowers will team well with cream pansies or cream-variegated ivies. Plant the bulbs 5cm (2in) apart in lavish groups. Other good blue alliums: *A. beesianum* (bright purplish blue); *A. cyaneum* (bright turquoise); *A. sikkimense* (rich deep blue).

Allium carinatum subsp. pulchellum Keeled garlic
○ ◊ ↓↓ 🍂❖ MID- to LATE SUMMER
H 45cm (18in) S 5cm (2in)

This grassy plant is almost evergreen and has loose heads of dainty, reddish-amethyst flowers. Grow with blue flowers and grey foliage. Plants self-seed happily without becoming invasive, and soon bulk up into drifts and threads among their neighbours. The graceful form f. *album* is one of the loveliest white alliums (also shown above).

Allium flavum Small yellow onion
○ ◊ ↓↓ 🍂❖ MID- to LATE SUMMER
H 15–30cm (6–12in) S 5cm (2in)

This is a variable species, blooming at different heights, with loose heads of up to 60 rich lemon-yellow, scented flowers with darker prominent stamens. The flowers face the sky at first and then trail casually downwards. Another yellow allium is *A. moly* (golden garlic), which is boisterous and bears lots of sparkling gold flowers in early summer; 'Jeannine' self-seeds less than other varieties.

Allium 'Globemaster'
○ ◊ ↓↓ ❖ EARLY to MIDSUMMER
H 90cm (3ft) S 20cm (8in)

A huge onion bred from the outrageous *A. giganteum*, 'Globemaster' has broad, robust leaves and magnificent, densely packed, 20cm (8in) spheres of long-lasting, intense violet-purple stars. Team it with forget-me-nots and white tulips in a border, or let it naturalize in a wild garden. Other eye-catching giants: 'Gladiator' (rosy purple; H 1.5m/5ft); 'Mont Blanc' (creamy white; H 60cm/2ft); 'Round and Purple' (deep mauve).

Amaryllis belladonna
Belladonna lily
○ ❄ ↓↓ 🍂❖ EARLY AUTUMN
H 75cm (30in) S 15cm (6in)

A. belladonna, not to be confused with the indoor amaryllis (*Hippeastrum, see* page 89), likes a hot summer baking followed by a good soak before the flower stems appear. These bear from six to ten pink, flaring trumpets with a fresh scent. Mulch if temperatures fall below -5°C (23°F), or grow under glass in large pots. Good varieties: 'Hathor' (white flowers, yellow throats); 'Johannesburg' (pale pink; free flowering).

Anemone blanda
○ ◊ ↓↓ pH+ 🍂❖ EARLY to MID-SPRING
H 15cm (6in) S 30cm (12in)

The earliest spring anemone, this species carpets the ground for between six and eight weeks in a range of cheerful colours. The tuber-like rhizomes naturalize well among primroses and dwarf daffodils in rock gardens and borders. Good varieties: 'Atrocaerulea' or 'Ingramii' (both deepest violet blue); 'Charmer' (clear pink); var. *rosea* 'Radar' (rich magenta, white eye); *A. b.* 'White Splendour' (white flowers, pink reverse).

Anemone coronaria
Poppy anemone
○ ◊ ↓↓ 🍂❖ LATE WINTER to EARLY AUTUMN
H up to 45cm (18in) S 15cm (6in)

With its 8cm (3in) flowers in bright shades of red, blue, mauve and white, this is a parent of the florists' strains sold as cut flowers. The De Caen Group bears single flowers. Good varieties: 'Die Braut' (white; shown above); 'Hollandia' (scarlet); 'Mister Fokker' (rich blue). The Saint Bridgid Group, a race of doubles or semi-doubles, includes 'Mount Everest' (white, green eye); 'The Admiral' (violet).

Anemone nemorosa
Wood anemone
◐ ● 🌢 🍂 ✣ EARLY to MID-SPRING
H 15cm (6in) S 30cm (12in)

The wood anemone has white flowers, often flushed with pink and mauve, and rhizomes that quickly spread in all but the driest soils. Plant them on their sides among arums, cyclamen, primroses and muscari. Good varieties: 'Blue Bonnet' (large, rich blue flowers); 'Robinsoniana' (lavender); 'Rosea' (pink buds, white flowers aging to deep pink).

Anthericum liliago
St Bernard's lily
○ 🌢 ↓↓ pH↓ ✣ LATE SPRING, EARLY SUMMER
H 60cm (2ft) S 30cm (12in)

Although very hardy, this alpine native benefits from a gravel mulch in winter; alternatively, plant the rhizomes in deep pots placed in a bulb frame. The species produces tall spikes of small, starry, white flowers; 'Major' (syn. *A. algeriense*) has larger, sweetly scented flowers with prominent golden anthers (H 90cm/3ft).

Arum creticum
○ ◐ ❄ ↓↓ 🍂 ✣ LATE SPRING, AUTUMN
H 45cm (18in) S 15cm (6in)

The glory of the arum race, this uniquely coloured Greek species needs warmth and sunshine; otherwise keep the tubers in deep pots under glass. With its glossy rich green, arrowhead leaves (appearing in autumn) and sweetly scented, lemon-yellow spathe surrounding a prominent central golden spadix, this is a star of the spring border or light woodland. Spikes of poisonous orange-red berries follow in autumn.

Anomatheca laxa
○ ◐ ❄ ↓↓ ✣ SUMMER
H 30cm (12in) S 5cm (2in)

A close South African freesia relative, this is a heat-loving species widely naturalized in the Isles of Scilly. In colder districts plant corms every spring and lift in autumn to keep dry over winter, or grow in pots under glass. Slender, arching stems carry up to 12 flat-faced trumpets in rich shades of carmine, flecked with maroon and all facing the same way. Var. *alba* is pure white with maroon spots.

Arisaema
◐ 🌢 ↓↓ pH↓ 🍂 ✣ EARLY SUMMER
H 30–60cm (12–24in) S 15cm (6in)

Arisaemas revel in cool, damp shade and look best with camassias, hostas and ferns. The 'flowers' are hooded spathes, the leaves and stems beautifully marked. Plant tubers at least 20cm (8in) deep and mulch every autumn. Good species: *A. candidissimum* (scented, white, pink- and green-veined spathes, shown above; orange berries); *A. erubescens* (slim, brownish-red spathes).

Arum italicum subsp. *italicum* 'Marmoratum' Marbled arum
○ ◐ ↓↓ 🍂 ✣ LATE SPRING
H 30cm (12in) S 15cm (6in)

This has bold, extravagant foliage from autumn until late spring. The pale yellow or greenish-white spathe is followed by a spike of poisonous vermilion berries. Other good varieties: subsp. *albispathum* (plain leaves; clear white spathe); subsp. *italicum* 'Tiny' (dwarf; neat, tiny leaves; H 15cm/6in); 'White Winter' (clear white marbling on the leaves; H 20cm/8in).

Asphodeline lutea
Yellow asphodel
○ ◊ ↕↕ 🍃 ❖ LATE SPRING
H 1.5m (5ft) S 30cm (12in)

This handsome species of Jacob's rod is a very hardy Mediterranean perennial with fleshy rhizomes that fatten into dense clusters in fertile soil. It produces long, furrowed, blue-green leaves and stout spires of closely packed, fragrant, bright yellow flowers that open after midday. 'Gelbkerze' (syn. 'Yellow Candle') has more conspicuous flowers.

Asphodelus albus White asphodel
○ ◊ ↕↕ 🍃 ❖ LATE SPRING
H 90cm (3ft) S 30cm (12in)

A yellow asphodel relative with similar rhizomes, this aristocrat of the spring border or wild garden has grassy foliage and striking, fat, white buds. These open to bright white, occasionally rose-pink, starry flowers with a green or deep-pink midvein on each petal. *A. aestivus* (H up to 2m/6ft) and *A. ramosus* (H 1.5m/5ft) are similar but semi-evergreen with multiple flower stems.

Babiana stricta Baboon flower
○ ❄ ◊ ↕↕ 🍃 ❖ EARLY SUMMER
H up to 30cm (12in) S 5cm (2in)

This is perfect for growing in pots of loam-based compost under glass. In mild areas it should survive in a sunny spot outdoors if planted at least 15cm (6in) deep or, where it is colder than -5°C (23°F), 25cm (10in) deep. Mulch over winter or lift the corms in autumn like gladioli. It is usually supplied as a mixture, with short spikes of fragrant, freesia-like flowers in brilliant shades of blue, creamy yellow, crimson and lilac.

Begonia (Non Stop Series)
◐ ❄ ◊ pH↓ 🍃 ❖ EARLY SUMMER to EARLY AUTUMN
H 20cm (8in) S 30cm (12in)

There are many attractive series of large-flowered bedding begonias (often classed as *Begonia × tuberhybrida*). This popular series is upright, compact and vigorous, with heart-shaped, fresh green foliage and a long display of 8cm (3in), fully double flowers in brilliant orange, pink, salmon, scarlet, white or yellow. Plant top-size tubers (5–6cm/2–2½in diameter) in pots in early spring and bed out after the last frost.

Begonia sutherlandii
◐ ❄ ◊ ↕↕ 🍃 ❖ SUMMER, EARLY AUTUMN
H 45cm (18in) S trailing to 75cm (30in)

Although usually grown in pots or baskets, this irresistible species is almost hardy and will grow outdoors until the first autumn frost. Small tubers produce slim, arching and branching red stems; deeply toothed, light green leaves veined in red; and pendent clusters of 2.5cm (1in) tangerine or orange-red single flowers. In late summer minute black bulbils appear in the leaf axils; collect these for planting in spring.

Belamcanda chinensis
Leopard lily
○ ◐ ◊ ↕↕ 🍃 ❖ SUMMER
H 75cm (30in) S 20cm (8in)

This showy Asian species, with creeping rhizomes and fans of iris-like leaves, does well in pots, borders and larger rock gardens. For several weeks, its stems bear wide-open, 5cm (2in) flowers in deep yellow or orange studded with red freckles. In autumn it produces seedpods that split to reveal black seeds. If these are sown the following spring, they will flower in their second year.

Bellevalia paradoxa
○ ◑ ‡‡ 🌿 ❖ MID-SPRING
H 30cm (12in) S 5cm (2in)

This looks like a robust grape hyacinth, and will self-seed in the same way when happy. Plant the bulbs 10cm (4in) deep, in drifts with primroses and cyclamen under deciduous shrubs and trees for a sumptuous spring display. The bell-like flowers in dense cones are blue-black with greenish-yellow rims and insides.

Brimeura amethystina
○ ◑ ‡‡ 🌿 ❖ LATE SPRING
H 25cm (10in) S 5cm (2in)

Daintier and less burly than bluebells, this close relative – sometimes known as the Spanish hyacinth – is a more suitable choice for rock gardens and gravel and scree beds. The bulbs produce thin, grassy leaves and slim, wiry stems loosely studded with up to 15, long-lasting, bright blue, indigo or white bells. 'Alba' is a fine, vigorous, pure white variety.

Bulbocodium vernum
○ ‡‡ 🌿 ❖ EARLY SPRING
H 8cm (3in) S 5cm (2in)

Although closely resembling an autumn crocus, this colchicum relative flowers in early spring, even late winter in bowls of bulb fibre. Each corm produces a single, large, goblet-shaped flower, usually pinkish purple, sometimes light mauve or white. As the flowers age, the broad petals open out and two or three slender, 15cm (6in) leaves follow. Plant in generous groups at the front of a border or naturalize in thin grass.

Bessera elegans Coral drops
○ ❄ ‡‡ ❖ EARLY AUTUMN
H 75cm (30in) S 5cm (2in)

This beautiful Mexican member of the lily family deserves to be better known for its pendent, brilliant orange-scarlet lanterns, ivory white inside with red veins. Up to a dozen open in sequence at the top of the tall, slim flower stem. Plant the slightly tender corms in the shelter of a warm, sunny wall and mulch deeply against frost, or grow them in pots of soil-based compost and keep completely dry while dormant.

Brodiaea californica
○ ◑ ❄ ◌‡‡ ❖ EARLY SUMMER
H 50cm (20in) S 8cm (3in)

This Californian plant revels in lighter, drier soils and makes an attractive display in gravel, thin grass or the dappled shade of deciduous trees. Up to 15 flowers appear just as the leaves die down, clustered like an allium or agapanthus in large, loose heads, in various shades of lilac, violet and lavender. Where temperatures fall below -5°C (23°F), mulch over winter or grow the corms in pots or a bulb frame.

Caladium bicolor Angel wings
◑ ◑ ● ❄ ◌ ‡‡ pH↓ 🌿 ❖ SPRING to AUTUMN
H up to 60cm (2ft) S 30cm (12in)

This tropical South American tuberous perennial is a magnificent foliage house plant, with large, arrow- or heart-shaped leaves splashed, marbled and veined in shades of red, pink, green, silver or white. Its 'flowers', 15cm (6in) greenish-white spathes, appear in spring. It needs a rest in winter, so keep tubers warm and almost dry from autumn, when leaves show signs of age, until they are repotted in early spring.

Calochortus venustus Cat's ears

○ ❄ ◌ ↕↕ ❖ EARLY SUMMER

H up to 45cm (18in) **S** 8cm (3in)

This is a showy tulip relative for warm, dry conditions; it is often better grown in pots of gritty, soil-based compost. Keep under glass to bake in the sun after flowering, and leave dry and undisturbed all winter. This extra care is rewarded by beautiful, 8cm (3in), white, yellow, purple or deep-red flowers, each with a complex contrasting centre. Bulbs may divide after flowering and need growing on for two years to flower again.

Canna hybrids

Canna lily, Indian shot

○ ◐ ❄ ◌ ◢ ❖ MIDSUMMER to EARLY AUTUMN

H up to 1.8m (6ft) **S** 50cm (20in)

These are rhizomatous plants, with big green, bronze or purple leaves, often with contrasting edges and stripes, and orchid-like flowers in dazzling shades of red and yellow. Varieties include: 'Golden Lucifer' (dwarf; rich yellow with red speckles); 'Striata' (orange with yellow-striped leaves); 'Wyoming' (orange with purple leaves; shown above).

Chionodoxa Glory of the snow

○ ↕↕ ◢ ❖ EARLY SPRING

H 15–30cm (6–12in) **S** 5cm (2in)

Chionodoxas are charming, irrepressible bulbs for planting in drifts. Commonest is *C. luciliae* (syn. *C. gigantea*; shown above), with soft violet-blue flowers, each with a small white eye, which last for up to a month; there are pink and pure white varieties. Don't confuse this with robust *C. forbesii*, with up to 12 intensely rich blue (sometimes violet or white) flowers per 25cm (10in) stem. *C. sardensis* is deep blue.

Camassia

○ ◐ ◌ ◢ ❖ LATE SPRING to EARLY SUMMER

H 60–75cm (24–30in) **S** 10cm (4in)

These stately North American bulbs bridge spring and summer displays, and make impressive clumps in damp, heavy ground. Plant at least 10cm (4in) deep; mulch in cold winters. Good species: *C. cusickii* (earliest to bloom; pale or deep blue; shown above); *C. leichtlinii* (blue, violet or creamy white; H 1.2m/ 4ft); *C. quamash* (syn. *C. esculenta*; bright blue or white, starry flowers).

Cardiocrinum giganteum

Giant lily

◐ ❄ ◌ ↕↕ pH↓ ◢ ❖ LATE SUMMER

H up to 4m (13ft) **S** 60cm (2ft)

This spectacular Himalayan woodland lily bears up to 20 downward-facing, white, very fragrant trumpets, striped maroon inside and green outside. Then the plant dies, leaving daughter bulbs to repeat the show three to five years later. The bulbs grow near the surface, so add a mulch at least 8cm (3in) deep to prevent frost forcing them out of the ground and damaging spring growth.

Chlidanthus fragrans

○ ❄ ↕↕ ◢ ❖ EARLY SUMMER

H 30cm (12in) **S** 15cm (6in)

This solitary, beautiful species from the Peruvian Andes only survives outdoors against a warm wall in frost-free gardens; elsewhere, dig up bulbs in autumn for storing cool and dry over winter. Alternatively, grow them under glass, three or four per 15cm (6in) pot, planted in spring with their noses just above the surface. Their intensely fragrant, golden-yellow trumpets are followed by long, grey-green leaves.

Clivia miniata

✳ ⬙⬙ 🍀 ❖ LATE WINTER to LATE SPRING

H 45cm (18in) **S** 30cm (12in)

This South African evergreen, grown as a house plant in cooler regions, has fans of robust, strap-shaped leaves and thick stems topped by heads of 12–20 funnel-shaped blooms in strong shades of cream, orange, scarlet or yellow. Keep plants pot bound and nearly dry until flower stems are growing strongly. Watering too early may result in mis-shapen blooms. Water and feed freely from flowering time until mid-autumn.

Codonopsis grey-wilsonii

◯ ◐ ⬙⬙ 🍀 ❖ LATE SUMMER, EARLY AUTUMN

H up to 2m (6ft)

Although thin and frail in appearance, this charming Chinese climber is hardy and easily grown in light soils sheltered from strong winds. Elongated tubers produce slender, twining stems that hoist themselves through neighbouring shrubs to reveal neat, 5cm (2in) wide, azure-blue or white flowers, nodding gently in the breeze.

Colchicum speciosum
Autumn crocus

◯ ◌ ⬙⬙ 🍀 ❖ EARLY to MID-AUTUMN

H 25cm (10in) **S** 10cm (4in)

Possibly the finest autumn-flowering colchicum, this is magnificent in every respect, with its goblet-shaped blooms, and in spring broad, 25cm (10in) leaves. It looks wonderful with silver or purple ground-cover plants. Good varieties: 'Album' (shown above); 'Atrorubens' (pinkish purple; red stems). *C. autumnale* (meadow saffron) is similar, but earlier to flower (late summer and early autumn).

Colchicum 'Waterlily'
Autumn crocus

◯ ◌ ⬙⬙ 🍀 ❖ EARLY AUTUMN

H 15cm (6in) **S** 10cm (4in)

This extravagant double variety has up to eight crowded heads of pinkish-lilac petals. Its weighty blooms, though, may collapse in heavy rain unless supported by ground-cover plants or naturalized in grass. Other popular varieties: 'Autumn Queen' (rose pink, white throats); 'Glory of Heemstede' (reddish purple); 'Rosy Dawn' (pinkish violet); 'The Giant' (robust; violet-purple; H 20cm/8in).

Commelina tuberosa Coelestis
Group Day flower

◯ ◐ ✳ ◌ ⬙⬙ ❖ LATE SUMMER to MID-AUTUMN

H 90cm (3ft) **S** 45cm (18in)

Commelina tuberosa is a plain, tender ground-cover plant 20cm (8in) high, while its hardier form, Coelestis Group (shown above), is quite different, with upright growth and spires of vivid blue (occasionally white) flowers grouped in green leafy bracts, each opening for a day. Mulch deeply in winter, or lift and store the tubers like dahlias.

Convallaria majalis
Lily-of-the-valley

◐ ◑ ◌ 🍀 ❖ LATE SPRING

H 23cm (9in) **S** 30cm (12in)

The neat, pendent flowers of this spreading rhizomatous perennial are renowned for their sweet, heady scent. Each arching stem can bear up to 15 waxy, pure white bells. The simple species is hard to beat. Good varieties: 'Bordeaux' and 'Géant de Fortin' (syn. 'Fortin's Giant') are taller (30cm/12in) with larger flowers; 'Flore Pleno' (double flowers); 'Hardwick Hall' and 'Variegata' (gold-striped leaves).

Corydalis solida
Fumitory
○ ◐ ◖ ♦ ↓↓ ❖ SPRING
H 25cm (10in) S 20cm (8in)

This is a typical rhizomatous fumitory, with ferny, grey-green leaves and dense spikes of spurred trumpets in shades of mauve, purple, pink or white. It is great for naturalizing under shrubs or in grass. Subsp. *solida* 'Beth Evans' has coral-pink flowers with white spurs, but the brightest variety is 'George Baker', with deep rosy-red flowers (shown above).

Crinum
○ ❄ ◖ ♦ ↓↓ 🍂 ❖ LATE SUMMER
H 60–90cm (2–3ft) S 15–30cm (6–12in)

Give these stately tropical bulbs a sheltered site with a lavish winter mulch, or keep them in large pots to move indoors in late autumn. Towering stems are topped with numerous, often sweetly scented blooms. *C. × powellii* (shown above) is the best for outdoors, with up to a dozen 10cm (4in) pink blooms; 'Album' is pure white. Allow lots of room, as the bulbs are 15cm (6in) across and the leaves long and untidy.

Crocosmia × crocosmiiflora
Montbretia
○ ◐ ◖ ♦ ↓↓ 🍂 ❖ MIDSUMMER to EARLY AUTUMN
H 60cm (2ft) S 23cm (9in)

The common montbretia produces late colour just when border displays can flag. In cold gardens its shallow corms may need a winter mulch, but elsewhere growth is vigorous, even invasive. It has shapely, sword-like leaves and striking, vivid orange flowers, dozens per arching stem. Lift and divide clumps every three or four years before overcrowding depresses flowering.

Crocosmia hybrids
○ ◐ ◖ ♦ ↓↓ 🍂 ❖ MIDSUMMER to EARLY AUTUMN
H 60–120cm (2–4ft) S 23–30cm (9–12in)

The many eye-catching hybrids tend to be slightly less hardy than common montbretia, so shelter them against a warm wall or under shrubs, and mulch in cold winters. Outstanding varieties: 'Emily McKenzie' (bright orange); 'Lucifer' (vermilion, upward-facing flowers); 'Late Lucifer' (flowers a month later); 'Solfatare' (apricot yellow; midsummer; shown above); 'Zambesi' (golden yellow with orange markings).

Crocus (large-flowered)
○ ◐ ◖ ↓↓ ❖ LATE WINTER to LATE SPRING
H 8–12cm (3–5in) S 5cm (2in)

These are all robust hybrids to naturalize or grow in generous, irregular drifts, where most multiply freely. Popular varieties include: 'Ard Schenk' (pure white); 'Blue Pearl' (lilac-blue and white with yellow throats); 'Flower Record' (light violet); 'Jeanne d'Arc' (white, purple base and feathering); 'Pickwick' (white with pale and dark lilac stripes). *C. ancyrensis* 'Golden Bunch' and *C. × luteus* 'Golden Yellow' (shown above) are brilliant rich yellow.

Crocus speciosus
○ ◐ ◖ ◊ ↓↓ ❖ EARLY to MID-AUTUMN
H 15cm (6in) S 5cm (2in)

This is a dramatic late-flowering crocus, each corm producing a single, tall, violet-blue flower with deep-blue veins and a startling orange stigma; the leaves appear after flowering has finished. The corms naturalize and self-seed readily throughout the garden. Good varieties: 'Albus' (pure white); 'Conqueror' (deep lavender blue); 'Oxonian' (violet).

Crocus tommasinianus
◯ ⬇⬇ ✧ LATE WINTER to EARLY SPRING
H 8cm (3in) S 2.5cm (1in)

The earliest crocus in bloom, this flowers and self-seeds readily anywhere in full sun. It has slender, grass-like foliage and one or two gold-centred, lilac or bluish-mauve flowers. Good varieties: 'Albus' (pure white); 'Barr's Purple' (silvery purple); 'Ruby Giant' (large; reddish purple; non-seeding); 'Whitewell Purple' (deep rich purple; spreads rapidly; shown above).

Cyclamen coum
◑ ● ◍ ◢ ✧ EARLY WINTER to EARLY SPRING
H 8cm (3in) S 10cm (4in)

This cyclamen is a winter-flowering treasure that blooms for several weeks. It is available in shades of red, pink or white, often with darker colouring at the mouth. The rounded, deep-green leaves appear with the flowers and last for many more weeks. Good forms include: subsp. *coum* f. *c.* Pewter Group (vigorous; leaves richly silvered); subsp. *c.* f. *pallidum* 'Album' (white, deep-pink mouth).

Cyclamen hederifolium
◑ ● ◍ ◢ ✧ LATE SUMMER to MID-AUTUMN
H 12cm (5in) S 15cm (6in)

This vigorous, late-flowering cyclamen often starts to bloom at summer's end, before its large, triangular- or heart-shaped leaves with silver patterns emerge. Flower colour ranges from white to rich magenta. Good varieties: var. *h.* f. *albiflorum* (white); 'Rosenteppich' (deep magenta pink); var. *h.* f. *hederifolium* 'Ruby Glow' (rosy purple; shown above); var. *h.* f. *h.* 'Silver Cloud' (pink; leaves wholly silver).

Cyclamen persicum (large-flowered)
◑ ❄ ⬇⬇ ✧ EARLY AUTUMN to LATE SPRING
H 10–30cm (4–12in) S 15–30cm (6–12in)

Florists' cyclamen, sold as house plants or winter bedding, range from hearty to miniature and even 'micro' specimens. Keep the corky tubers nearly dry for three months after flowering, then repot. Good varieties: Laser Series (large; nine colours); Midori Series (micro range); Miracle Series (miniature); 'Scentsation' (large; fragrant, pink or red); 'Victoria' (large; ruffled petals; white, cherry red).

Cypella herbertii
◯ ❄ ⬇⬇ ◢ ✧ SUMMER
H 30–45cm (12–18in) S 5cm (2in)

Grow this beautiful South American iris in a sunny spot or in pots of loam-based compost under glass. Bulbs produce a succession of curiously shaped flowers, each with three spreading 'claws' and ranging in colour from chrome yellow to apricot with purple stripes or spots. Keep dry while dormant.

Cyrtanthus elatus
Scarborough lily
◯ ❄ ⬇⬇ ◢ ✧ LATE SUMMER
H 45–60cm (18–24in) S 10cm (4in)

This elegant South African bulb, still commonly known as *Vallota*, is almost hardy in mild, sheltered gardens if protected with a generous winter mulch; otherwise grow under glass in pots of well-drained compost. Bulbs produce stout stems crowned with between six and nine immaculate, 8–10cm (3–4in) trumpets, usually brilliant scarlet – although 'Cream Beauty' and 'Pink Diamond' are attractive variants.

Dahlia 'Bishop of Llandaff'

○ ◑ ❄ ⬇⬇ 🍂 ❖ MIDSUMMER to MID-AUTUMN
H 90–120cm (3–4ft) S 60cm (2ft)

Possibly the most famous dahlia of recent years, this has fiery-red blooms and deep-purple, almost black foliage. Like all dahlias, it is easy from seed, producing subtle colour shades between amber and crimson; 'Bishop's Children' is a seed mixture derived from this variety, with a wider range of rich flower colours and the same dark leaves.

Dahlia hybrids

○ ◑ ❄ ⬇⬇ 🍂 ❖ MIDSUMMER to MID-AUTUMN
H 23cm–1.5m (9in–5ft) S 30–60cm (12–24in)

Dahlias come in every colour except blue and green. They are divided into groups according to their flower shape, which includes single daisies to collerette (a central group of tiny petals against a large outer ring) and various doubles including the short, vivid orange semi-cactus D. 'Ruskin Marigold' (shown above). Plant tubers in late spring and dig them up for drying and storing after frost has blackened their stems.

Dichelostemma ida-maia

Californian firecracker

○ ❄ ⬇⬇ ❖ EARLY SUMMER
H 30–45cm (12–18in) S 5cm (2in)

The firecracker is a truly cracking plant and makes an excellent cut flower. Its gracefully arching stems are crowned with numerous pendent, crimson (occasionally yellow) blooms, each tipped with a greenish-cream frill. The corms need a dry rest after flowering, so provide very good drainage or keep dormant plants in a bulb frame.

Dierama pulcherrimum

Wandflower

○ 💧 ⬇⬇ 🍂 ❖ LATE SUMMER
H 90cm–1.5m (3–5ft) S 60cm (2ft)

The long, slender stems of this semi-evergreen plant bow gracefully under the weight of their bell-shaped flowers, gathered in pendent tassels in shades of pink or purple, occasionally white, and look most dramatic arching over water. The corms multiply into dense clumps that prefer to be left undisturbed. Good varieties: var. album (white); 'Blackbird' (deep violet); and pink-flowered 'Slieve Donard' hybrids (shown above).

Dietes iridioides

○ ◑ ❄ 💧 ❖ MID-SPRING to EARLY SUMMER
H 45–60cm (18–24in) S 30cm (12in)

These African plants bear a long sequence of short-lived blooms, each an extravagant confection of white, yellow and lilac or pale blue. The rhizomes can survive -5°C (23°F) outdoors; otherwise, grow in pots of loam-based compost under glass. Flower stems are perennial and must not be cut back. Other species: D. bicolor (yellow and burnt orange; almost hardy; H 90cm/3ft); D. grandiflora (white; H 1.2m/4ft).

Dracunculus vulgaris

Dragon arum

○ ◑ ❄ 💧 ⬇⬇ 🍂 ❖ EARLY SUMMER
H up to 1.5m (5ft) S 60cm (2ft)

This is a fantastic but oddly compelling arum. Each tuber produces a thick, trunk-like stem and a fan of large, dark green leaves with purple-spotted stalks. The flower is an intriguing, slightly malodorous spathe, sometimes 90cm (3ft) long and rich maroon inside, greenish outside, with a sharp, nearly black central spadix. Plants look best in a wild or woodland setting.

Eranthis hyemalis Winter aconite
◯ ◗ ↕ ✿ MIDWINTER to EARLY SPRING
H 8cm (3in) S 5cm (2in)

These winter stalwarts quickly self-seed in bare ground to form carpets of shiny, bright yellow flowers set in ruffs of frilly green leaves. Buy plants 'in the green' or grow from seed. Cilicica Group has bolder flowers and bronzy foliage; Tubergenii Group is larger with very bronze, feathery foliage, especially in the form 'Guinea Gold'.

Eremurus Desert candle, Foxtail lily
◯ ◊ ↕ ✿ LATE SPRING to MIDSUMMER
H 90cm–2.5m (3–8ft) S 90–120cm (3–4ft)

These rhizomatous perennials are aristocrats of borders and wild gardens. The towering flower spikes, packed with yellow, pink, red or white stars, erupt above basal rosettes of leaves. They need very sharp drainage and cold winters to flower well. Reliable kinds: *E. himalaicus* (white; shown above); *E. × isabellinus*, especially 'Cleopatra' (deep orange); *E. robustus* (pink); *E. stenophyllus* (yellow).

Erythronium dens-canis
European dog's-tooth violet
◗ ◊ ↕ ✿ SPRING
H 10–15cm (4–6in) S 10cm (4in)

This charming woodland species has purple-mottled leaves and pendent flowers, wide open and starry, with petals turned sharply upwards. Never allow the bulbs to dry out of the ground completely. Good varieties: 'Frans Hals' (purple); 'Lilac Wonder' (lavender); 'Pink Perfection' (clear soft pink); 'Purple King' (plum-purple); 'Rose Queen' (deep pink); 'Snowflake' (pure white).

Erythronium 'Pagoda'
Dog's-tooth violet
◗ ◊ ↕ ✿ MID- to LATE SPRING
H 30cm (12in) S 15cm (6in)

This vigorous plant has large, sulphur-yellow blooms and glossy green leaves. It multiplies freely from offsets. Other good hybrids: 'Citronella' (clear yellow; mottled leaves); 'Jeanette Brickell' (white; free-flowering); 'Kondo' (lemon yellow, brown centres; mottled leaves). *E. californicum* 'White Beauty' and *E. revolutum* 'Rose Beauty' are also lovely.

Eucharis amazonica Amazon lily
◗ ✤ ↕ ✿ EARLY AUTUMN
H 50–60cm (20–24in) S 30cm (12in)

This choice bulb from the tropics has long been a greenhouse favourite. Up to eight, elegant, pure white flowers arch from the top of the sturdy stem to fill the room with their intense perfume. Grow in pots of loam-based compost, always above 10°C (50°F), and keep almost dry in winter. Eucharis can be misidentified: if yours blooms in early summer, it may not be a eucharis at all.

Eucomis Pineapple lily
◯ ❄ ◊ ↕ ✿ MID- to LATE SUMMER
H 15–75cm (6–30in) S 15–20cm (6–8in)

Eucomis is Greek for 'lovely hair', referring to the flowers' distinctive topknot of leaves. Protect from frost or lift in autumn, or treat as pot plants. Good forms: *E. bicolor* (green with maroon edges; shown above); *E. comosa* (white with purple markings); *E. c.* 'Sparkling Burgundy' (cream and purple); *E. pallidiflora* (greenish white); *E. vandermerwei* 'Octopus' (maroon flowers; chocolate-spotted leaves).

Freesia

○ ❄ ● ‼ ❖ LATE WINTER to LATE SUMMER
H 40–45cm (16–18in) S 5cm (2in)

The florists' freesia is a celebrated, intensely fragrant cut flower in a range of lovely shades and bicolours. Plant corms of large-flowered mixtures and varieties in a cool greenhouse from late summer until late winter for a succession of flowers. Special 'retarded' corms will flower outdoors in summer from a mid-spring planting. Freesias are easy to propagate from seed.

Fritillaria imperialis
Crown imperial

○ ◑ ‼ pH↑ 🌿 ❖ MID- to LATE SPRING
H 1.2–1.5m (4–5ft) S 25cm (10in)

The giant of the genus, with impressive stems topped with a whorl of between six and eight large, yellow, orange or red bells and a crown of green leafy bracts. Good varieties: 'Aureomarginata' (rusty orange; gold-edged leaves); 'Aurora' (bright orange red; shown above); 'Maxima Lutea' (bright butter yellow); 'Rubra' (large, bright red flowers).

Fritillaria meleagris
Snakeshead fritillary

○ ◑ ● pH↑ 🌿 ❖ MID-SPRING
H 25–30cm (10–12in) S 5–8cm (2–3in)

This is one of the easiest fritillaries, increasing steadily into clumps when happy. The species' small, fragile bulbs produce pure white or pink-and-purple-chequered bells. Fine varieties: 'Jupiter' (small, pale mauve flowers, darker check); 'Mars' (very large, rich purple, chequered flowers); var. *unicolor* subvar. *alba* 'Aphrodite' (large; gleaming white).

Fritillaria persica

○ ‼ pH↑ 🌿 ❖ MID-SPRING
H 60–120cm (2–4ft) S 30cm (12in)

This robust, variable species is best as the popular, reliable variety 'Adiyaman' (shown above), which has brooding damson-purple bells above a feathering of blue-grey leaves. This Turkish fritillary prefers a hot, sunny site where the bulbs are baked in summer. 'Ivory Bells' is a soft greyish-white variety.

Galanthus nivalis
Single common snowdrop

○ ◑ ● ‼ 🌿 ❖ LATE AUTUMN to MID-SPRING
H 10–25cm (4–10in) S 5–8cm (2–3in)

The best-known snowdrop in this large, popular genus is the easy, common single *G. nivalis*. Like all snowdrops, it is best planted 'in the green'. Other good single kinds: *G.* 'Atkinsii' (vigorous; early; large outer petals); *G. elwesii* (robust; broad leaves; fat blooms); *G. reginae-olgae* (autumn flowering; needs a dry, sheltered site); *G.* 'S. Arnott' (large; vigorous; honey-scented; shown above).

Galanthus nivalis f. pleniflorus 'Flore Pleno'
Double common snowdrop

◑ ● ‼ 🌿 ❖ LATE WINTER to EARLY SPRING
H and S 10cm (4in)

Double snowdrops might not have the simple grace of their single cousins but they make a greater impact, especially when naturalized. This double version of the common snowdrop is robust and spreads steadily from offsets. Other good doubles: 'Lady Elphinstone' (yellow staining on inner petals); 'Pusey Green Tip' (green tips on petals).

Galtonia candicans
Summer hyacinth
○ ◐ ♦ ↨↨ 🍂 ❖ LATE SUMMER
H 1.2m (4ft) S 10–15cm (4–6in)

Invaluable in the late-summer border, this bulb produces strong, imposing spires of drooping, greenish-white bells. Grow with agapanthus, dahlias and lilies for a stunning display that will help hide galtonia's untidy foliage. Plant the bulbs 15–20cm (6–8in) deep in small groups for maximum impact and leave undisturbed. 'Moonbeam' is a vigorous and handsome double variety, widely grown for cut flowers (H 2m/6ft).

Geranium tuberosum
○ ◐ ♦ ↨↨ 🍂 ❖ MID-SPRING to EARLY SUMMER
H 25cm (10in) S 30cm (12in)

This pretty, easy-going plant has attractive, deeply cut leaves that emerge in autumn, dying down again after flowering – plants are dormant in summer, so partner them with late annuals or silvery artemisias to prolong interest. The pinkish-purple, wide-open flowers are prettily notched and veined with crimson. Plants spread gently into satisfying clumps.

Gladiolus communis subsp. *byzantinus* Byzantine gladiolus
○ ❄ ◊ ↨↨ ❖ EARLY SUMMER
H 60–90cm (2–3ft) S 8cm (3in)

This elegant species is vigorous and easy to grow, rapidly spreading by its numerous cormlets in a warm, free-draining spot. Its arching, eye-catching flower spikes bear up to 20 funnel-shaped, deep-magenta flowers with paler streaks and blotches. The forms 'Albus' (fine white) and 'Ruber' (vivid cerise) are occasionally available.

Gladiolus (large-flowered hybrids)
○ ❀ ◊ ↨↨ ❖ MIDSUMMER to EARLY AUTUMN
H 1.2–1.8m (4–6ft) S 15cm (6in)

These gladioli from the Grandiflorus group supply bold, almost tropical glamour in every colour except blue. Taller kinds with giant blooms need staking up the lower half of flower spikes. Lovely varieties include: 'Amsterdam' (pure white); 'Black Jack' (deepest purple); 'Green Woodpecker' (lime yellow, red throat; shown above).

Gladiolus murielae
Abyssinian sword lily
○ ❀ ◊ ↨↨ ❖ LATE SUMMER to EARLY AUTUMN
H 1m (40in) S 8cm (3in)

Still better known as acidanthera, this is an East African gladiolus with a unique personality. The corms produce tall, arching stems with 10–12 sweetly scented, wide open stars, pure white with wine-red or purple throats. Planting is best left until late spring to avoid cold weather, or you can plant earlier in pots in frost-prone districts; lift, dry and store in autumn as for other gladioli.

Gladiolus (small-flowered hybrids)
○ ❀ ◊ ↨↨ ❖ EARLY SUMMER to LATE SUMMER
H 50cm–1.2m (20in–4ft) S 15cm (6in)

These have dainty flowers in a kaleidoscope of colours. Nanus group varieties have two or three slim spikes of loose blooms in early summer; Primulinus group are later, with one stem of up to 24 blooms. Good varieties: 'Amanda Mahy' (orange pink, violet lip); 'Bizar' (white, scarlet markings); 'Impressive' (rose pink, crimson markings; shown above); Leonore (butter yellow).

Gloriosa superba Glory lily

○ ◐ ❄ ↓↓ ❖ MIDSUMMER to EARLY AUTUMN

H up to 1.8m (6ft) S 30cm (12in)

This tropical climber needs 10°C (50°F), so plant the thin tubers under glass in pots of gritty, loam-based compost; in frost-free gardens try a warm, sunny, well-drained spot. Slender stems bear glossy, oval leaves tipped with tendrils. The large, exotic, red, purple or yellow flowers have crisped edges and spidery stamens. 'Rothschildiana' is scarlet with gold base and edges (shown above).

Haemanthus

○ ❄ ↓↓ ❖ EARLY AUTUMN

H 10–38cm (4–15in) S 15cm (6in)

These tender South African bulbs make excellent house and greenhouse plants. They are noted for their small but extraordinary brush-like 'flowers', dozens of which appear on each established plant. Reduce water after flowering, but don't dry off altogether in winter. Best species: *H. albiflos* (white); *H. coccineus* (Blood lily; coral or scarlet; shown above).

Hemerocallis lilioasphodelus

○ ◐ ♦ ↓↓ 🍂 ❖ EARLY SUMMER

H and S 90cm (3ft)

Most daylilies are border perennials with fleshy roots, but this is a true rhizomatous species and one of the best. Its 60cm (2ft) sword-like foliage is semi-evergreen, over-topped in early summer by slender flower spikes of 8–12 elegant, lemon-chrome blooms, 8cm (3in) long and strongly fragrant. Longer-lasting than most daylilies, each bloom stays open for 16 hours or more.

Habranthus

○ ❄ ❄ ♦ ↓↓ pH ❖ MIDSUMMER to EARLY AUTUMN

H 10–30cm (4–12in) S 5cm (2in)

These dainty South American bulbs may survive winter in paving cracks or at the base of sun-drenched walls; otherwise, grow in pots of loam-based compost. Plant in autumn, and dry off after plants die down. Each bulb bears a solitary red, pink or yellow trumpet. *H. tubispathus* (copper-orange flowers, yellow within) is the best for outdoors; *H. robustus* is larger and more vigorous (huge, soft-pink flowers; shown above).

Hedychium Ginger lily

○ ◐ ❄ ♦ ↓↓ 🍂 ❖ MIDSUMMER to EARLY AUTUMN

H 60cm–3m (2–10ft) S 60–90cm (2–3ft)

These exotic giants with fragrant flowers make superb dot plants in big pots or summer bedding for tropical schemes. Plant the fleshy rhizomes with their tips at the surface; water well in growth. Dry off after flowering. Popular species: *H. coccineum* (red, orange, pink or white); *H. coronarium* (white with yellow markings); *H. densiflorum* (orange or yellow; 'Assam Orange' is shown above).

Hermodactylus tuberosus

Widow iris

○ ♦ ↓↓ pH ❖ LATE WINTER, EARLY SPRING

H 30–40cm (12–16in) S 5cm (2in)

This iris relative has finger-like tubers that creep steadily into broad mats. It is noted for its subtle and unusual early flowers, mainly olive green in colour with velvety brownish-black or purple outer petals. They are very fragrant and popular for cutting. The leaves die down in summer, when plants need a long, hot baking to ensure good flowers the following year.

Hippeastrum Amaryllis

○ ❄ ↕↕ 🍂 ❖ LATE WINTER to LATE SPRING

H 45–60cm (18–24in) S 30cm (12in)

Amaryllis (*Hippeastrum*) are usually large-flowered hybrids that flower indoors and are not to be confused with *Amaryllis belladonna* (*see* page 76). Dry off in late summer and rest for three months; repot every three to four years. Good varieties: 'Apple Blossom' (white, pink tips); 'Red Lion' (vivid scarlet); *H. papilio* (orchid-like; yellow brushed with maroon); *H. picotee* (white, red-edged; shown above).

Homeria

○ ❄ ◐ ↕↕ 🍂 ❖ MID-SPRING to MIDSUMMER

H 15–60cm (6–24in) S 5–8cm (2–3in)

As natives of hot, sandy regions, these fragrant South African and Australian species need winter protection or pot culture. Plant corms in autumn and spring for a sequence of wide, pastel-coloured blooms. *H. collina* is the most familiar species, with gold or peachy flowers (shown above). Others include: *H. flaccida* (peach with gold centres); *H. ochroleuca* (pale yellow and orange).

Hyacinthoides Bluebell

◐ ◐ ❖ 🍂 ❖ MID- to LATE SPRING

H 15–50cm (6–20in) S 8cm (3in)

The native English bluebell *H. non-scripta* (shown above) is the most graceful of the three main species, with violet-blue (sometimes white), slender bells on one side of arching stems. *H. hispanica*, the taller Spanish bluebell, has blue, white or pink bells all round its upright stems; be careful – if given a chance, it hybridizes with our own species, threatening its survival in our woodlands. Diminutive *H. italica* is different, with packed heads of lightly scented, upward-facing stars.

Hyacinthus orientalis (large-flowered) Hyacinth

○ ◐ ↕↕ 🍂 ❖ EARLY WINTER to MID-SPRING

H 20–30cm (8–12in) S 8cm (3in)

Varieties have large, single or double fragrant flowers packed in showy spikes. Pick top-size (15cm/6in) bulbs to grow indoors, smaller for the garden. Good varieties: 'Anna Marie' (soft pink); 'Blue Pearl' (rich blue); 'Carnegie' (white; shown above); 'City of Haarlem' (primrose yellow); 'Delft Blue' (soft blue); 'Gipsy Queen' (apricot orange); 'Jan Bos' (cerise); 'Woodstock' (purple).

Hyacinthus orientalis (multi-flowered) Roman hyacinth

○ ◐ ↕↕ 🍂 ❖ EARLY SPRING

H 30cm (12in) S 10cm (4in)

These prolific varieties, once called French or Multiflora hyacinths, have large multiple bulbs that produce up to a dozen stems, each with a loose, bushy spike of fragrant and long-lasting flowers. They are usually sold by colour (blue, pink or white), singly or as a mixture; the 'Festival' strain is a superior selection.

Hymenocallis × *festalis* Spider lily

○ ◐ ❄ ◐ ↕↕ 🍂 ❖ EARLY to MIDSUMMER

H 75cm (30in) S 30cm (12in)

This semi-evergreen has five or six huge blooms like white, spidery daffodils and a sweet fragrance. The bulbs are best planted in autumn in large pots of gritty compost, although in warm, sheltered gardens they may be planted 12–15cm (5–6in) deep outside in spring to flower in late summer; mulch over winter or lift in late autumn for storing indoors. *H.* 'Sulphur Queen' is creamy yellow with darker, green-striped centres (H 60cm/2ft).

Ipheion uniflorum
Spring starflower
○ ❄ ◊ ⅱ ➡ 🍂 ❖ EARLY to MID-SPRING
H 12–15cm (5–6in) S 5–8cm (2–3in)

These cheery bulbs from South America do best in a sunny rock garden or at the foot of a warm wall. The species (shown above) has several slender stems holding fragrant stars, generally silvery blue with darker midveins. Good varieties: 'Album' (larger white flowers); 'Charlotte Bishop' (lilac pink); 'Froyle Mill' (deep violet); 'Wisley Blue' (pale lilac blue, deeper tips).

Iris (Bearded)
○ ⅱ pH↓ pH➡ 🍂 ❖ MID-SPRING to EARLY SUMMER
H 10–75cm (4–30in) S 15–40cm (6–16in)

The sun-loving Bearded irises are truly glorious. All have spreading surface rhizomes and elaborate flowers, ranging from early miniatures and dwarfs to the many gorgeous tall varieties, flowering last, in early summer. Good varieties include: 'Curlew' (soft yellow); 'Gingerbread Man' (brown and purple); 'Night Owl' (deep purple, shown above).

Iris ensata (Beardless)
Japanese water iris
○ ◊ pH↓ 🍂 ❖ MIDSUMMER
H 90cm (3ft) S 45–60cm (18–24in)

Beardless irises are mainly forms of violet-blue *I. sibirica* (Siberian iris) and the even lovelier, reddish-purple *I. ensata*. These revel in boggy, acid soil. Good varieties of *I. ensata*: 'Flying Tiger' (pale mauve, veined purple; shown above); 'Moonlight Waves' (white, lime-green centres); 'The Great Mogul' (purple-black); 'Variegata' (purple; leaves striped white).

Iris reticulata
○ ◊ ⅱ ❖ LATE WINTER to EARLY SPRING
H 8–15cm (3–6in) S 5cm (2in)

This is the most familiar of the dwarf bulbous irises, often called Reticulata Group from the netted tunic enclosing the bulbs. The species, often supplied as mixed seedlings, has fragrant, violet-blue or purple flowers with yellow-crested midribs. Good varieties: 'Cantab' (pale blue, yellow crest); 'George' (rich purple); 'J.S. Dijt' (rich red-purple, gold crest); 'Joyce' (deep sky blue); 'Katharine Hodgkin' (soft blue, darker veins, yellow crest; shown above).

Iris unguicularis (Beardless)
Algerian iris
○ ◊ ⅱ pH↑ ❖ LATE AUTUMN to EARLY SPRING
H and S 30cm (12in)

A few fragrant blooms appear in autumn (especially after a hot, dry summer) on this vigorous iris, but the majority open from midwinter on. These are pale lavender with deeper veins and a central yellow band on each fall. Good varieties: 'Mary Barnard' (intense violet purple; tidy foliage); 'Oxford Dwarf' (deep blue, purple veins, orange band; H 10cm/4in).

Ixia species Corn lily
○ ❄ ⅱ 🍂 ❖ LATE SPRING to EARLY SUMMER
H 45–60cm (18–24in) S 5–8cm (2–3in)

Ixia species are slightly more frost-sensitive than hybrids, but grow well in pots. With tall, wiry stems and long-lasting blooms with extraordinary colouring, they are perfect for cutting. Good species include: *I. maculata* (orange, deep-purple centres); *I. paniculata* (creamy pink or yellow, tinged with red; H up to 90cm/3ft); *I. viridiflora* (star-shaped, soft sea-green flowers with deep-red centres; shown above).

Ixia hybrids Corn lily

○ ❄ ‖ 🍂 ❖ LATE SPRING to LATE SUMMER

H 40–50cm (16–20in) S 5–8cm (2–3in)

Ixias are exuberant and inexpensive plants that tend to revert to their South African internal clock and try to grow in winter, so lift them when the leaves and flowers die down in autumn or pot them up in autumn for spring and summer blooms indoors. Although often bought as a mixture, individual varieties are available, including: 'Blue Bird' (white, purple veins and centre; shown above); 'Venus' (magenta, purple eye); 'Vulcan' (orange and red).

Ixiolirion tataricum

○ ❄ ‖ 🍂 ❖ LATE SPRING, EARLY SUMMER

H 30–40cm (12–16in) S 5cm (2in)

These bulbs come from rocky hillsides in Central Asia where hot summers and fast drainage prevail, so plant them at the foot of a warm wall or in gravelly scree; otherwise, grow in pots under glass and keep dry while dormant. This is the only species normally available, with grassy leaves and blue or violet-blue reflexed trumpets; Ledebourii Group has bright violet blooms.

Lachenalia Cape cowslip

○ ❄ ‖ ❖ EARLY WINTER to MID-SPRING

H 8–45cm (3–18in) S 5cm (2in)

Once popular but now mysteriously neglected, lachenalias can be easily grown indoors where their crowded spikes of tubular blooms last for up to two months. The late winter-flowering *L. aloides* (shown above) is the usual species, with purple-spotted leaves and flowers in vibrant yellows. Good varieties: var. *luteola* (bright yellow); var. *quadricolor* (scarlet, apricot, gold); var. *vanzyliae* (grey, white and olive green).

Leucocoryne

○ ❄ 💧 ‖ ❖ MID-SPRING to EARLY SUMMER

H 45–50cm (18–20in) S 8cm (3in)

These long-flowering bulbs from Chile start growing at the turn of the year, and then die down and go dormant after producing loose heads of scented, funnel-shaped blooms. *L. ixioides* (Glory of the sun; shown above) is the usual species, bearing purple-veined, white, lilac-blue or lavender flowers with white throats. *L. purpurea* is rich lilac, aging to magenta, with purple centres. Mixtures are often available in a range of blues.

Leucojum Snowflake

○ ❖ LATE WINTER to EARLY AUTUMN

H 10–90cm (4in–3ft) S 10–20cm (4–8in)

These are superficially similar to snowdrops, but more robust. *L. vernum* has chubby, green-tipped flowers in late winter and early spring. *L. aestivum* flowers from mid- to late spring (the best form is 'Gravetye Giant'; shown above). *L. vernum* and *L. aestivum* like damp, heavy ground. *L. autumnale* has slender bells from late summer and prefers well-drained, sandy soil.

Lilium auratum

Golden-rayed lily of Japan

○ 💧 ‖ pH↓ 🍂 ❖ LATE SUMMER to EARLY AUTUMN

H 90cm–2m (3–6ft) S 30cm (12in)

This gorgeous, wild, stem-rooting species bears 12–30 sweetly scented blooms, waxy white with carmine-red spots and a yellow midstripe. Var. *platyphyllum* (syn. 'Gold Band') is larger and spotless, with a wider band; it is a parent of the Oriental hybrids, which include 'Casa Blanca' (pure white, orange anthers, very fragrant) and 'Star Gazer' (red flowers, white-edged).

Lilium (lily)

Lilium 'African Queen' has large, trumpet-shaped, fragrant flowerheads.

Growing lilies

Generally, lilies are easy to grow in the garden or in pots. The majority have bulbs made of overlapping scales; a few have creeping rhizomes or stolons. Most lilies are happy planted at about 10–15cm (4–6in) deep, although stem-rooting varieties (which develop roots on the buried stem) need planting about 20cm (8in) deep and others, such as *L. candidum*, prefer to be just under the surface. Lilies tend to prefer acid soils, but several tolerate lime and a few, such as *L. henryi*, need alkaline soil. All lilies with true bulbs do well in pots of well-drained, loam-based compost. Beware lily beetles (*see* page 71).

Choosing lilies

Qualities to check include: colour (every shade except blue); height, from the dwarf, scarlet *L. pumilum* (15–30cm/6–12in) to statuesque Bellingham hybrids like the orange-yellow 'Shuksan', 2.2–2.5m (7–8ft) or more; and flowering time, from late spring (the rose-pink *L. mackliniae*) to early autumn (the white or pink

L. speciosum), although most flower in early or midsummer. Scent is important, but variable and, as ever, a matter of personal taste.

Flower form

Lilies are officially classified into nine Divisions, but are also grouped more simply according to their flower forms. Trumpet-shaped varieties have long blooms that open wide at the mouth. Bowl-shaped flowers are more cupped or bell-like, with reflexed petals that sometimes open into a star. Turkscap lilies have very reflexed petals that often curl backwards and tend to hang downwards.

> **MORE GOOD LILY VARIETIES**
>
> *L.* 'African Queen' (*see* above) – apricot, trumpet
>
> *L.* 'Centerfold' – white with purple markings, bowl-shaped
>
> *L.* 'Connecticut King' – yellow, bowl-shaped
>
> *L. formosanum* – white, trumpet
>
> *L. lancifolium* (tiger lily) – orange-red, black-spotted, turkscap
>
> *L.* 'Pink Perfection' – purple-pink, trumpet

Lilium longiflorum Easter lily
○ ✧ ⇊ 🍂 ❖ MIDSUMMER
H 75–90cm (30–36in) S 23cm (9in)

Widely grown for florists because of its intense perfume and pure white colour, this is a lime-tolerant and stem-rooting species that needs warmth and shelter from cold winds; it does well in pots, and can be forced for early blooms. It is easy from seed, often flowering the following year. Selected forms include: 'Triumphator' (large flowers, deep-burgundy centres); 'White American' (green-tipped petals); 'White Heaven' (larger trumpets, very fragrant).

Lilium martagon Turkscap lily
○ ◑ ⇊ 🍂 ❖ EARLY to MIDSUMMER
H 90cm–2m (3–6ft) S 30cm (12in)

Although found wild on limestone, this lovely but malodorous, stem-rooting species tolerates any well-drained soil. Purplish-green stems bear leaves in whorls and 20 or more nodding, dusky purple-pink lanterns with brown flecks. Var. *album* is white with carmine spots; var. *cattaniae* is more vigorous than the species, with spotless, wine-red blooms.

Lilium regale Royal lily

◯ ‖ 🍃 ❖ MIDSUMMER

H 90–120cm (3–4ft) S 23cm (9in)

This vigorous, stem-rooting species is perhaps the most fragrant of all lilies. Very hardy, lime-tolerant and long-lived, it is easy-going and looks good in bold drifts. Buy top-size bulbs, stake the leaning stems, and beware of its indelible orange pollen. Plants produce 15–25 horizontal trumpets, waxy white with rosy backs and yellow throats. 'Album' is all white and 'Royal Gold' all yellow.

Lycoris

◯ ❄ ‖ 🍃 ❖ LATE SPRING to EARLY AUTUMN

H 30–75cm (12–30in) S 20cm (8in)

These slightly tender bulbs are best grown in warm borders where summers are dry, or in pots under cool glass. The following three species are hardier than others: *L. aurea* (golden spider lily; early heads of slim, golden flowers; shown above); *L. radiata* (red spider lily; later; rose or deep red); *L. squamigera* (resurrection lily; fragrant; nodding, rose flowers flushed and veined purple).

Moraea

◯ ❄ △ ‖ ❖ EARLY SUMMER

H 45–90cm (18–36in) S 8cm (3in)

Plant these African irises outdoors in spring and lift in autumn, or grow in pots of gritty compost. *M. huttonii* and *M. spathulata* (shown above) are yellow with dark flecks. The moraeas known as Peacock have three large, bright petals and contrasting, ringed centres; they include: *M. aristata* (white with green, blue and black rings); *M. villosa* (cream, pink, orange or purple, with dark eyes).

Muscari armeniacum

Grape hyacinth

◯ ◑ ● ‖ ❖ EARLY SPRING

H 20–25cm (8–10in) S 5cm (2in)

These jaunty, mostly spring-flowering bulbs generally have bold blue flowers with a sweet musky fragrance, and slightly untidy foliage. This species is reliable and prolific, with dense heads of rounded bells, bright blue with pale rims. Dead-head to prevent lavish seeding. Choice varieties: 'Blue Spike' (rich blue, double flowers in profuse bunches); 'Cantab' (soft Cambridge blue; strong-growing).

Muscari comosum

Tassel grape hyacinth

◯ ● ‖ ❖ MID-SPRING

H 30–40cm (12–16in) S 8cm (3in)

M. comosum stands out from other grape hyacinths because of its loose spikes of creamy purple-brown flowers topped by a cheeky blue tuft like a miniature French lavender. Its variety 'Plumosum' is a curiosity, all its flowers transformed into a feathery mop of sterile violet tassels. More robust than it appears, it looks stunning in bold clumps.

Muscari macrocarpum

◯ ● ‖ ❖ EARLY SPRING

H 15cm (6in) S 8cm (3in)

This sun-loving species is an oddball, its loose flower spikes starting out greyish violet-blue but soon changing to bright yellow, fading to soft purple. Perhaps the most fragrant of all grape hyacinths, it needs a hot, dry summer to bake its dormant bulbs into flowering well the following year. 'Golden Fragrance' (shown above) is an improved selection, robust and cold-tolerant, with golden-yellow spikes (H up to 23cm/9in).

Narcissus bulbocodium
Hoop petticoat daffodil

○ ◑ ◊ ↓↓ pH↓ 🐛 ❖ EARLY SPRING
H 10–15cm (4–6in) S 5cm (2in)

The horizontal, widely-flared trumpets of this dainty wild species are instantly recognizable. Like most wild daffodils its solitary flowers appear early, while the leaves are merely slender threads. There are several lovely forms with colours ranging from pale sulphur to deep gold, all prefering acid soils. Other good acid-loving species: *N. asturiensis* (full sun only), *N. cyclamineus*, *N. triandrus*.

Narcissus (double)

○ ◑ ◊ ↓↓ 🐛 ❖ EARLY to MID-SPRING
H 15–45cm (6–18in) S 8–15cm (3–6in)

They might look like spectacular designer flowers, but several wild species do produce double variants. The most famous is *N.* 'Telamonius Plenus' (syn. 'Van Sion') with partially or fully double, greenish-yellow blooms. Others include soft lemon-yellow 'Eystettensis' (Queen Anne's double daffodil; shown above), and the strongly fragrant double Campernelle jonquil (*N. × odorus*). All of these naturalize well.

Narcissus (daffodil)

With its prominent, bright yellow trumpet, 'King Alfred' is the classic, ever-popular daffodil.

Growing daffodils

There are thousands of varieties of these beautiful bulbs ('daffodils' are large-trumpeted narcissi). Most do well in any well-drained garden soil in full sun or light shade. Varieties are available for every conceivable use, including beds and borders, rock and wild gardens, naturalized in grass, in pots and for cutting. The flowering period runs from late autumn to early summer, with spring the main season of glory. Very early varieties are best grown under glass.

Colour and form

Daffodils are available in a host of shades and combinations of yellow, orange, pink, red and white, and a range of different forms. The official system recognizes 13 *Narcissus* Divisions, but they are often divided into three main groups according to their flower shape. Trumpet daffodils have the classic daffodil form, with a pronounced central tube as long as, or longer than, the outer ring of six petals. Cupped varieties have trumpets that are shorter than the outer petals and can be flaring or almost flat. Reflexed varieties (which can have trumpets or cups) have outer petals that bend backwards, either gently or strongly swept back.

MORE GOOD NARCISSUS VARIETIES

N. 'Charity May' – yellow, reflexed

N. 'Cragford' – white and orange, cupped

N. 'February Silver' – white and lemon-yellow, reflexed

N. 'Golden Harvest' – yellow, trumpet

N. 'Jack Snipe' – white and yellow, trumpet, dwarf

N. 'Jetfire' – yellow and orange, reflexed

N. 'Jumblie' – yellow, reflexed

N. 'King Alfred' (*see* above) – yellow, trumpet

N. minor 'Little Gem' – yellow, trumpet, dwarf

N. 'Mount Hood' – white, trumpet

N. 'Mrs R.O. Backhouse' – shell-pink and white, trumpet

N. papyraceus – white, cupped

N. pseudonarcissus – yellow and cream, trumpet, dwarf

N. 'Rip van Winkle' – yellow, double, dwarf

N. 'Sun Disc' – yellow, cupped

Narcissus (large-cupped)

○ ◑ ◊ ↕↓ 🍂 ❖ MID-SPRING

H 30–60cm (12–24in) S 10cm (4in)

The trumpets of large-cupped (trumpet) daffodils vary in shape from rounded to almost flat, and in colour from white to rich red. Mainly flowering mid-season, they add unique charm and symmetry to garden and indoor displays. Good varieties: 'Carlton' (clear yellow, paler cup); 'Ice Follies' (soft white, cup wide, crinkled, primrose fading to white); 'Professor Einstein' (frosty white; flat, vivid orange cup; shown above).

Narcissus (multi-headed)

○ ◑ ◊ ↕↓ 🍂 ❖ EARLY to MID-SPRING

H 15–45cm (6–18in) S 8–15cm (3–6in)

Narcissi with several blooms per stem offer extra impact for no extra cost. Most are hybrids of species *N. jonquilla*, *tazetta* and *triandrus*, with small, sometimes highly fragrant blooms. *Tazetta* hybrids, often used for forcing, are slightly tender. Good varieties: 'Pipit' (yellow, white cup); 'Suzy' (yellow, orange cup); 'Geranium' (white, orange-red cup); 'Grand Soleil d'Or' (gold, orange cup); 'Minnow' (creamy yellow, yellow flat cup); 'Hawera' (bright yellow; shown above); 'Ice Wings' (white).

Nectaroscordum siculum

Sicilian honey garlic

○ ◑ ↕↓ 🍂 ❖ EARLY SUMMER

H 90cm (3ft) S 10cm (4in)

This unusual woodland bulb is robust enough to naturalize successfully in grass and wild gardens. Stout stems are crowned with clusters of pendulous bells, greenish cream with a purple flush and opening over a long period. It seeds happily from prominent seedpods that turn upwards as they develop and make a unique contribution to dried flower arrangements. Subsp. *bulgaricum* is off-white with pink or green markings.

Nerine bowdenii

○ ❄ ↕↓ ❖ EARLY AUTUMN

H 45–60cm (18–24in) S 8cm (3in)

Nerines flower best when established and overcrowded, producing glowing heads of shimmering pink, lightly fragrant flowers, each a star-burst of long wavy petals. The leaves emerge after flowering. Grow them against a warm, sheltered wall. Fine varieties include: 'Alba' (white, pink flush); 'Mark Fenwick' (cyclamen pink; vigorous; early); 'Mollie Cowie' (fuchsia pink; cream-edged leaves); 'Pink Triumph' (deep silvery pink).

Nerine sarniensis Guernsey lily

○ ❀ ↕↓ ❖ EARLY AUTUMN

H 45–60cm (18–24in) S 8cm (3in)

The Guernsey lily is a handsome, frost-tender species that is best grown in a pot as it needs drying off in summer. It has tight heads of up to 20 deep-red, rich orange or white blooms with prominent stamens. Glossy, strap-like leaves follow. There are many good Exbury hybrids with pink, white, red, purple or orange flowers. Other good species: *N. flexuosa* (dark veined, pink or white); *N. undulata* (nodding, clear-pink or white flowers).

Nomocharis saluenensis

◑ ◊ ↕↓ pH↓ 🍂 ❖ EARLY SUMMER

H 90cm (3ft) S 10cm (4in)

Nomocharis are graceful Himalayan lilies that enjoy moist, peaty soil in cool shade. This easy species bears five or six broad, pendent, pink or white stars, embellished with wavy edges, maroon spots and a dark, contrasting throat. Plant bulbs at least 15cm (6in) deep, never letting them dry out. *N. aperta* (shown above) has larger, pink, speckled blooms 15cm (6in) across; *N. pardanthina* has many soft pink flowers, fringed and spotted.

Notholirion
◐ ◌ ⇊ pH⇊ ❧ ❖ MIDSUMMER

H 45cm–1.5m (18in–5ft) S 15cm (6in)

These graceful bulbs from Chinese alpine meadows are monocarpic, dying after flowering and leaving behind bulbils that take from three to four years to reach flowering size. The giant of the genus is *N. bulbuliferum* (shown above), whose tall stems carry 20–30 pale lilac trumpets; easiest, smallest and most colourful is *N. macrophyllum*, with a few clear-pink or mauve, speckled trumpets.

Ornithogalum thyrsoides
Chincherinchee
○ ❄ ⇊ ❖ LATE SPRING or LATE SUMMER

H 60–75cm (24–30in) S 10cm (4in)

This best-known tender species is a florists' favourite for its large and very long-lasting flowers. Plant the bulbs under glass, six to a 15cm (6in) pot of soil-based compost, or start in pots in autumn for bedding out in spring to flower in late summer. The 45cm (18in) spikes of 20–30 creamy-white flowers last for weeks if cut in bud. *O. dubium*, with orange, red or yellow blooms, needs similar care (H 30cm/12in).

Ornithogalum umbellatum
Star of Bethlehem
○ ◐ ⇊ ❧ ❖ LATE SPRING to EARLY SUMMER

H 15–30cm (6–12in) S 10cm (4in)

This hardy ornithogalum is reliable and happy in any fertile soil or grass, and spreads rapidly. A cluster of upturned stars, brilliant white with green-striped backs, appears as the white-veined leaves wither. *O. nutans* is neat and silver-white (H 60cm/2ft); *O. narbonense* is taller, with larger milky-white flowers (H 90cm/3ft). All tolerate light shade, although flowering is then less profuse.

Oxalis adenophylla
○ ⇊ ❧ ❖ EARLY SUMMER

H 10–15cm (4–6in) S 15cm (6in)

This well-behaved cousin of wood sorrel and shamrock is a neat, clump-forming bulb with pleated, grey-green leaves composed of pretty, heart-shaped leaflets. Its purplish-pink, 2.5cm (1in) flowers have darker veins and a purple-spotted, silvery throat. *O. × enneaphylla* is a lovely rhizomatous, deep reddish-pink species; a fine hybrid between the two species; 'Matthew Forrest' has large, mauve blooms with a dark eye.

Pancratium illyricum
○ ❄ ⇊ ❧ ❖ EARLY SUMMER

H 30–45cm (12–18in) S 20cm (8in)

This stunning Mediterranean bulb makes a wonderful indoor plant. Grow in pots of very gritty, loam-based compost. Its 10 to 15 pure white blooms are deliciously fragrant and can reach 8cm (3in) across. Water freely while in leaf, give a high-potash feed every month and keep quite dry after the foliage dies down.

Paradisea Paradise lily
○ ◐ ◌ ⇊ ❧ ❖ LATE SPRING to EARLY SUMMER

H 45cm–1.5m (18in–5ft) S 30–45cm (12–18in)

These rhizomatous, grassy-leaved perennials from alpine or damp meadows naturalize well in informal and wild gardens and in grass. The roots must never dry out. Numerous fragrant white trumpets line one side of the wiry stems. *P. liliastrum* (shown above) is dainty and flowers early; *P. lusitanicum* is more robust and later-flowering, with 20–25 blooms on tall stems.

Physalis alkekengi Chinese lantern
○ ◐ ‡‡ ❖ MIDSUMMER to MID-AUTUMN
H 60–90cm (2–3ft) S 90cm (3ft)

This familiar herbaceous perennial has creeping rhizomatous roots that can spread to produce a thicket of vigorous leafy stems. Small, nodding, creamy-white bells appear in the leaf axils in summer, followed by gold or orange papery 'lanterns' enclosing large, bright scarlet berries. At this point stems can be cut for dried-flower arrangements. Good varieties: 'Gigantea' (very large lanterns); 'Variegata' (gold-splashed foliage).

Polianthes tuberosa Tuberose
○ ✿ ‡‡ 🍃 ❖ MIDSUMMER
H 90–120cm (3–4ft) S 15cm (6in)

Few bulbs smell as seductive as this centuries-old species, unknown in the wild. It needs a minimum of 15°C (59°F), so grow it in pots of soil-based compost and water freely once the rosette of slender leaves appears. Each tuber produces several spikes crowded with waxy, white, tubular flowers. Reduce watering after flowering; keep warm and dry until mid-spring. 'The Pearl' (shown above) is fully double and shorter.

Polygonatum × hybridum
Solomon's seal
◐ ● ◕ ‡‡ 🍃 ❖ LATE SPRING
H 90–120cm (3–4ft) S 30cm (12in)

Solomon's seal is a garden hybrid between two wild species, inheriting large flowers from one and soft scent from the other. It is a choice plant for full shade and moist soils. Its rhizomes produce graceful arching stems, strung with pendent, creamy-white bells with green tips. Good varieties: 'Betberg' (young leaves purple, then deep green); 'Flore Pleno' (double flowers); 'Striatum' (leaves striped with cream).

Puschkinia scilloides Striped squill
○ ◐ ‡‡ 🍃 ❖ EARLY SPRING
H 20cm (8in) S 5cm (2in)

This trouble-free bulb loves mountain grassland and stony meadows, so makes a good choice for rock gardens and for naturalizing in lawns and wild gardens. Stems carry dense heads of between six and ten bluish-white, starry flowers, with a central dark blue stripe down each petal. Var. libanotica has smaller, slimmer flowers, often without the characteristic stripe; var. l. 'Alba' is pure white.

Ranunculus ficaria
Lesser celandine
◐ ● ◕ ‡‡ ❖ EARLY SPRING
H 5cm (2in) S 30cm (12in)

Unlike the large-flowered, florists' ranunculus (R. asiaticus), this is a variable small, tuberous buttercup that can be rampant but has many lovely, well-behaved offspring for shady, moist sites. They include: var. aurantiacus (copper, single; silvery-bronze leaves); 'Brazen Hussy' (glossy, chocolate leaves; gold flowers); 'Collarette' (yellow, double); 'Double Mud' (greyish cream, double); 'Salmon's White' (pale bluish cream).

Rhodohypoxis baurii
○ ‡‡ pH↓ 🍃 ❖ LATE SPRING to LATE SUMMER
H and S 10cm (4in)

This little alpine gem is sold in bulb catalogues often as a mixture of red, pink and white varieties. It is tougher than it looks, provided the soil is acid and very well drained to avoid winter waterlogging. Good varieties: 'Albrighton' (deep red); 'Harlequin' (pink, flushed with white); 'Helen' (large white flowers); 'Lily Jean' (creamy pink, double); 'Margaret Rose' (clear pink); 'Pintado' (soft pink, red edges).

Romulea bulbocodium

○ ↓↓ 🍃 ❖ MID-SPRING

H 10cm (4in) **S** 5cm (2in)

Romuleas are crocus relatives with small, lopsided corms and funnel-shaped flowers that open flat in full sun. This is the commonest and hardiest species, with large, lavender blooms and contrasting yellow throats; the smaller *R. ramiflora* is pale lilac. Keep the tender South African species such as *R. atranda* (purple and rich rose) and *R. sabulosa* (scarlet or ruby red) under glass in pots of gritty, loam-based compost.

Roscoea

◑ ❄ ◔ ↓↓ pH↓ 🍃 ❖ EARLY to MIDSUMMER

H 30–60cm (12–24in) **S** 15cm (6in)

These ginger relatives have exotic, orchid-like flowers and prefer cool, shady sites on leafy, acid soil. Plant the tubers at least 15cm (6in) deep and cover with a thick winter mulch. *R. purpurea* produces rich purple or occasionally white flowers with deep-purple markings. For yellow flowers, try *R. cautleyoides* 'Jeffrey Thomas' (cream and primrose; shown above) and 'Kew Beauty' (soft yellow).

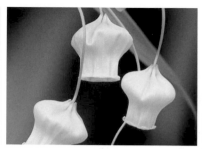

Sandersonia aurantiaca
Lantern lily

○ ❄ ↓↓ 🍃 ❖ EARLY to LATE SUMMER

H 75–90cm (30–36in) **S** 10–15cm (4–6in)

This solitary species of a short tuberous climber from South Africa is barely hardy, so protect from frost outdoors or lift tubers in the autumn. Under glass it bears its glowing, yellow-orange, 2.5cm (1in) lanterns almost all summer. Grow in pots of gritty, loam-based compost with support for its tiny tendrils, water and feed freely while in growth; keep dry from late autumn to mid-spring.

Sanguinaria canadensis
Bloodroot

◑ ● ◔ ↓↓ 🍃 ❖ MID-SPRING

H 15cm (6in) **S** 30cm (12in)

This creeping rhizomatous perennial comes from moist North American woodlands and makes a dependable choice for damp, shady spots, its clear white or pink-tinted flowers, up to 8cm (3in) across, illuminating the gloomiest corner. By late summer, growth dies back out of sight. Its variant f. *multiplex* 'Plena' (shown above) has densely double, longer-lasting, white flowers.

Scadoxus multiflorus Blood lily

○ ◑ ❄ ↓↓ 🍃 ❖ MIDSUMMER

H 60–75cm (24–30in) **S** 15cm (6in)

The dandelion-like leaves of this large African bulb give no hint of the blooms to come – extraordinary 15cm (6in) spheres of up to 200 narrow, blood-red trumpets with spidery stamens, erupting at the top of tall, stout stalks and lasting for many weeks. Keep in pots under glass, above 10°C (50°F) with high humidity. *Subsp. katherinae* is taller than the species, with wavy-edged leaves (H 1.2m/4ft).

Schizostylis coccinea River lily

○ ◔ ↓↓ 🍃 ❖ EARLY to LATE AUTUMN

H 45–60cm (18–24in) **S** 30cm (12in)

A solitary, clump-forming species with many gorgeous varieties, this star of the autumn border flowers up to the first frosts and is almost evergreen in mild areas. The species has red, pink or white blooms on spikes. Good varieties: f. *alba* (white, tinged pink); 'Major' (deep red); 'Mollie Gould' (warm pink, deeper streaks); 'Mrs Hegarty' (soft pink; early); 'Professor Barnard' (dusky red); 'Viscountess Byng' (pale pink; later).

Scilla Squill
○ ◐ ↓↓ 🌿 ❖ SPRING, SUMMER, AUTUMN, WINTER
H 8–40cm (3–16in) S 5–8cm (2–3in)

The spring-flowering squills are best-known, especially for naturalizing, but some flower at other times of the year. Best species: *S. autumnalis* (lilac or pink; late summer to mid-autumn); *S. bifolia* (purple-blue; late winter to early spring); *S. mischtschenkoana* (silvery blue, dark stripes; late winter); *S. scilloides* (mauve; late summer); *S. siberica* (Siberian squill; bright blue; early to mid-spring; shown above) and its variety 'Alba' (white).

Scilla peruviana
○ ❄ ↓↓ 🌿 ❖ EARLY SUMMER
H 30–40cm (12–16in) S 10cm (4in)

An almost evergreen, clump-forming squill for mild gardens; elsewhere grow in pots of loamless (soilless) compost with added grit. Unlike other species, it has large, round heads of up to 100 deep-blue or purple, star-shaped flowers that open in sequence. 'Alba' is white with a green stripe. Divide every few years to maintain vigour and flowering.

Sinningia speciosa
Florists' gloxinia
◐ ❄ ↓↓ pH→ 🌿 ❖ SUMMER
H and S 30cm (12in)

This gorgeous greenhouse and conservatory plant flowers all summer if tubers are started in late winter. It is often sold by colour or in mixtures. Outstanding varieties: 'Blanche de Méru' (white, pink fringe); 'Gregor Mendel' (bright red, white edge, double); 'Kaiser Friedrich' (red, white fringe); 'Kaiser Wilhelm' (purple, white edge); 'Mont Blanc' (pure white).

Sisyrinchium
○ ↓↓ pH ❖ SPRING, SUMMER
H 10–60cm (4–24in) S 15cm (6in)

Most of these self-seeding, rhizomatous perennials are dainty, with fans of tiny, iris-like leaves and starry or trumpet-shaped blooms in bright colours. Popular hardy species: *S. angustifolium* (blue, yellow centres); *S. californicum* (bright yellow); *S. graminoides* (blue with yellow throats); *S. idahoense* (violet). Good hybrids: 'Biscutella' (yellow, purple veins); 'E.K. Balls' (mauve); 'Californian Skies' (silvery-striped mauve; shown above).

Sisyrinchium striatum
○ ↓↓ 🌿 ❖ EARLY to MIDSUMMER
H 60–90cm (2–3ft) S 25cm (10in)

This dramatic evergreen species has bold fans of long, grey-green leaves and tall spikes of up to 20 wide, cup-shaped, creamy-yellow flowers, clearly veined with purple-brown. It is an undemanding but effective perennial for any well-drained border or gravel garden. 'Aunt May' is less vigorous, with slender flower spikes and cream-striped leaves.

Sparaxis Harlequin flower
○ ❄ ◌ ↓↓ 🌿 ❖ LATE SPRING or LATE SUMMER
H 15–45cm (6–18in) S 8cm (3in)

In their native South Africa, these tender plants start growing in autumn, and in colder regions often die over winter. Either plant new corms in spring for late summer display, and then discard them, or pot them up in autumn for spring blooms indoors. The various species are usually sold in a cheerful mixture of vibrant colours – white, yellow, orange, red and purple – with bright, contrasting throats and markings.

Sprekelia formosissima
Jacobean lily

○ ❄ ⬇⬇ ❖ LATE SPRING

H 30–35cm (12–14in) S 15cm (6in)

This stunning plant has an exotic, orchid-like bloom, usually velvet crimson but occasionally scarlet or white, which appears before or with its long, slender leaves. Grow outdoors in frost-free gardens, or keep at temperatures above 7°C (45°F) in pots. Allow the leaves to wither in autumn before withholding water, then keep the pot dry all winter.

Sternbergia Autumn daffodil

○ ◊ ⬇⬇ pH↑ pH→ ❖ EARLY to MID-AUTUMN

H 8–15cm (3–6in) S 8cm (3in)

Sternbergias have small, funnel-shaped or goblet-shaped flowers and are ideal for a sunny rock garden. All species resent winter wet, so grow in pots if drainage is imperfect. The hardiest outdoors are S. lutea (free-flowering, large, yellow goblets; shown above) and S. sicula (deep yellow). The larger-flowered S. clusiana (waxy yellow blooms) needs warmth and shelter.

Tecophilaea cyanocrocus
Chilean blue crocus

○ ❄ ⬇⬇ ❖ MID-SPRING

H 10cm (4in) S 5cm (2in)

This is one of the most dramatic spring bulbs, with its intense gentian-blue flowers. Growth starts very early, so grow it outdoors only in the mildest gardens in well-drained, sandy soil topped with plenty of shingle. Otherwise, plant the corms in pots of gritty compost in a frame or cold greenhouse. 'Leichtlinii' has paler blue flowers with white throats; 'Violacea' is deep violet blue.

Tigridia Peacock flower

○ ❄ ⬇⬇ ❖ LATE SUMMER, EARLY AUTUMN

H 45–60cm (18–24in) S 10cm (4in)

These ancient Aztec bulbs are grown for their large, exotic and vividly coloured blooms. They are frost tender so plant in spring and lift like gladioli in autumn, or grow them in pots of gritty compost in a cool greenhouse. They are usually sold as a mixture of T. pavonia varieties (shown above), in brilliant shades of yellow, orange, pink, red and white, with speckled or blotched throats.

Tricyrtis Toad lily

◐◑●◊ ⬇⬇ pH↓ pH→ 🍂

❖ LATE SUMMER to MID-AUTUMN

H 30–75cm (12–30in) S 30cm (12in)

These graceful Himalayan perennials need shade, lime-free soil, plenty of humus and shelter from wind to do well. Their long-lasting blooms (which are good for cutting) are waxy and subtly coloured, often with elaborate contrasting purple, maroon or chocolate speckles. Good species include: T. flava (yellow, purple spots); T. formosana (pink, purple and white; shown above); T. hirta (white, speckled with maroon).

Trillium Wood lily

◐◑●◊ pH↓ pH→ 🍂 ❖ MID- to LATE SPRING

H 15–60cm (6–24in) S 25–30cm (10–12in)

Shade-loving woodland gems for deep, moist, acid soils, these all have leaves and flowers made up of three parts. T. grandiflorum (shown above) is easy and showy, with 8cm (3in) wide white flowers; 'Flore Pleno' is a double form. Other good species: T. cuneatum (musky scent, deep-maroon flowers); T. luteum (upright, sweetly scented, rich gold).

Triteleia

○ ◊ ‡‡ 🍃 ❖ LATE SPRING, EARLY SUMMER
H 15–60cm (6–24in) S 8cm (3in)

The prolific flowers of these North American grassland gems are good for cutting, and supply colour after other spring bulbs have finished. They like plenty of sunshine, sandy soil and good drainage; or grow the corms in pots of gritty compost under glass. Good varieties include: *T. ixioides* 'Starlight' (yellow with a chocolate stripe; shown above); *T. laxa* (syn. *Brodiaea laxa*) 'Königin Fabiola' (purple blue).

Tritonia

○ ❄ ◊ ‡‡ ❖ LATE SPRING to LATE SUMMER
H 20–90cm (8–36in) S 5–8cm (2–3in)

Two species of these montbretia relatives are suitable for growing outdoors in cooler gardens. *T. disticha* has orange, pink or red flowers; its outstanding form subsp. *rubrolucens* (syn. *T. rosea*; shown above) is dusky pink. *T. crocata* (orange or red) and 'Princess Beatrix' (vivid orange-scarlet) are slightly less hardy and often grown in pots.

Tropaeolum

○ ❄ ‡‡ pH↓ pH→ 🍃
❖ MIDSUMMER to MID-AUTUMN
H 3–5m (10–16ft) S 90cm (3ft)

Perennial nasturtiums with tubers need warm, sheltered sites with good drainage and a thick mulch. The most reliable is *T. speciosum* (the flame flower; shown above), with a long display of vermilion flowers. *T. tuberosum*, with russet-yellow blooms, is less hardy; lift its tubers in late autumn for storing like dahlias; var. *lineamaculatum* 'Ken Aslet' has earlier orange flowers and more cold tolerance.

Tulbaghia

○ ❄ ‡‡ 🍃 ❖ MIDSUMMER to EARLY AUTUMN
H 45–60cm (18–24in) S 25cm (10in)

Where frost is rare, these charming South African corms will survive outdoors in warm, sheltered sites with a dry mulch over winter; otherwise, grow them under glass. The easiest species is *T. violacea* (shown above), vigorous with slender, garlic-scented leaves and large clusters of pleasantly fragrant, lilac flowers; the lovely form 'Silver Lace' (syn. 'Variegata') has larger flowers and attractive, cream-edged leaves.

Tulipa clusiana Lady tulip

○ ◊ ‡‡ 🍃 ❖ MID-SPRING
H 30–45cm (12–18in) S 5cm (2in)

This is a beautiful tulip, both outdoors and as a cut flower. Its slender, white bowls open wide to reveal their deep-purple throats and almost black anthers. Plants spread by underground stolons and naturalize freely. The form var. *chrysantha* (shown above) has golden-yellow flowers stained with reddish purple; *T. clusiana* 'Cynthia' is creamy yellow with a red flush and green edge.

Tulipa (Lily-flowered)

○ ❄ ‡‡ ❖ LATE SPRING
H 45–60cm (18–24in) S 8–12cm (3–5in)

These tulips are incredibly elegant, their slim, reflexed blooms the perfect choice for formal bedding and cutting. They are brightly coloured, often with a contrasting edge, 'flame' or 'feathering'. Good varieties: 'Ballerina' (orange; shown above); 'China Pink' (pink, white base); 'Marilyn' (cream, strawberry edge and feathers); 'Mona Lisa' (gold, red edge and flame); 'West Point' (primrose yellow); 'White Triumphator' (white).

Tulipa (tulip)

Planted *en masse*, multicoloured Parrot tulips cannot fail to make a striking display.

Choosing tulips

Tulips make a wonderful, colourful display in beds and borders, and many are suitable for containers and rock gardens, or for cutting. Selecting from hundreds of glorious varieties is always difficult. Important criteria include flowering time, which ranges from late winter almost until early summer; height, anything from 10cm (4in) to 75cm (30in); and colour, from white to nearly black, often combined with streaks, 'flames' and 'feathers'.

There are four main tulip forms. Cupped varieties have elegant, single blooms taller than they are wide. Bowl-shaped tulips are the more open singles or broader doubles. Goblet varieties have tall, tapering or fluted flowers. The fringed group consists of goblet-shaped tulips with feathered or ruffled edges and include the multicoloured Parrot tulips (*see* above).

Growing tulips

Leave planting until late autumn, after all other spring bulbs; this also helps prevent tulip fire (*see* page 72). Most tulips resent cool summers and wet soils, so it is usual to lift bedding tulips after their leaves turn yellow, and store them dry until late autumn. Many developed from wild species, however, including *T. humilis*, *T. sylvestris* and *T. turkestanica*, can be left in over winter.

MORE GOOD TULIP VARIETIES

T. 'Antoinette' – yellow, multi-flowered, bowl-shaped

T. 'Apeldoorn' – cherry-red, cupped

T. 'Bellona' – yellow, cupped

T. 'Blue Diamond' – blue-purple, bowl-shaped

T. 'Blushing Lady' – bicoloured, goblet-shaped

T. 'Estella Rijnveld' – pink-and-white, fringed, Parrot tulip

T. 'Fringed Beauty' – vermilion-and-gold, fringed

T. 'Green Wave' – mauve-and-green, fringed, Parrot tulip

T. 'Humming Bird' – green-tinted, bowl-shaped

T. 'Monte Carlo' – yellow, bowl-shaped

T. 'Oranje Nassau' – orange, bowl-shaped

T. 'Palestrina' – rose-pink, goblet-shaped

T. 'Queen of Night' – velvety maroon, cupped

T. 'Stresa' – red-striped, bowl-shaped

Tulipa sylvestris

○ ◕ ↨↨ 🐛 ❖ MID-SPRING

H 45cm (18in) S 5cm (2in)

Nobody knows where this dainty and very hardy species came from, but it has escaped from gardens all over Europe, Asia and North Africa. Vigorous and easy to grow, its underground stolons stray far and wide. Try growing it in borders, under hedges or in short grass, where it can wander at will. Its large, slightly drooping, fragrant flowers are gold or creamy yellow, with green and maroon markings.

Tulipa (Triumph Group)

○ ❄ ↨↨ ❖ MID-SPRING

H 35–60cm (14–24in) S 8–12cm (3–5in)

These mid-season hybrids between the Single Early and Darwin tulips share their parents' strong stems and large, cup-shaped blooms. Good varieties: 'Abu Hassan' (deep mahogany, gold edges); 'Bing Crosby' (scarlet); 'Garden Party' (white, carmine edges and 'feathers'); 'Golden Melody' (buttercup yellow); 'Prinses Irene' (orange and buff, purple 'flames'; shown above); 'White Dream' (ivory white).

Uvularia Merrybells

◐ ● ◆ ↕↕ pH↓ pH→ 🍂 ❖ LATE SPRING

H 60–75cm (24–30in) S 30cm (12in)

These North American woodland plants are shade-lovers for damp, leafy soils, where their creeping rhizomes spread to form crowded clumps. They look charming growing near water. The species usually offered is *U. grandiflora* (shown above), with glossy leaves and 5cm (2in), slightly twisted pendent bells in bright yellow with green shading; the form var. *pallida* is soft pale yellow.

Veltheimia

○ ❄ ◇ ↕↕ ❖ LATE WINTER, EARLY SPRING

H 45cm (18in) S 30cm (12in)

There are just two species of these tender South African bulbs, both with rosettes of thick, wavy leaves and dense, crowded spikes of long-lasting, drooping flowers that resemble those of kniphofia. They make good pot plants in gritty, loam-based compost at a minimum of 5°C (41°F). *V. bracteata* (shown above) is very sturdy with yellow-spotted pink-and-green flowers. Less robust, *V. capensis* is white with pink speckles.

Veratrum

◐ ● ◆ ↕↕ 🍂 ❖ MID- to LATE SUMMER

H 60cm–2m (2–6ft) S 60cm (2ft)

These imposing woodland plants have thick, poisonous rhizomes that revel in moist, organic soils. They have fans of pleated leaves and several stout stems bearing radiating spikes of numerous star-shaped, slightly malodorous flowers. Good species: *V. album* (white, greenish tints; shown above); *V. nigrum* (deep reddish brown); *V. viride* (Indian poke; yellowish green; tolerates very wet soils).

Watsonia

○ ❄ ◇ ↕↕ 🍂 ❖ LATE SUMMER

H 45cm–2m (18in–6ft) S 10–15cm (4–6in)

In mild areas, watsonias thrive and multiply outdoors given a protective winter mulch; elsewhere, lift and dry the corms in autumn or grow in pots of gritty, loam-based compost. Best species: *W. borbonica* (bright pink) and its pure white form 'Arderne's White'; *W. fourcadei* (pink, orange or vermilion); *W. pillansii* (tall and prolific; peach, pink or orange-red; shown above).

Zantedeschia aethiopica Arum lily

○ ◐ ❄ ◆ 🍂 ❖ LATE SPRING to MIDSUMMER

H 60–90cm (2–3ft) S 60cm (2ft)

Spectacular white spathes, up to 25cm (10in) long, and eye-catching leaves are the main features of this relatively hardy arum lily (also known as calla lily); 'Crowborough' is extra cold-tolerant. Grow them as marginal and bog garden plants, submerged in planting baskets as shallow aquatics, or in pots indoors for earlier flowers. Most coloured arum lilies are tender hybrids from golden *Z. elliottiana* or pink *Z. rehmannii*, needing at least 10°C (50°F) to grow well.

Zephyranthes candida Zephyr lily

○ ❄ ◆ ↕↕ 🍂 ❖ MIDSUMMER to EARLY AUTUMN

H 10–20cm (4–8in) S 8cm (3in)

An enchanting name for a dainty bulb, the Zephyr lily bears a succession of pure shining white, crocus-like flowers over several weeks. This is the only kind hardy enough to grow outdoors. Tender species for pots in a frame or cool greenhouse include: *Z. citrina* (bright yellow); *Z. grandiflora* (bright pink, white throat); *Z. rosea* (rose pink).

Challenging sites

Bulbs, like many garden plants, have learned to adapt to sites with hostile conditions; as a result, there's a wide range of bulbs that will grow in gardens that fall into the 'difficult' category – shady, wet, dry, windy or cold, perhaps. There is plenty you can do to improve your soil and to provide protection and the all-important good drainage, but the real key to success is to choose the right bulb for the right place in your garden so it can fulfil its potential.

Shady sites

Anyone who has been gardening for more than a few years will recognize shade as an opportunity, not a problem, and even the gloomiest spot can be made to sparkle with flowers. Whereas unashamed sun-lovers live and metabolize fast, burning up energy in bright light, plants that grow in shady situations survive on meagre light levels and may even scorch or dehydrate if hot sun beats down on them.

Planting bulbs with light flowers, such as these gleaming lilac-and-white *Crocus vernus* 'Pickwick', is an effective way to relieve shade.

Types of shade

There are many degrees of shade, ranging from the dappled sunlight under deciduous trees and shrubs that would please most woodland bulbs, or the partial shade of a hedge bottom where crocuses and snowdrops thrive, to the gloomy shadow cast by neighbouring buildings, where hardy cyclamen and epimediums will grow, just as long as they're given a little extra organic matter.

Lightening the darkness

Check the kind of shade in your garden. Is it there constantly or only at certain times of the year? Does it move during the day as the sun travels round? Is it total or only partial? Then explore practical solutions that might alleviate conditions. Trees can be pruned to thin or raise the canopy and admit more light without ruining their shape. Hedges can be lowered or reduced in width. Walls and fences can be painted or lime-washed to reflect more light.

Improving the soil

In a really disastrous situation, most light-loving bulbs can be grown in containers, which you can move as seasonal light levels change. But before giving up, remember that shade tolerance tends to increase if you can satisfy other growth needs such as adequate fertility, moisture and freedom from competition. Adding plenty of garden compost or leaf mould next to dry walls or between tree roots will raise fertility and help to hold moisture, as will an organic mulch applied after planting and topped up once or twice during the year (especially in autumn for slightly tender bulbs).

More shade-loving bulbs

Anemone nemorosa	Lilium martagon
Arisaema	Nomocharis
Begonia	Polygonatum
Cardiocrinum	Ranunculus ficaria
Convallaria majalis	Roscoea
Erythronium	Sanguinaria
Galanthus	Tricyrtis
Hyacinthoides	Trillium
Iris foetidissima	Uvularia
Lilium hansonii	Veratrum

Don't forget

Shade can also imply shelter. An open, sunny spot might be affected by winter frosts that could prove lethal to borderline-hardy species better grown with protection from nearby shrubs or a warm wall.

The pure white flowers of *Lilium longiflorum*, always happiest when growing in dappled shade, help lighten the darkness underneath a tree canopy.

Wet sites

Too much water can be just as damaging for plants as too little, except for those members of natural wetland communities that have adapted to soggy soils. Most true bulbs and corms must have good drainage, even those that require plenty of moisture at critical times during their life cycles, but bulbous plants with rhizomes and even some that produce tubers have learned to cope with wet conditions. Plant these and you'll find you no longer curse your wet and boggy ground.

The challenge

In the majority of gardens, saturated ground is a transient event brought to an end when drainage and evaporation manage to shed the excess water the soil can't absorb. Trouble occurs when bogginess becomes endemic, whether through poor drainage, a locally high water-table, or a heavy, sticky type of soil that hangs on to water long after others have dried out.

The main problem for plants is that roots need air as well as moisture to grow well. Soil particles are separated by tiny cavities that normally contain a balanced mix of air and water, but in waterlogged ground these spaces are flooded, and all air is then excluded. This denies roots vital access to oxygen, and also encourages the kind of bacteria that thrive in airless conditions. Since many of these bacteria are organisms that are carrying diseases, submerged roots and storage organs such as bulbs are likely to start rotting.

Zantedeschia 'Odessa', like all arum lilies, is a tuberous perennial that loves moist and swampy soils.

Dependable irises

The remarkable *Iris* genus includes over 300 species that have colonized a range of different habitats. Many have fibrous root systems and fall outside the scope of this book, but a large number grow from bulbs or rhizomes, the latter being a typical adaptation to wet ground. Most of the Beardless irises, for example, revel in constantly moist soil, while some are characteristic plants of really wet places such as ditches, swamps and water courses throughout Europe, Asia and North America.

Irises will grow contentedly in any bog garden or pond margin, as long as you give them an autumn mulch of compost or leaf mould to supply the humus-rich conditions they enjoy (but check whether your choice prefers acid or alkaline soil). Their fans of sword-shaped foliage provide good contrast for the generally large or sprawling leaves of many other marginal plants. Try the following species, some of which have several lovely varieties: *Iris ensata* (syn. *I. kaempferi*), *I. laevigata*, *I. orientalis* (syn. *I. ochroleuca*), *I. pseudacorus*, *I. sibirica*, *I. versicolor* or *I. virginica*.

The yellow flag, *Iris pseudacorus*, is a sound choice for wet sites beside ponds and streams or in a bog garden.

How some plants cope

Plants from the kind of wet habitats that challenge many other species have evolved a number of ways to shrug off these problems. The submerged rhizomes of many true water plants contain large spaces that are filled with air by the aerial parts; others can source oxygen from the water itself.

The water requirements and tolerance of different species vary considerably, so that some (such as water lilies) are truly aquatic, living in permanently wet surroundings; others, including skunk cabbage (*Lysichiton*) and many irises, grow at the water's edge with just their 'toes' dipped below the surface; while plants such as daylilies (*Hemerocallis*) and *Schizostylis* resent any kind of submersion, even though they prefer permanently moist conditions.

Understanding this type of 'zoning' is important when you are trying to match bulbs and their allies to the sites where they will grow with the least trouble.

As the common name river lily implies, *Schizostylis coccinea* prefers plenty of moisture at its roots and thrives best when the soil is never allowed to dry out.

Adapting wet ground

The best strategy with challenging soils is to recruit plants from the natural community found in that sort of habitat. Wetlands are a rich and precious resource favoured by a host of lovely species, but it must be admitted few of these are true bulbs. Only *Galanthus elwesii* and *Narcissus bulbocodium* are likely to thrive in very wet soils, and even these prefer drier conditions when dormant.

There are a number of ways of amending boggy soils to expand the plant repertoire without destroying the unique wetland character. First, check that the waterlogging is not caused by some easily remedied disorder, such as a blocked drain or compaction. If this is the case, you can cure this by deep digging. If it is a more serious problem, you could install drainage (*see* page 49; you may need professional help). Or, you could raise the surface level by spreading 60–90cm (2–3ft) of good topsoil over a drainage layer of rubble, either in informal bands and mounds or enclosed within low walls to make permanent raised beds. Another option would be to contour the ground into a series of small pools, sodden spots and seasonally wet locations separated by drier ridges, islands and causeways so as to create a diverse mix of specialized habitats for aquatic, marginal, bog and damp-loving plants.

More bulbs for bog gardens

Arisaema	Fritillaria meleagris
Arum	Hemerocallis
Camassia	Leucojum aestivum
Convallaria	Schizostylis
Dierama	Zantedeschia

Don't forget

Some moisture-loving plants are quite specific about the depth of water and the amount of saturation they can tolerate, so always try to find out exactly where best to plant your choice for good results, bearing in mind that many rhizomatous plants will gradually spread into the most favourable spots.

Don't forget

You can minimize the risks to bulbs on heavier ground by planting them on a bed of grit at least 5cm (2in) deep and surrounding them with more grit. Planting naked bulbs such as lilies (see pages 10–11) on their sides is a further precaution against waterlogging in heavy soil.

Dry sites

Excessively dry soil comes in various guises. It might be light and sandy – pleasant to work but demanding watering only a few days after heavy rain – or unimproved clay – which bakes hard and cracks in hot sun. New-build gardens made with a dressing of topsoil over builders' rubble can dry out fast, and gravelly soil holds very little water. While no dry soil is beyond improvement, there are many bulbs that have adapted to these conditions.

Making the most of dry soil

Impeccable drainage suits the majority of bulbs, which have evolved to grow in cooler, wet weather and then retreat into safe dormancy underground when the going gets tough. In fact, many are so used to this routine that lying in wet soil while they rest can be lethal; tulips are the most familiar example, which is why they are usually lifted and dried off over summer.

Problems arise with light, sandy soils, which are essentially inert and rapidly lose soluble nutrients and minerals; the fine particles of clay soil, on the other hand, set hard in dry weather, denying plants air and rain. The solution in both cases is to work plenty of humus-forming organic material, such as compost or leaf mould, into the soil when cultivating planting areas. Top the prepared soil with a mulch to protect the surface from drying sunshine and wind (*see* page 58).

Agapanthus is typical of many bulbous plants that enjoy the enhanced drainage of dry ground but welcome a gravel mulch to help retain some moisture at their roots.

This will be enough to make most bulbs comfortable without compromising the soil's excellent drainage. It's particularly important to improve the soil's water retention for summer-flowering bulbs, such as camassias, galtonias and lilies, as they make most of their growth after spring rain and need consistent moisture at their roots to grow and flower well. Bulbs like erythroniums, snowdrops and species anemones from woodland habitats prefer a mulch of leaf mould, whereas those from dry hillsides, rocky habitats and mountain regions, for example Spanish irises (*Iris xiphium*), winter aconites (*Eranthis*) or wild cyclamen, are best mulched with coarser material such as chipped bark or gravel. As always, get to know your bulbs and where they come from, so you can make them comfortable.

Mediterranean bulbs like these golden sternbergias cannot tolerate wet conditions, especially during their summer rest, and thrive in hot, dry soils.

Bulbs for hot spots

Dry doesn't necessarily mean sun-baked, but if you do have an area that is both well drained and sunny, it would be a prime spot for a range of bulbs from hot, dry places; if it's also sheltered from frost and cold winds, you could try borderline-hardy species too. Try growing *Amaryllis belladonna*, nerines, *Ornithogalum thyrsoides* (chincherinchee) and, for cutting and fragrance, freesias. Add ixias, sternbergias, tigridias, tulbaghias and zephyranthes. If you're prepared to water in really dry weather and watch out for hard winter frosts, you might succeed with pancratium, later-flowering schizostylis varieties (especially varieties such as 'November Cheer' and 'Viscountess Byng') and even aspidistra, the indoor 'cast-iron plant', which is almost hardy. Winter-flowering *Iris unguicularis* is also a good choice.

A hot, sunny position at the foot of a dry wall is an ideal spot for slightly tender nerines, encouraging the iridescent blooms that complement autumn leaf tints.

More drought-tolerant bulbs

Agapanthus	Gladiolus
Allium	Habranthus
Arum	Homeria
Asphodeline	Ipheion
Asphodelus	Leucocoryne
Babiana	Moraea
Belamcanda	Narcissus
Calochortus	Sparaxis
Colchicum	Veltheimia
Fritillaria (some)	Watsonia

Don't forget

The soil under paving slabs often stays moist all summer, so experiment with miniature bulbs, such as oxalis and species crocus, as pavement plants grown in pockets of soil in the joints between the slabs.

Shallow chalk

Gardens with shallow soils over chalk or limestone subsoil are often stony and dry in summer. Adding plenty of humus can improve water retention, but there are many bulbs that appreciate the natural free drainage that reduces the risks of rotting even in a wet winter, as well as the dry surroundings during their summer dormancy.

Most Mediterranean and Californian bulbs, including bellevalias, chionodoxas, crocuses, muscari and scillas, will positively rejoice in these conditions, while gladiolus and tulip species such as *Gladiolus communis* or *Tulipa humilis* should be reliably perennial and spread into good clumps. Don't assume all lime-lovers will automatically thrive in shallow chalk. Lilies, for example, need plenty of moisture in summer (even *Lilium candidum*, despite preferring lime-rich alkaline soil). Almost all benefit from additional organic matter.

Many tulip species, including dainty *Tulipa humilis* from sunny Turkish hills, are reliably perennial in dry, stony soil.

Windy sites

At the confluence of four major weather systems, the British Isles is one of the windiest places in Europe. Wind varies in strength and direction, with local and unpredictable effects that cause injury to our plants. Fortunately, there are ways to relieve the problem of gardening on an exposed site.

The challenges

The most obvious threat posed by wind is structural damage. Stems may be snapped, blooms torn off, leaves and shoots damaged by rubbing against each other or (near the sea) by salt and sand abrasion. Wind dries out the ground and can carry off bare topsoil. In frosty weather it can 'scorch' soft foliage and, in hot dry conditions, can cause plants to wilt and desiccate.

Overcoming problems

Top priority is to shelter plants by deflecting or filtering the wind, to reduce its ferocity. Erect a windbreak of permeable fencing, evergreen hedging or tough plants like tamarix, cotoneaster, escallonia, euonymus, griselinia, olearia or sea buckthorn (all good for coastal gardens), and plant bulbs in the lee of these.

Support is essential for taller bulbs such as galtonias, gladioli and lilies. Use stout stakes, wires and rings or, best of all, neighbouring plants that will filter the wind, physically prevent collapse and shade the ground to help retain moisture and humidity (*see also* pages 58–9). In the wild, shorter bulbs in really exposed positions suffer injury unless sheltered by ferns, grasses like *Stipa* and *Miscanthus* varieties, open dwarf bushes such as hypericums and shrubby potentillas, or strategic rocks and boulders.

You can protect the whole garden, or individual beds, by contouring the ground to baffle the prevailing wind; lower the level in some parts, and move the surplus topsoil to make low ramparts on the windward side, planting the lee side with shelter-belt grasses and shrubs.

Choosing bulbs

With adequate shelter, most hardy bulbs should grow well. Tall-growing types are more at risk, unless supported or integrated among obliging neighbours – for example gladioli with stout ferns, or camassias

Here, tall *Allium sphaerocephalon* survives exposure shielded by nearby grasses.

'Star of the East' is one of many crocosmias so robust they escaped from gardens to become wild flowers.

and bluebells (*Hyacinthoides*) in tall grass – as are most double forms with their heavier burden of petals.

Bulbs with wiry or flexible stems, such as daylilies (*Hemerocallis*), have spread from gardens to the wild. Native species may also prove more resilient than cultivated varieties, especially if grown in hard, poor soil. Try spring and autumn crocuses, grape hyacinths (*Muscari*), lily-of-the-valley (*Convallaria*), scillas and snowdrops (*Galanthus*).

Don't forget

Ground-cover plants can delay the soil drying out in exposed places and also support shorter bulbs; try growing crocuses or dwarf narcissi through mats of sedum and thrift, or grape hyacinths and chionodoxas among violets and *Alyssum montanum*.

More bulbs for windy sites

Allium schoenoprasum	*Narcissus pseudonarcissus*
Allium triquetrum	*Ornithogalum umbellatum*
Anthericum liliago	*Sisyrinchium angustifolium*
Gladiolus illyricus	*Tulipa sylvestris*
Iris reticulata (varieties)	

Cold sites

Bulbs that originated in hot climates may well be at risk in extremely cold weather, with frost being the biggest threat. Site vulnerable bulbs in the warmest spots and supply them with protection when necessary. You could even re-design parts of your garden to create safe havens for them.

Choosing the right bulbs

Most hardy bulbs won't raise their heads above ground until it is safe. Snowdrops may flower very early, but if there's a long, cold winter they can wait indefinitely before making a move. Other hardy or native bulbs, and those from areas with similar seasonal weather patterns, can also adapt. Don't assume bulbs from arctic and mountain habitats are frost resistant: most are used to an insulating blanket of snow or grow near the surface to avoid almost permanently frozen subsoil.

It is species from warmer climates that are likely to suffer, but even these can succeed in cold gardens if planted and protected carefully. More sensitive kinds, such as allium, iris and crocus species from warmer climes, respond to the protection of gravel or scree beds (see pages 30–3). Really frost-tender bulbs like eucharis, haemanthus and sprekelias are best grown in a bulb frame (see page 61) or cool greenhouse, where you can adjust ventilation and provide frost protection as needed.

Coping with frost

You can't prevent frost, but there are a number of ways to limit its impact.

Don't plant the earliest bulbs where early-morning sun reaches them, because a rapid thaw is often more harmful than freezing. Plant borderline-hardy bulbs close to a wall that will provide shelter and radiate stored heat, and put shade-tolerant bulbs under trees: their canopies can block heat-loss from the ground.

Delay pruning perennials and shrubs near bulbs until spring, as pruning in autumn removes material that might protect the ground underneath. Increase the depth of cover by applying an autumn mulch (see page 58), then don't disturb the ground around them until spring: hoeing 2cm (¾in) deep can cool the surface overnight by 2–3°C (3.5–5°F).

Moist soil can hold four times more heat than dry so, if frost is forecast, water sensitive bulbs in the day, then cover with fleece.

See box (left) for how to deal with any 'frost pockets' you might have.

Iris reticulata and snowdrops (here, *Galanthus nivalis*) will brave the cold.

Don't forget

Soil is a good insulator, so make sure bulbs are planted at the right depth (see pages 50–1). In light ground, add an extra few centimetres.

Frost pockets

Cold air is dense and heavy, and drains downhill where ground is uneven. If it meets a hollow or obstacle that blocks its flow, it collects close to the ground, trapped by lighter, warmer air above. Penetrating frost will occur more often and lingers longer in this 'frost pocket'.

Remedial action is simple. If the depression is small or shallow, level out the ground to prevent cold air collecting there. If you have a solid barrier like a wall, fence or hedge, make a hole in it so the air can continue escaping downhill. Alternatively, block or divert the flow of cold air by siting a hedge or row of trees or shrubs at the top of the slope.

More bulbs for cold sites

Allium	Colchicum
Anemone	Cyclamen coum
Asphodeline lutea	Eranthis hyemalis
Chionodoxa	Ipheion

Fully hardy bulbs like these golden crocuses can be trusted to survive harsh weather unaided.

Season by season

There is no season of the year when there isn't something to catch the eye and stimulate the interest of the keen bulb gardener. With each species adapted to growing and blooming at a particular time of year, from the tiniest midwinter snowdrops to dramatic late-summer cannas, there is a stunning array of bulbous plants to enhance our gardens as well as keep us busy virtually all year round.

A flower for every day

It isn't difficult to plan a virtually non-stop display of bulbs and bulbous flowers in the garden. As with all gardening, of course, the reality is at the mercy of unpredictable factors like weather and plant ailments, but in a typical year it is possible to have a flower every day, even by concentrating on just a handful of familiar varieties. Add in slightly less common kinds – plus a little help from a bulb frame or an early start in pots to protect growth or extend the season – and continuity is almost assured.

Keeping bulbs happy

The first step in planning an unbroken rota is to assign bulbs to spots where they will be happy, especially those growing or flowering at extreme times of year, such as the depths of winter or in the midsummer heat. Find out what each kind likes, the amount of sunshine or drainage for example, and the type of soil or exposure, and where possible satisfy these preferences. The A–Z directory will give growing conditions required for each bulb (*see* pages 74–103).

If you get to know your garden well, you will discover its soil type and microclimates, such as where frost or shade stays for the longest, the wet patches and the hot spots (*see* pages 48–9). Match the best species to these sites, for example camassias in soggy areas, trilliums in shade and alliums in sun-baked gravel, and there will be much less remedial work or disappointment. Then look after the bulbs at key times of the year, particularly after flowering, and you're halfway there.

Widen your choice

The other key strategy is to venture beyond the familiar, widely stocked selection of varieties and explore less common kinds that could extend the range of flowering times. For example, most tulips flower between early and late spring, but plant *Tulipa biflora* and you could have blooms in late winter in a warm sheltered corner, while naturalized *Tulipa sprengeri* could take you into early summer. *Narcissus* 'Tête à Tête' often flowers in late winter, too, and the old pheasant's eye (*Narcissus poeticus* var. *recurvus*) is very late, frequently coinciding with the first gladioli (*Gladiolus tristis* and dainty Nanus hybrids, for instance *Gladiolus* 'Charm'), in very early summer.

Lily varieties can supply a sequence of flowers over several months. *Lilium* 'Gran Paradiso' is one of the first, blooming in early summer.

Flowers for all seasons

Given good soil and shelter from the worst of the elements, you could have flowers all year round from the basic programme shown below.

Midwinter	*Eranthis hyemalis, Galanthus*
Late winter	*Crocus, Scilla*
Early spring	*Anemone, Narcissus*
Mid-spring	*Fritillaria, Muscari*
Late spring	*Iris, Tulipa*
Early summer	*Allium, Camassia*
Midsummer	*Begonia, Lilium*
Late summer	*Canna, Crocosmia*
Early autumn	*Dahlia, Sternbergia*
Mid-autumn	*Colchicum, Nerine*
Late autumn	*Crocus* (autumn-flowering), *Schizostylis*
Early winter	*Cyclamen, Iris unguicularis*

Find out the earliest- and latest-flowering variety of the different genera you want to grow, bearing in mind that dwarf, wild or single-flowered species and varieties can behave differently from the more glamorous doubles or hybrids, and then see if you can overlap or double up on typical flowering seasons to insure against gaps occurring should one kind finish early or not bloom well. Remember, if you're prepared to cheat you can always put pots of bulbs in flower into the border to fill gaps.

Spring

This is the flowering season when bulbs take centre stage in the garden. Most are relatively short plants, with ready-formed buds that lie in wait all winter until a few mild days trigger rapid growth and flowering before they are shaded out by their less precocious neighbours. Enjoy their celebration of winter's end, and then plant summer bulbs to prolong the display.

Start planting up deep pots with summer bulbs now, using a supply of fresh, moist compost.

page 119). Take begonia and dahlia cuttings from tubers and corms started under glass during late winter (*see* page 69).

Sow fast-growing annuals, such as candytuft (*Iberis*) or love-in-a-mist (*Nigella*), over and around spring bulbs to conceal their dying foliage.

Dividing and lifting
Divide snowdrops (*Galanthus*) and winter aconites (*Eranthis*) while their foliage is still green, and replant

The yellows and golds of double daffodils and variegated iris foliage perfectly reflect the spring sunshine.

immediately. Lift spring bulbs after flowering if they're in the way of summer bedding, and heel them in elsewhere so they can finish dying down naturally.

Caring for outdoor bulbs
For bulbs to repeat the dramatic display they give you year after year, most have to follow flowering by restocking their underground storage organs with food to ensure survival during dormancy and also to develop the next generation of buds. So feeding them while their leaves are still green is essential basic

Don't forget

Early spring bulbs can quickly disappear from sight for the rest of the year, so label any that you want to move, divide or lift for drying after their top-growth has withered.

Planting and sowing
Early spring is the time to start begonias and dahlias into growth so that they're well rooted for planting out in late spring. Summer bulbs such as galtonias, sparaxis and tigridias should be planted in mid-spring, although in milder areas they can be planted slightly earlier. Plant lily bulbs outdoors *in situ* and in pots; transplant those in growth while stems are still short, but take a large rootball.

If you want to grow gladioli for cut flowers (*see* box, opposite) plant them from early spring, or start the corms in pots or trays of compost for planting later. Wait a few weeks before planting florists' anemones for cut flowers in late summer (*see*

Snowdrops are best divided straight after flowering, while their leaves are still green and their roots active.

care (*see* pages 56 and 117). New bulbs might skip the next season if they didn't store enough food first time round, or disappear altogether.

Give lawn bulbs a sprinkling of blood, fish and bone or high-potash (potassium) fertilizer in early spring (this won't stimulate grass growth).

Dead-head spring bulbs as they fade, pinching off solitary heads and stripping multiple blooms from their stalks (*see* page 60).

Caring for forced bulbs

Any bulbs that have been forced into bloom early (*see* page 55) will have exhausted their food stores, especially if kept in glasses of water, on trays of gravel or even dry on a windowsill, and are unlikely to be worth forcing next season. This is no reason to discard or neglect them, however: with appropriate post-flowering care they will go on to bloom again if they are planted outdoors in the garden the following year, although their flowers will almost certainly be smaller.

Caring for hardy indoor bulbs

In mild weather, hardy spring bulbs that are displayed indoors, such as crocuses, daffodils and hyacinths, can safely be moved straight outdoors after flowering and hardening off – remember to give them a full-strength high-potash feed – where they can complete their growth cycle. Water them when dry.

You can use pot-grown bulbs as instant fillers for gaps in a border if you plant them while in bud.

Planting gladioli for summer

Large-flowered gladiolus hybrids make stately and dramatic cut flowers for your tallest summer vases, and can be gathered in glorious succession from the longest day until early autumn if you stagger their planting.

The secret of growing gladioli is to grow the corms in rows in specially prepared ground, perhaps in a sheltered part of a vegetable plot. The autumn before planting, dig a strip at least one spit deep, adding plenty of compost or leaf mould, plus plenty of sharp sand or grit on heavier ground.

In early spring, apply a dressing of a general or slow-release fertilizer. Also in spring (about 11 or 12 weeks after New Year, to be precise) plant the corms 10–15cm (4–6in) deep according to size (the larger, the deeper) and 20cm (8in) apart. In cold areas, start these early corms in pots under glass and plant out in late spring. Carry on planting a batch every 10 to 14 days up to early summer. In an average year you can expect the spikes to be ready about 12 weeks later for small-flowered varieties, up to 14 weeks later for larger kinds.

Replant gladioli you have lifted in autumn (*see* pages 118–19) and remember the flowers of gladiolus may be slightly smaller in the second year, so always buy new top-size corms (*see* page 46) to grow for cutting.

Bulbs in flower in spring

Allium	Hippeastrum
Anemone	Homeria
Anthericum	Hyacinthoides
Arum	Hyacinthus
Asphodeline	Iris
Asphodelus	Ixiolirion
Brimeura	Leucojum
Brodiaea	Moraea
Camassia	Muscari
Chionodoxa	Narcissus
Clivia	Ornithogalum
Convallaria	Polygonatum
Corydalis	Puschkinia
Crocus	Ranunculus
Cyclamen	Romulea
Eranthis	Sanguinaria
Erythronium	Scilla
Freesia	Trillium
Fritillaria	Tulipa
Galanthus	Zantedeschia

Caring for tender indoor bulbs

After flowering, tender bulbs, such as amaryllis (*Hippeastrum*) and lachenalias, need regular watering and feeding indoors until their leaves die down and they are ready for their three- to four-month summer rest (*see* page 117).

Forced arum lilies (*Zantedeschia*) must be watered and fed indoors after flowering until late spring, then left to dry off until midsummer (*see* page 117).

Don't forget

Before mowing over naturalized bulbs, wait at least six weeks after flowering or until their foliage yellows and dies down; leave them until midsummer if you want them to self-seed.

Summer

Summer-flowering bulbs tend to be taller than spring bulbs, with quite differing growth cycles. For example, many need consistent moisture just when spring kinds are entering their dry dormancy. Some summer bulbs, such as camassias and lilies, are hardy perennials that are planted to settle down and multiply; many others are 'migrants', adding their seasonal contribution before being stored away for winter.

Planting and sowing

In mid- and late summer plant autumn-flowering colchicums, crocuses and sternbergias (see box, below right). Daffodils, erythroniums and grape hyacinths (*Muscari*) start rooting in late summer, so plant them as soon as they are available. The time to plant out begonias, dahlias and other tender bulbs is when you can be sure the last frost is past. Gather the ripe seeds of spring bulbs such as bluebells and fritillaries, and sow immediately (see pages 68–9).

Dividing and lifting

Summer is a busy time of year for bulb growers, because tending summer bulbs coincides with the need to lift and divide some spring species. If your daffodils are all leaf and no flower, they are almost certainly overcrowded and now is

Ornamental onions are stalwart summer-flowering bulbs; here, *Allium sphaerocephalon* flowers top a thicket of annual *Euphorbia stricta*.

As soon as the danger of spring frost is past, you can safely plant out tender species such as cannas and dahlias, but make sure they're fully hardened off first.

Planting bulbs for autumn interest

Most autumn-flowering bulbs are available in late summer and need planting straight away, in groups, to twice their depth and as much apart, in fertile, well-drained soil. You can plant them much closer in pots of gritty, loam-based compost, but transplant into the garden straight after flowering, when they start producing their roots. If well suited, they will multiply into fat clumps and after four to five years will benefit from splitting by lifting, dividing and promptly replanting the corms in late summer while still dormant.

Some of the bulbs for this time of year, such as colchicums and autumn crocuses, are difficult to place in the garden, because their naked flowers are vulnerable to wind and heavy rain unless supported by neighbouring plants. Try planting them among marbled arums, ferns, hostas, pulmonarias, or a carpet of purple bugle (*Ajuga*) or silvery-grey ground cover, which will also protect the blooms from splashes of soil. They grow well in grass, which is the native habitat of meadow saffron (*Colchicum autumnale*), but you can mow only between early and late summer to avoid injuring the spring foliage and autumn blooms.

the time to dig up and divide the clumps (*see* pages 60 and 66–7). Lift, dry and store hyacinths and tulips as soon as their foliage has shrivelled and died down.

Caring for bulbs

Feed spring bulbs growing in containers after flowering, plus any summer kinds growing with other plants, using half-strength, high-potash fertilizer at every watering. Cut down the faded foliage of all spring-flowering bulbs now that their goodness has been passed down into the bulb itself.

Leave the lids off bulb frames while summer bulbs flower until their leaves die down, then cover once more. After the leaves of

tender bulbs such as amaryllis (*Hippeastrum*) have died down, reduce watering and keep the plants dry in a warm spot for their vital resting period.

Arum lilies (*Zantedeschia*) can be repotted and grown on outdoors until a second dormant season occurs naturally in autumn (*see* page 119).

Watch out for pests and diseases, especially viruses (distorted flowers and mottled leaves) and lily beetles (bright scarlet adults with larvae that resemble bird droppings). (*See* pages 70–3.)

Cutting gladioli

Support the developing spikes of gladioli with canes and raffia, and cut them low down, early in the morning, when two to three blooms are fully open. Add one or two leaves if you wish, but make sure three to four full-size leaves are left to support new corm development.

Feeding bulbs with high-potash fertilizer is the best way to make sure they bloom again next year.

Forcing hyacinths

Late summer is the time to force hyacinths if you want to be certain of having an indoor display of flowers by Christmas. For bulbs in the new year and later, you could wait until early autumn. There are many bulbs that are suitable for forcing, including tulips, daffodils and crocuses (*see* page 55).

Don't forget

Watch out in late summer for ripening bulbils on the stems of lilies such as *Lilium bulbiferum* and *Lilium lancifolium* (tiger lily). Gather these before they fall and plant them straight away (see pages 66–7).

Plant autumn-flowering colchicums any time after midsummer, as their bulbs will be primed and ready for the shortening days to burst into life.

Don't forget

Spring bulb catalogues appear from midsummer, so prepare your wish lists in advance and then order as soon as possible, especially autumn bulbs and daffodils, which all do best if planted before early autumn.

Bulbs in flower in summer

Acidanthera	Hemerocallis
Allium	Homeria
Agapanthus	Iris
Begonia	Ixiolirion
Brodiaea	Lilium
Camassia	Moraea
Canna	Nomocharis
Cardiocrinum	Notholirion
Crinum	Sisyrinchium
Crocosmia	Sparaxis
Dahlia	Tigridia
Dierama	Tricyrtis
Eremurus	Triteleia
Galtonia	Tropaeolum
Gladiolus	Tulbaghia
Hedychium	Watsonia

Autumn

Far from being the end of the gardening year, for a bulb enthusiast autumn is just the beginning. With most garden bulbs flowering in spring, a key task now is to tuck new ones safely under ground in good time for their roots to get going while the soil is still relatively warm. Autumn is also an important flowering season – almost an alternative spring – so make time to enjoy the many bulbs blooming now, just when nearly everything else is at an end.

Like all dahlias, the variety 'David Howard' is a star of the autumn border until the first frosts.

Planting and potting up

Bulb suppliers have done the job of raising the bulbs to the point of flowering, so you can feel confident that a few hours of work now will virtually guarantee colour and beauty in a few months (and every year thereafter in many cases). So press on with planting spring-flowering bulbs, finishing in late autumn with tulips and outdoor hyacinths. Plant *Anemone coronaria* hybrids in a cold frame or greenhouse for spring cutting (*see* box, opposite). If you want early indoor hyacinths, plant them up now in pots or bulb bowls (*see* page 55).

Both notholirions and little *Iris danfordiae* (*see* page 120) are a treat the first year and then promptly split into tiny bulblets which take a season or two to bulk up; the trick is to plant annually in autumn until you have a regular sequence.

Care and preparation

Apply mulch to shallow and frost-sensitive bulbs such as crinums and crocosmias as soon as their growth dies down.

Collect ripe seeds and bulbils from lilies (*see* pages 66–9), and dry for storage or plant straight away (*see* pages 62–3).

Bulbs that are being forced need regular checks for watering and general progress.

Lifting tender bulbs

To flower well the following year, all bulbs need to generate and store the maximum amount of potential energy before growth ceases and they become dormant. For this reason, tender summer-flowering subjects such as dahlias, gladioli and ixias are left outdoors until the very last moment, when the first frost occurs, which may be early autumn in some seasons or a couple of months later if it is mild.

As the days shorten and temperatures begin to fall, it is time to lift tender bulbs such as these cannas before they are injured by the first frosts.

If potted up now, dwarf irises such as *Iris reticulata* will give welcome colour in late winter and early spring.

After lifting, dahlia tubers dry off best if arranged stem downwards in boxes or trays under glass.

Start amaryllis (*Hippeastrum*) in pots of damp compost now. Do not water until the flower bud emerges.

Growing anemones for early-spring vases

If poppy or florists' anemones (*Anemone coronaria*) are successively planted, their flowers can be available almost all year round. This obliging bulb looks glorious in pots and blooms over several weeks, although it produces a lot of leaf and insufficient flowers at any one time to fill a vase. For this you need to grow them in a greenhouse border, where they can use space that might lie empty all winter. Plant them about 5cm (2in) deep and 10–15cm (4–6in) apart in a light, sandy soil mix or loam-based potting compost, keep at 10°C (50°F) minimum, and they'll flower three to six months later. Plant in early autumn for early spring, early spring for early to midsummer, and midsummer for autumn.

Bulbs in flower in autumn

Agapanthus	Gladiolus
Amaryllis	Hedychium
Begonia	Leucojum
Canna	Lilium
Colchicum	Nerine
Crinum	Schizostylis
Crocosmia	Sternbergia
Crocus	Tigridia
Cyclamen	Tulbaghia
Dahlia	Zephyranthes

Dig up plants as soon as frost has blackened the foliage. Spread bulbs in a warm, sunny spot, under glass if necessary, for two to three weeks until you can rub off soil, roots and papery skins, and then store the bulbs in paper bags in a dry, cool, frost-free place.

Cut dahlia stems down to 10–15cm (4–6in) high, turn the tubers upside down to dry off (*see* above), and when they're quite dry trim off any fibrous roots; cut the dry stem down to about 2.5cm (1in) and then store the tubers in boxes of dry sand or compost at around 5°C (41°F).

Tender tropical plants, for instance begonias and cannas, should be brought in just before the first frosts. Pack these in boxes of compost and reduce watering to encourage them to die down naturally. Clean off the dry dead top-growth and then store

Tender tropical bulbs (here, cannas) are best stored in a frost-free place, packed in barely moist compost.

in dry sand or sawdust at 5°C (41°F). Dusting begonia tubers with sulphur helps to prevent fungal problems.

Divide and pot up arum lilies (*Zantedeschia*) and amaryllis (*Hippeastrum*) from mid-autumn to encourage early flowers under glass.

Winter

There might be little to see in the bulb garden right now, but below ground life has been stirring since the autumn – dig up a spring bulb in early winter and you'll find plenty of roots and even a shoot just below the surface. Summer-dormant *Iris unguicularis* flowers throughout the winter, while the shortest day is the cue for aconites, snowdrops, *Cyclamen coum* and early crocuses to emerge. Celebrate their brave beauty, but also remember to order summer bulbs for planting soon.

The distinctive lemon-yellow flowers of *Iris danfordiae* are among the first to greet the new year.

Dividing and potting on

Move or divide snowdrops (*Galanthus*) and winter aconites (*Eranthis*) while they have green leaves, and replant immediately (*see* page 114).

Continue potting up amaryllis (*Hippeastrum, see* page 119) and pot up lilies (*Lilium*) for early flowers indoors or transplanting in spring.

Care and preparation

Check forced bulbs like crocuses, hyacinths and narcissi frequently, and move any that are ready into light and warmth (*see* page 55). If you want begonia and dahlia cuttings (*see* page 69), start tubers and corms into growth in late winter.

Ordering summer bulbs

Order begonias, cannas, dahlias, gladioli and many more bulbs for spring delivery and planting. Look

It's important to ventilate the greenhouse for short spells during the day to keep mildew at bay.

for less common bulbs, such as crinum lilies, gloriosa and fragrant polianthes, as well as stalwarts like alstroemerias, crocosmias and schizostylis. Lilies can be planted any time between mid-autumn and early spring.

Bulbs under glass

In winter, it's important to ventilate as much as possible by day, except during severe frost and damp, misty weather. Little watering of bulbs under glass will be necessary unless

plants are actually growing, such as *Crocus laevigatus*, which could be in leaf any time between mid-autumn and late winter.

In a greenhouse with a minimum temperature of 7°C (45°F), it's possible for lachenalias, freesias (potted in late summer), ixias and sparaxis to bloom from New Year onwards. Water only if the compost is dry. Ventilate cautiously in cold or windy weather – ten minutes per day is enough.

To protect recently planted bulbs in pots from mice and squirrels, place wire mesh over the top. Mice are particularly fond of tulip bulbs.

Bulbs in flower in winter

OUTDOORS	INDOORS
Anemone	*Clivia*
Chionodoxa	*Crocus*
Crocus	*Cyclamen*
Cyclamen	*Freesia*
Eranthis	*Hippeastrum*
Galanthus	*Hyacinthus*
Iris	*Iris*
Narcissus	*Lachenalia*
Scilla	*Narcissus*

At-a-glance planting calendar

A number of influences determine when bulbs start growing – soil temperature, for example, or how long they have been dormant – and many will wait until conditions are just right. Gardeners, however, have to keep things simple and go by the calendar.

Although there is often some leeway (and it's always better to take a gamble if you're late rather than not plant at all), every bulb has its ideal planting season. This is an approximate guide only, as the climate varies from year to year and from one region to another.

PLANT	PLANTING TIME
Achimenes	late winter to early spring
Agapanthus	mid- to late spring
Albuca	late autumn
Allium	early to mid-autumn
Amaryllis	early to midsummer
Anemone	early autumn
Anemone coronaria	early autumn, early spring or early summer
Anomatheca	mid-spring
Anthericum	early autumn or early spring
Arisaema	early autumn
Arum	late summer to early autumn
Asphodeline	late summer to early autumn
Asphodelus	mid-autumn or early spring
Babiana	mid-spring
Begonia	early spring
Belamcanda	early to mid-spring
Bellevalia	early to mid-autumn
Bessera	mid-spring
Brimeura	early to mid-autumn
Brodiaea	early autumn
Bulbocodium	mid-autumn
Caladium	early spring
Calochortus	early autumn
Camassia	early to mid-autumn
Canna	early spring
Cardiocrinum	mid-autumn
Chionodoxa	early autumn
Chlidanthus	mid-spring
Clivia	mid-spring
Codonopsis	late spring
Colchicum	mid- to late summer
Commelina	mid- to late spring
Convallaria	mid-autumn or early spring
Corydalis	early to mid-spring
Crinum	late spring
Crocosmia	early to mid-spring
Crocus	midsummer (autumn-flowering), early to late autumn (spring-flowering)
Cyclamen	late summer (large-flowered), midsummer to mid-autumn (wild)
Cypella	mid-autumn or mid-spring

PLANT	PLANTING TIME
Cyrtanthus	early summer
Dahlia	late spring
Dichelostemma	mid-autumn
Dierama	mid- to late autumn
Dietes	mid-autumn
Dracunculus	late summer to early autumn
Eranthis	early autumn
Eremurus	early autumn
Erythronium	late summer
Eucharis	mid-spring
Eucomis	mid-spring
Freesia	late summer to late winter (indoors), mid-spring (outdoors)
Fritillaria	early to mid-autumn
Galanthus	early to mid-autumn
Galtonia	mid-spring
Geranium	early to mid-spring
Gladiolus	late spring
Gloriosa	midwinter to early spring
Habranthus	mid-autumn
Haemanthus	mid-spring
Hedychium	mid-spring
Hemerocallis	early to mid-spring
Hermodactylus	mid-autumn
Hippeastrum	mid-autumn to mid-spring
Homeria	mid-autumn or mid-spring
Hyacinthoides	early to mid-autumn
Hyacinthus	early autumn (indoors), early to mid-autumn (outdoors)
Hymenocallis	mid-autumn or early spring
Ipheion	early autumn
Iris	early to mid-autumn (bulbs), late summer (rhizomes)
Ixia	mid-autumn, early spring
Ixiolirion	early autumn
Lachenalia	late summer
Leucocoryne	mid-autumn
Leucojum	early to mid-autumn
Lilium	late summer to mid-spring
Lycoris	mid-autumn
Moraea	mid-spring
Muscari	early to mid-autumn
Narcissus	late summer to early autumn

PLANT	PLANTING TIME
Nectaroscordum	early to mid-autumn
Nerine	mid-spring or late summer
Nerine sarniensis	early autumn
Nomocharis	late autumn
Notholirion	mid-autumn
Ornithogalum	mid-autumn or mid-spring
Oxalis	early autumn or mid-spring
Pancratium	early spring
Paradisea	early autumn or mid-spring
Physalis	early autumn or mid-spring
Polianthes	early spring
Polygonatum	early to late spring
Puschkinia	mid-autumn
Ranunculus	early to mid-spring
Rhodohypoxis	late spring
Romulea	early autumn or early spring
Roscoea	late winter to mid-spring
Sandersonia	mid-spring
Sanguinaria	early to mid-spring
Scadoxus	mid-spring
Schizostylis	mid-spring
Scilla	late summer to mid-autumn
Sinningia	late winter to mid-spring
Sisyrinchium	early to mid-autumn
Sparaxis	late autumn (indoors), mid-spring (outdoors)
Sprekelia	mid-spring
Sternbergia	mid- to late summer
Tecophilaea	early autumn
Tigridia	mid- to late spring
Tricyrtis	early spring
Trillium	early autumn
Triteleia	mid-autumn
Tritonia	early autumn or early spring
Tropaeolum	mid-spring
Tulbaghia	mid-spring
Tulipa	mid- to late autumn
Uvularia	early autumn or early spring
Veltheimia	early autumn
Veratrum	mid-autumn or early spring
Watsonia	mid- to late spring
Zantedeschia	mid-autumn (indoors), mid-spring (outdoors)
Zephyranthes	mid-spring

Index

Page numbers in *italics* refer to plants described in the A–Z directory of recommended bulbs.

A

Abyssinian sword lily *87*
Achimenes 75
  A. 'Ambroise Verschaffelt' *75*
  A. 'Stan's Delight' *75*
acid soil 43
African blue lily *see Agapanthus*
Agapanthus 10, 36, *75*, 108
  A. 'Blue Giant' 17
  A. campanulatus var. *albidus 75*
  A. Headbourne Hybrids *75*
  A. patens 75
Albuca 60, *75*
  A. canadensis 75
  A. humilis 75
  A. shawii 75
Algerian iris *90*
alkaline soil 42
Allium 9, 10, 60, 111
  A. azureum 17
  A. beesianum 75
  A. bulgaricum 17
  A. caeruleum 75
  A. carinatum subsp.
    pulchellum 76
  A. cristophii 26, 32, 60
  A. cyaneum 75
  A. flavum 16, *76*
  A. giganteum 76
  A. 'Gladiator' *76*
  A. 'Globemaster' 17, 21, *76*
  A. × *hollandicum* 13
  A. 'Mars' 17
  A. moly 76
  A. 'Mont Blanc' *76*
  A. obliquum 16
  A. oleraceum 52
  A. 'Round and Purple' *76*
  A. sikkimense 75
  A. sphaerocephalon 16, 110,
    116
  A. triquetrum 52
  A. tuberosum 26
  A. ursinum 52
  A. vineale 52
    A.v. 'Hair' 16
alpine troughs 31

Alstroemeria 60
amaryllis *see Hippeastrum*
Amaryllis belladonna 14, 58, 66,
  76, 109
  A.b. 'Hathor' *76*
  A.b. 'Johannesburg' *76*
Amazon lily *85*
Anemone 108, 119
  A. apennina 21
  A. blanda 17, 21, 29, 33, 37,
    76
    A.b. 'Atrocaerulea' *76*
    A.b. 'Charmer' *76*
    A.b. 'Ingramii' *76*
    A.b. var. *rosea* 'Radar' *76*
    A.b. 'White Splendour' 29,
      76
  A. coronaria 41, *76*, 118, 119
    A.c. 'The Admiral' *76*
    A.c. De Caen Group 16,
      76
    A.c. 'Die Braut' *76*
    A.c. 'Hollandia' *76*
    A.c. 'Mister Fokker' *76*
    A.c. 'Mount Everest' *76*
    A.c. Saint Bridgid Group
      76
  A. nemorosa 10, 17, *77*
    A.n. 'Blue Bonnet' *77*
    A.n. 'Robinsoniana' *77*
    A.n. 'Rosea' *77*
  A. ranunculoides 16
angel wings *79*
animal pests 73, 120
Anomatheca laxa 77
Anthericum liliago 77
  A.l. 'Major' *77*
aphids 70
Arisaema 77
  A. candidissimum 77
  A. erubescens 77
  A. griffithii 17
Arum
  A. 'Chameleon' 13
  A. creticum 77
  A. italicum
    A.i. subsp. *albispathum 77*
    A.i. subsp. *italicum*
      'Marmoratum' 13, 29,
      77
    A.i. subsp. *italicum* 'Tiny'
      77
    A.i. subsp. *italicum* 'White
      Winter' *77*

arum lily *see Zantedeschia*
Asparagus setaceus 41
aspect 48
Asphodeline lutea 78
  A.l 'Gelbkerze' *78*
Asphodelus 60
  A. aestivus 78
  A. albus 78
  A. ramosus 78
Aspidistra elatior 41, 109
autumn 14, 116, 118–19
autumn crocus *see Colchicum*
autumn daffodil *see Sternbergia*

B

Babiana stricta 78
baboon flower *78*
balconies and roof gardens 35
beds and borders 18–22
  cutting bed 27
  dot plants 19
  lifting bulbs 22
  mixed borders 20–2
  permanent plantings 21–2
  seasonal bedding schemes
    18–19
  temporary plantings 21
bees, bulbs for 42
Begonia
  B. 'Memory Scarlet' 16
  B. 'Orange Cascade' 16
  B. sutherlandii 17, *78*
  Non Stop Series *78*
begonias
  lifting 62, 119
  planting 116
  propagation 69, 120
  see also Begonia
Belamcanda chinensis 60, *78*
Belladonna lily *see Amaryllis belladonna*
Bellevalia paradoxa 79, 109
Bessera elegans 16, *79*, 111
bird damage 73
Bletilla striata 11
blindness 73
blood lily *98*
blood root *98*
bluebells *see Hyacinthoides*
botrytis 72
Brimeura amethystina 79
Brodiaea californica 79
bulb frames 57, 61, 117

bulb planters 47
Bulbocodium vernum 79
bulbous plants 9–11
  corms 10, 11
  pseudobulbs 11
  rhizomes 10, 11
  true bulbs 10, 11
  tubers 10, 11
buying bulbs 45–6, 70, 75
Byzantine gladiolus *see Gladiolus communis* subsp. *byzantinus*

C

Caladium bicolor 41, *79*
Californian firecracker *84*
calla lily *103*
Calochortus venustus 17, *80*
Camassia 60, *80*, 108
  C. cusickii 17, 25, *80*
  C. leichtlinii 80
    C.l. 'Semiplena' 16
    C.l. subsp. *suksdorfii* 30
  C. quamash 24, 25, *80*
Campernelle jonquil *94*
Canna 10, 19, *80*, 118, 119
  C. 'Assaut' 16
  C. 'Durban' 19
  C. 'Golden Lucifer' *80*
  C. 'Striata' 19, *80*
  C. 'Wyoming' *80*
Cape cowslip *see Lachenalia*
capsid bugs 70
Cardiocrinum giganteum 12,
  29, *80*
caterpillars 71
cat's ears *80*
chalky soil 48, 49, 109
challenging sites 57, 104–11
Chilean blue crocus 33, 61,
  100
chincherinchee *96*
Chinese lantern *97*
Chionodoxa 18, 21, *80*, 109
  C. forbesii 80
    C.f. 'Pink Giant' 17
  C. luciliae (syn. *C. gigantea*)
    80
  C. sardensis 17, 22, *80*
chipping 67
Chlidanthus fragrans 80
clay soil 48
Clivia miniata 41, *81*
Codonopsis grey-wilsonii 81

Colchicum 14, 28, 116, 117
  C. 'Autumn Queen' 81
  C. autumnale 25, 81, 116
  C. 'Glory of Heemstede' 81
  C. luteum 33
  C. 'Rosy Dawn' 81
  C. speciosum 81
    C.s. 'Album' 17, 81
    C.s. 'Atrorubens' 81
  C. 'The Giant' 81
  C. 'Waterlily' 17, 81
cold sites 111
collections of bulbs, forming
  38–9
colour schemes 12, 16–17
Commelina
  C. coelestis 17, 81
  C. tuberosa 81
containers 34–7, 53–4
  balconies and roof gardens
    35
  composts and additives 53–4
  container size 34–5
  feeding and top-dressing 56
  moving containers 35
  planting 53–4
  planting schemes 36–7
  spring bulbs 54
  storing 63
  watering 57
  winter protection 54, 58
Convallaria majalis 10, 41, 52,
  60, 81, 110
  C.m. 'Bordeaux' 52, 81
  C.m. 'Flore Pleno' 81
  C.m. 'Géant de Fortin' (syn.
    'Fortin's Giant') 81
  C.m. 'Hardwick Hall' 81
  C.m. 'Variegata' 81
coral drops 79
corms 10, 11
corn lily 90–1
Corydalis solida 17, 82
  C.s. 'Beth Evans' 82
  C.s. 'George Baker' 82
Crinum 14, 21, 58, 82, 118
  C. 'Album; 82
  C. × powellii 82
Crocosmia 52, 60, 82, 118
  C. × crocosmiliflora 82
    C. × c. 'Harlequin' 16
  C. 'Emily McKenzie' 82
  C. 'Late Lucifer' 82
  C. 'Lucifer' 82

C. 'Orange Devil' 16
C. 'Solfatare' 82
C. 'Star of the East' 110
C. 'Zambesi' 82
Crocus 10, 82, 109
  C. ancyrensis 33
    C.a. 'Golden Bunch' 82
  C. 'Ard Schenk' 82
  C. banaticus 17
  C. 'Blue Pearl' 82
  C. chrysanthus
    C.c. 'Blue Bird' 17
    C.c. 'Cream Beauty' 16
    C.c. 'Dorothy' 16
  C. flavus subsp. flavus 29
  C. 'Flower Record' 82
  C. 'Jeanne d'Arc' 82
  C. laevigatus 120
  C. × luteus 'Golden Yellow'
    16, 82
  C. pulchellus 14
  C. 'Ruby Giant' 17
  C. sativus 14
  C. speciosus 14, 82
    C.s. 'Albus' 82
    C.s. 'Conqueror' 82
    C.s. 'Oxonian' 82
  C. tommasinianus 29, 52, 83
    C.t. 'Albus' 83
    C.t. 'Barr's Purple' 83
    C.t. 'Ruby Giant' 83
    C.t. 'Whitewell Purple' 83
  C. vernus
    C.v. 'Flower Record' 17
    C.v. 'Grand Maître' 24
    C.v. 'Pickwick' 24, 82
  C. zonatus 14
crocus
  division 60
  forcing 55
  planting and growing 50, 51,
    111, 116
crown imperial see Fritillaria
  imperialis
cutting, bulbs for 26–7, 43
cuttings 69
Cyclamen 9, 14, 46, 50, 66, 108
  C. coum 22, 28, 83
    C.c. subsp. coum f. c.
      Pewter Group 83
    C.c. subsp. coum f. pallidum
      'Album' 83
  C. graecum 41, 65
  C. hederifolium 83

C.h. var. h. f. albiflorum 83
C.h. var. h. f. hederifolium
  'Ruby Glow' 83
C.h. var. h. f. hederifolium
  'Silver Cloud' 83
C.h. 'Rosenteppich' 83
C. persicum 83
  C.p. Laser Series 83
  C.p. Midori Series 83
  C.p. Miracle Series 83
  C.p. 'Scentsation' 83
  C.p. 'Victoria' 83
Cypella herbertii 83
Cyrtanthus elatus 39, 83
  C.e. 'Cream Beauty' 83
  C.e. 'Pink Diamond' 83

D
'daffodil slime' 27
daffodils 10, 15, 21, 57
  colour and form 94
  cut flowers 26, 27
  dead-heading 60
  division 60
  forcing 55
  growing in water 65
  naturalizing 24, 25
  planting and growing 24,
    94, 116
  seed 63
  see also Narcissus
Dahlia 10, 84
  D. 'Bishop of Llandaff' 84
  D. 'Bishop's Children' 84
  D. 'David Howard' 118
  D. 'Kenora Sunset' 16
  D. 'Nuit d'Eté' 16
  D. 'Peach Delight' 17
  D. 'Promise' 16
  D. 'Radiance' 17
  D. 'Ruskin Marigold' 84
  D. 'Swan Lake' 16
  D. 'Wittemans Superba' 16
dahlias
  lifting and drying 62, 119
  planting 116
  propagation 69, 120
  staking 59
  see also Dahlia
day flower 81
daylily see Hemerocallis
dead-heading 52, 60, 115
deformed flowers 73
desert candle see Eremurus

designing with bulbs
  beds and borders 18–22
  colour schemes 12, 16–17
  containers 34–7
  cut flowers 26–7, 43
  foliage 13
  grass, bulbs in 23–5
  gravel, rockeries and scree
    30–3, 42
  incorporating bulbs 14–15
  indoor bulbs 40–1, 43
  plants for a purpose 42–3
  scent 15, 43
  trees, bulbs under 28–9, 42
Dichelostemma ida-maia 84
Dierama pulcherrimum 84
  D.p. var. album 84
  D.p. 'Blackbird' 84
  D.p. 'Merlin' 16
  D.p. 'Slieve Donard' 84
Dietes
  D. bicolor 84
  D. grandiflora 84
  D. iridioides 84
diseases 72–3
division 60, 66–7, 114, 116–17,
  120
dog's-tooth violet 85
dot plants 19
Dracunculus vulgaris 17, 84
dragon arum 84
drainage 106, 108
dry sites 108–9

E
Easter lily see Lilium longiflorum
eelworms 71
Eranthis hyemalis 60, 85, 108,
  114
  E.h. Cilicia Group 85
  E.h. 'Guinea Gold' 85
  E.h. Tubergenii Group 85
Eremurus 10, 12, 85
  E. bungei 26
  E. himalaicus 26, 32, 85
  E. × isabellinus 'Cleopatra'
    42, 85
  E. robustus 26, 85
  E. stenophyllus 16, 85
Erythronium 58, 108, 116
  E. californicum 'White Beauty'
    16, 85
  E. dens-canis 85
    E.d.-c. 'Frans Hals' 85

E.d.-c. 'Lilac Wonder' 17, 85
E.d.-c. 'Pink Perfection' 85
E.d.-c. 'Purple King' 85
E.d.-c. 'Rose Queen' 85
E.d.-c. 'Snowflake' 85
E. 'Jeanette Brickell' 85
E. 'Pagoda' 16, *85*
E. revolutum 'Rose Beauty' 85
Eucharis amazonica 85, 111
Eucomis 85
   E. autumnalis 16
   E. bicolor 85
   E. comosa 85
     E.c. 'Sparkling Burgundy'
     85
   E. pallidiflora 22, 85
   E. vandermerwei 'Octopus' 85

F

feeding 56, 65, 114–15, 117
flame flower 101
florists' gloxinia *99*
flowering performance 48
foliage 13
   after flowering 59
forcing bulbs 55, 115, 117
foxtail lily *see Eremurus*
Freesia 10, 15, 55, *86*, 120
Fritillaria 10, 60
   F. imperialis 16, 21, *86*
     F.i. 'Aureomarginata' 86
     F.i. 'Aurora' 86
     F.i. 'Lutea' 16, 21
     F.i. 'Maxima Lutea' 86
     F.i. 'Rubra' 86
   F. liliacea 38
   F. meleagris 25, 37, *86*
     F.m. 'Mars' 86
     F.m. var. *unicolor* subvar.
     alba 'Aphrodite' 86
   F. michailovskyi 17, 33
   F. persica 86
     F.p. 'Adiyaman' 17
     F.p. 'Ivory Bells' 16, 86
frost 54, 58, 111
frost pockets 111
fumitory 82
fungicides 70

G

Galanthus 108, 110
   G. 'Atkinsii' 22, 28, 86
   G. communis subsp.
     byzantinus 28

G. elwesii 29, 86, 107
G. gracilis 38
G. 'Modern Art' 38
G. nivalis 17, *86*, 111
   G.n. f. *pleniflorus* 'Flore
     Pleno' 86
   G.n. 'Lady Elphinstone' 86
   G.n. 'Pusey Green Tip' 86
   G.n. Sandersii Group 38
G. 'Ophelia' 38
G. plicatus 28
   G.p. 'Trym' 38
G. reginae-olgae 86
G. 'S. Arnott' 86
Galtonia 108
   G. candicans 17, *87*
     G.c. 'Moonbeam' 87
   G. viridiflora 16
Geranium tuberosum 87
giant lily *see Cardiocrinum*
   giganteum
ginger lily *88*
gladioli
   cutting 117
   planting 114, 115
   staking 59, 117
   see also Gladiolus
Gladiolus 9, 10, 19, *87*
   G. 'Amanda Mahy' 87
   G. 'Amsterdam 87
   G. 'Bizar' 87
   G. 'Black Jack' 87
   G. 'Charm' 113
   G. communis subsp.
     byzantinus 17, 22, 25, 30,
     87, 109
   G. 'Green Star' 16, 59
   G. 'Green Woodpecker' 16,
     87
   G. 'Impressive' 87
   G. 'Jester' 16
   G. 'Leonore' 87
   G. murielae 35, *87*
   G. 'Ovation' 16
   G. 'Purple Flora' 17
   G. 'Silvana' 17
   G. 'The Bride' 17
   G. tristis 15, 113
Gloriosa
   G. 'Rothschildiana' 40, 88
   G. superba 88
glory lily *88*
glory of the snow *see*
   Chionodoxa

glory of the sun 91
golden spider lily 93
golden-rayed lily of Japan *91*
grape hyacinth *see Muscari*
grass, bulbs in 23–5
   lawns 23–4, 42
   mowing regimes 24, 115
   planting 50, 51
   tall grass 42
   wildflower meadows 24–5
gravel, bulbs in 30–2, 42
greenhouse and conservatory
   bulbs 39, 40–1, 43, 64–5,
   120
grey mould 72
growing conditions 48–9
Guernsey lily *95*

H

Habranthus 88
   H. robustus 88
   H. tubispathus 88
Haemanthus 60, *88*, 111
   H. albiflos 88
   H. coccineus 88
Harlequin flower *99*
harvest beetles 72
healthy bulbs 46
Hedychium
   H. coccineum 88
   H. coronarium 88
   H. densiflorum 'Assam
     Orange' 88
height 12
Hemerocallis 21, 107, 110
   H. 'Frans Hals' 16
   H. lilioasphodelus 16, *88*
Hermodactylus tuberosus 17, *88*
Hippeastrum 9, 39, 55, 63, 64,
   68, *89*, 117, 119, 120
   H. 'Apple Blossom' 89
   H. 'Benfica' 16
   H. 'Black Pearl' 17
   H. 'Bolero' 17
   H. 'Darling' 17
   H. 'Lemon Lime' 16
   H. papilio 89
   H. picotee 89
   H. 'Red Lion' 16, 89
Homeria 89
   H. collina 89
   H. flaccida 89
   H. ochroleuca 89
hoop petticoat daffodil 24, *94*

hot water plant *75*
house plants 41, 43
hyacinth fire 72
Hyacinthoides 60, *89*
   H. hispanica 52, 89
   H. italica 89
   H. non-scripta 17, 52, 89
hyacinths
   bulb size 46
   forcing 55, 117
   growing in water 65
   lifting 117
   see also Hyacinthus orientalis
Hyacinthus orientalis 89
   H.o. 'Anna Lisa' 17
   H.o. 'Anna Marie' 89
   H.o. 'Blue Pearl' 29, 89
   H.o. 'Carnegie' 89
   H.o. 'City of Haarlem' 89
   H.o. 'Delft Blue' 89
   H.o. 'Gipsy Queen' 16, 17, 89
   H.o. 'Jan Bos' 89
   H.o. 'Pink Pearl's 17
   H.o. 'Purple Sensation' 17
   H.o. 'Sky Jacket' 17
   H.o. 'White Pearl' 17
   H.o. 'Woodstock' 16, 89
hydroculture 65
Hymenocallis × *festalis* 17, *89*
   H. × *f.* 'Sulphur Queen' 89

I

'in the green' 46
Indian poke 103
Indian shot *see Canna*
indoor bulbs 40–1, 43
   growing bulbs in water 65
   half-hardy and tropical
     species 64–5
   hardy bulbs 64, 115
   light 64, 73
   pests 73
   problems 73
   temperature requirements
     65
   watering and feeding 65,
     73, 115
insects, beneficial 70
invasive bulbs 52
Ipheion uniflorum 60, *90*
   I.u. 'Album' 90
   I.u. 'Charlotte Bishop' 90
   I.u. 'Froyle Mill' 90
   I.u. 'Wisley Blue' 17, 90

Iris
  Bearded 10, *90*
  Beardless *90*, 106
  I. 'Apollo' 16
  I. 'Curlew' 90
  I. danfordiae 12, 16, 118, 120
  I. ensata 13, *90*
    I.e. 'Flying Tiger' 90
    I.e. 'The Great Mogul' 90
    I.e. 'Moonlight Waves' 90
    I.e. 'Variegata' 90
  I. foetidissima 16
  I. germanica 'Titan's Glory' 17
  I. 'Gingerbread Man' 90
  I. histrioides 12
  I. 'Jane Phillips' 17
  I. japonica 13
  I. 'Joyce' 33
  I. 'Langport Wren' 16
  I. 'Night Owl' 90
  I. pallida 13
    I.p. 'Argentea Variegata' 32
    I.p. 'Variegata' 21
  I. pseudacorus 13, 106
    I.p. 'Variegata' 13
  I. reticulata 53, *90*, 111, 119
    I.r. 'Cantab' 90
    I.r. 'George' 90
    I.r. 'Harmony' 17
    I.r. 'J.S. Dijt' 90
    I.r. 'Katharine Hodgkin' 90
    I.r. 'Purple Gem' 17
  I. sibirica 90
    I.s. 'Shirley Pope' 17
  I. unguicularis 21, *90*, 109,
    120
    I.u. 'Mary Barnard' 90
    I.u. 'Oxford Dwarf' 90
  I. xiphium 108
iris mosaic virus 72
irises
  planting and growing 50,
    111
  propagation 60, 68
  wet sites 106, 107
  see also Iris
Ixia *90–1*, 109, 120
  I. 'Blue Bird' 91
  I. maculata 90
  I. paniculata 90
  I. 'Venus' 91
  I. viridiflora 90
  I. 'Vulcan' 91
Ixiolirion tataricum 91

J, K
Jacobean lily 39, *100*
Japanese water iris *90*
keeled garlic *76*
Kniphofia 10

L
Lachenalia 65, *91*, 120
  L. var. *luteola* 91
  L. var. *quadricolor* 17, 91
  L. var. *vanzyliae* 91
lady tulip *101*
lantern lily *98*
Lent lily *see Narcissus*
    pseudonarcissus
leopard lily *78*
lesser celandine *97*
Leucocoryne
  L. ixioides 17, 91
  L. purpurea 91
Leucojum 91
  L. aestivum 29, 91
    L.a. 'Gravetye Giant' 91
  L. autumnale 91
  L. vernum 91
lifting bulbs 22, 56, 60, 62,
    116–17, 118
  drying and storing 63
lilies
  choosing 92
  in containers 37, 54
  flower forms 92
  planting and growing 50, 92,
    107, 108, 109, 114
  pollen 26
  potting up 120
  propagation 67, 117
  shade tolerance 28
  staking 59
  see also Lilium
Lilium 10, 22
  L. 'African Queen' 92
  L. auratum 91
    L.a. var. *platyphyllum* (syn.
      'Gold Band') 91
  L. bulbiferum 117
  L. canadense 29
  L. candidum 17, 50, 92, 109
  L. 'Casa Blanca' 91
  L. 'Centerfold' 92
  L. ciliatum 28
  L. 'Connecticut King' 92

  L. 'Ebony' 16
  L. 'Fire King' 16
  L. formosanum 37, 92
  L. 'Golden Stargazer' 16
  L. 'Gran Paradiso' 113
  L. henryi 92
  L. 'Lady Alice' 17
  L. lancifolium 92, 117
  L. longiflorum 37, 40, *92*,
    105
    L.l. 'Triumphator' 92
    L.l. 'White American' 92
    L.l. 'White Heaven' 92
  L. 'Luxor' 16
  L. mackliniae 14, 92
  L. martagon 21, 24, *92*
    L.m. var. *album* 92
    L.m. var. *cattaniae* 92
  L. 'Nerone' 15
  L. pardalinum 16, 24, 37
  L. parryi 37
  L. Pink Perfection Group
    17, 92
  L. pumilum 92
  L. pyrenaicum 66
  L. regale 19, 22, 37, *93*
    L.r. 'Album' 93
    L.r. 'Royal Gold' 37, 93
  L. rubellum 28
  L. 'Saboneta' 17
  L. 'Shuksan' 92
  L. speciosum 14, 22, 92
  L. 'Star Gazer' 91
  L. sulphureum 37
  L. superbum 29, 37
  L. 'Vivendum' 16
lily beetles 71
lily-of-the-valley *see Convallaria*
    majalis
loam 48
Lycoris 93
  L. aurea 93
  L. radiata 93
  L. squamigera 93

M
Madonna lily *see Lilium*
    candidum
marbled arum *see A. italicum*
    subsp. *italicum*
    'Marmoratum'
meadow saffron 81, 116
mealy bugs 73
merrybells *103*

mice and squirrels 120
microclimates 48
mites 71
monbretia *see Crocosmia*
Moraea 93
  M. aristata 93
  M. huttonii 93
  M. spathulata 93
  M. villosa 93
mulching 58, 111
Muscari 10, 38, 52, 60, 109,
    110, 116
  M. armeniacum 17, 52, *93*
    M.a. 'Blue Spike' 93
    M.a. 'Cantab' 93
    M.a. 'Valerie Finnis' 17,
      34
  M. botryoides 52
    M.b. 'Album' 17
  M. comosum 93
    M.c. 'Plumosum' 93
  M. macrocarpum 93
    M.m. 'Golden Fragrance'
      93
  M. neglectum 52
  M. plumosum 17

N
Narcissus 94–5
  double *94*
  large-cupped *95*
  multi-headed *95*
  N. 'Actaea' 15
  N. asturiensis 94
  N. bulbocodium 24, *94*, 107
  N. 'Canaliculatus' 33
  N. 'Carlton' 24, 95
  N. 'Charity May' 94
  N. 'Cheerfulness' 55
  N. 'Cragford' 94
  N. cyclamineus 94
  N. 'Dove Wings' 16
  N. 'Dutch Master' 16
  N. 'Eystettensis' 94
  N. 'February Gold' 39
  N. 'February Silver' 94
  N. 'Geranium' 95
  N. 'Golden Harvest' 94
  N. 'Grand Soleil d'Or' 15, 55,
    95, 118
  N. 'Hawera' 26, 36, 95
  N. 'Ice Follies' 36, 95
  N. 'Ice Wings' 95
  N. 'Jack Snipe' 29, 33, 39, 94

N. 'Jetfire' 37, 94
N. jonquilla 26
N. 'Jumblie' 94
N. 'King Alfred' 94
N. 'Martinette' 36
N. x *medioluteus* 25
N. 'Minnow' 33, 95
N. minor 39
   N.m. 'Little Gem' 94
N. 'Mount Hood' 94
N. 'Mrs R.O. Backhouse' 94
N. obvallaris 24
N. × *odorus* 94
N. 'Orangery' 16
N. papyraceus ('Paper White')
   15, 55, 94
N. 'Peeping Tom' 39
N. 'Pipit' 95
N. poeticus 23, 25
   N.p. var. *recurvus* 15, 113
   N.p. 'Tamar Double White'
      15
N. 'Professor Einstein' 57, 95
N. pseudonarcissus 25, 29, 94
N. 'Rip van Winkle' 94
N. 'Sinopel' 16
N. 'Sun Disc' 94
N. 'Suzy' 95
N. tazetta 95
N. 'Telamonius Plenus' (syn.
   'Van Sion') 24, 94
N. 'Tête-a-tête' 12, 37, 64,
   113
N. 'Trevithian' 16
N. triandrus 94
   N.t. 'Petrel' 36
narcissus bulb fly 71
narcissus fire 72
narcissus white streak 72
nasturtium *110*
native bulbs 25
naturalizing bulbs 23–5, 28, 46
   mowing regime 24, 115
Nectaroscordum siculum 16,
   30, *95*
   N.s. subsp. *bulgaricum* 95
Nerine 14, 21, 35, 58, 60, 109
   N. bowdenii 17, *95*
      N.b. 'Alba' 95
      N.b. 'Mark Fenwick' 95
      N.b. 'Mollie Cowie' 95
      N.b. 'Pink Triumph' 95
   N. flexuosa 95
   N. 'Maria' 17

N. sarniensis 95
N. undulata 95
Nomocharis
   N. aperta 95
   N. pardanthina 95
   N. saluensis 95
Notholirion 96, 118
   N. bulbuliferum 17, 96
   N. macrophyllum 96

O
offsets 66, 67
orchids 11
Ornithogalum 60
   O. dubium 96
   O. narbonense 96
   O. nutans 16, 52, 96
   O. thyrsoides 96, 109
   O. umbellatum 52, *96*
Oxalis
   O. acetosella 52
   O. adenophylla 96
   O. × *enneaphylla* 96
   O. 'Matthew Forrest' 96
   O. oregana 52
   O. versicolor 16
   O. violacea 52

P
Pancratium illyricum 96, 109
paradise lily *96*
Paradisea 96
   P. liliastrum 96
   P. lusitanicum 96
pavement plants 109
peacock flower *see Tigridia*
peat 48
pesticides 70
pests 70–2
pheasant's eye *see Narcissus
   poeticus* var. *recurvus*
Physalis alkekengi 16, *97*
   P.a. 'Gigantea' 97
   P.a. 'Variegata' 97
pineapple lily *85*
planting
   in autumn 118
   in containers 53–4
   depths/distances 50, 51, 53
   in grass 50, 51
   groups of bulbs 50
   growing conditions 48–9
   individual bulbs 50
   right way up 51

   in spring 114
   in summer 116
planting calendar 121
planting tools 47
Pleione formosana 11
poet's daffodil *see Narcissus
   poeticus*
Polianthes tuberosa 40, *97*
   P.t. 'The Pearl' 97
Polygonatum × *hybridum* 16,
   36, *97*
   P. × *h.* 'Betberg' 97
   P. × *h.* 'Flore Pleno' 97
   P. × *h.* 'Striatum' 97
poppy anemone *76*
problems and remedies 70–3
propagation 66–9
   chipping 67
   cuttings 69
   division 60, 66–7, 114, 116,
      120
   offsets 66, 67
   scaling 67
   scooping 67
   seed 68–9
pseudobulbs 11
Puschkinia scilloides 17, *97*
   P.s. var. *libanotica* 97
   P.s. var. *l.* 'Alba' 97

R
Ranunculus ficaria 97
   R.f. var. *aurantiacus* 97
   R.f. 'Brazen Hussy' 97
   R.f. 'Collarette' 97
   R.f. 'Double Mud' 97
   R.f. 'Salmon's White' 97
red spider lily 93
red spider mite 73
red-hot poker 10
resurrection lily 93
rhizomes 10, 11
   cuttings 69
Rhodohypoxis baurii 97
   R.b. 'Albrighton' 97
   R.b. 'Douglas' 61
   R.b. 'Harlequin' 97
   R.b. 'Helen' 97
   R.b. 'Lily Jean' 97
   R.b. 'Margaret Rose' 97
   R.b. 'Pintado' 97
   R.b. 'Tetra Red' 16
river lily *see Schizostylis
   coccinea*

rock gardens 33, 42
Romulea
   R. atranda 98
   R. bulbocodium 98
   R. ramiflora 98
   R. sabulosa 98
Roscoea 98
   R. cautleyoides 98
      R.c. 'Jeffrey Thomas' 98
      R.c. 'Kew Beauty' 98
   R. purpurea 98
rots 72
royal lily *see Lilium regale*

S
St Bernard's lily *77*
Sandersonia aurantiaca 98
sandy soil 48, 49, 108
Sanguinaria canadensis 98
   S.c. f. *multiplex* 'Plena' 98
Scadoxus multiflorus 39, *98*
   S.m. subsp. *katherinae* 98
scale insects 73
scaling 67
Scarborough lily 39, *83*
scent 15, 43
Schizostylis 14, 60, 107
S. coccinea 52, 98, 107
   S.c. f. *alba* 98
   S.c. 'Major' 98
   S.c. 'Mollie Gould' 98
   S.c. 'Mrs Hegarty' 98
   S.c. 'November Cheer' 109
   S.c. 'Professor Barnard' 98
   S.c. 'Salome' 17
   S.c. 'Viscountess Byng' 98,
      109
sciarid flies 73
Scilla 60, 99, 109, 110
   S. autumnalis 99
   S. bifolia 52, 99
   S. mischtschenkoana 17, 99
   S. peruviana 17, 32
   S. scilloides 99
   S. siberica 18, 99
      S.s. 'Alba' 99
      S.s. subsp. *armena* 18
      S.s. 'Spring Beauty' 17,
         18, 99
   S. verna 33
scooping 67
scree gardens 32–3, 42
seasonal bulbs 13–14, 113–21
seeds 68–9

collecting 68
germination 68
seedlings 68–9
sowing 68
storing 63
self-seeding 60
shady sites 49, 105
  see also trees, bulbs under
Siberian iris 90
Siberian squill 99
Sicilian honey garlic 95
Sinningia speciosa 99
  S.s. 'Blanche de Méru' 99
  S.s. 'Gregor Mendel' 99
  S.s. 'Kaiser Friedrich' 99
  S.s. 'Kaiser Wilhelm' 99
  S.s. 'Mont Blanc' 99
Sisyrinchium 99
  S. angustifolium 9
  S. 'Biscutella' 99
  S. 'Californian Skies' 17, 99
  S. californicum 99
  S. 'E.K. Balls' 99
  S. graminoides 52, 99
  S. idahoense 99
  S. striatum 16, 52, *99*
    S.s. 'Aunt May' 99
size, bulb 46
skin irritation 47
slugs and snails 71
snakeshead fritillary *see*
  Fritillaria meleagris
snowdrops 111
  division 114, 120
  'in the green' 46, 120
  seed 63, 68
  see also Galanthus
snowflake *91*
soft-tip cuttings 69
soil
  drainage 49
  improvement 49, 105
  texture 48
  types 48, 49
soil pH 48–9
Solomon's seal 36, *97*
Spanish bluebell 52, 89
Spanish iris 108
Sparaxis 16, *99*, 120
spider lily *89*
Sprekelia formosissima 39, 68,
  100
spring 13, 114–15
spring bedding schemes 18–19

spring starflower *90*
squill *see Scilla*
stakes and supports 58–9,
  110
star of Bethlehem *96*
Sternbergia 100, 108, 109,
  116
  S. clusiana 100
  S. lutea 16, 100
  S. sicula 100
  S. 'West Point' 16
storing bulbs 63
striped squill *97*
summer 13–14, 116–17
summer bedding schemes 19
summer hyacinth *87*
summer protection 57

T
tassel grape hyacinth *93*
Tecophilaea cyanocrocus 33,
  61, *100*
  T.c. 'Leichtlinii' 100
  T.c. 'Violacea' 100
Tenby daffodil 24
thrips 72
thunder bugs 72
tiger lily 92
Tigridia 19, *100*, 109
  T. pavonia 16, 100
toad lily *100*
tools and equipment 47
toxic plants 26, 46
trees, bulbs under 28–9, 42
Tricyrtis 100
  T. flava 100
  T. formosana 100
  T. hirta 100
Trillium 10, *100*
  T. cuneatum 100
  T. erectum 16
  T. grandiflorum 17, 100
    T.g. 'Flore Pleno' 100
  T. luteum 100
Triteleia 101
  T. ixioides 'Starlight' 16, 101
  T. laxa 'Königin Fabiola' 32,
    101
Tritonia 101
  T. crocata 101
  T. disticha 101
    T.d. subsp. *rubrolucens*
      (syn. *T. rosea*) 101
  T. 'Princess Beatrix' 101

Tropaeolum 101
  T. var. *lineamaculatum* 'Ken
    Aslet' 101
  T. speciosum 101
  T. tuberosum 101
tuberose *97*
tubers 10, 11
  cuttings 69
Tulbaghia 101, 109
  T. violacea 17, 101
    T.v. 'Silver Lace' (syn.
      'Variegata') 101
tulip fire 72
tulip necrosis 72
Tulipa 10
  lily-flowered *101*
  T. 'Abu Hassan' 102
  T. 'Antoinette' 102
  T. 'Apeldoorn' 102
  T. 'Ballerina' 16, 18, 101
  T. 'Bellona' 102
  T. biflora 113
  T. 'Bing Crosby' 102
  T. 'Black Parrot' 16
  T. 'Blue Diamond' 37, 102
  T. 'Blushing Lady' 102
  T. 'Burgundy' 34
  T. 'Cape Cod' 16
  T. 'China Pink' 17, 22, 101
  T. clusiana 101
    T.c. var. *chrysantha* 101
    T.c. 'Cynthia' 101
  T. 'Doll's Minuet' 18
  T. 'Estella Rijnveld' 102
  T. 'Fringed Beauty' 102
  T. 'Garden Party' 102
  T. 'Generaal de Wet' 34
  T. 'Golden Melody' 102
  T. 'Green Wave' 17, 102
  T. humilis 14, 33, 102, 109
  T. 'Humming Bird' 102
  T. linifolia Batalinii Group 59
  T. 'Little Beauty' 33
  T. 'Little Princess' 16, 33
  T. 'Madame Lefeber' 16
  T. 'Marilyn' 22, 101
  T. 'Mona Lisa' 101
  T. 'Monte Carlo' 102
  T. 'Orange Emperor' 16
  T. 'Oranje Nassau' 102
  T. 'Palestrina' 17, 102
  T. 'Peach Blossom' 17
  T. 'Prinses Irene' 17, 102
  T. 'Queen of Night' 37, 102

T. 'Sapporo' 29
T. 'Scarlet Baby' 33
T. 'Shakespeare' 16
T. sprengeri 14, 16, 113
T. 'Spring Green' 16, 37
T. 'Stresa' 102
T. sylvestris 25, *102*
T. tarda 16
T. Triumph Group *102*
T. turkestanica 16, 32, 102
T. 'Uncle Tom' 34
T. 'West Point' 16, 20, 101
T. 'White Dream' 102
T. 'White Triumphator' 101
T. 'Yellow Spring Green' 37
tulips
  in borders 21
  choosing 102
  in containers 21, 36
  cut flowers 26, 27
  flower forms 102
  forcing 55
  growing 102
  lifting 56, 117
  propagation 68
  see also Tulipa
Turkscap lily *see Lilium*
  martagon

U
uncommon bulbs 60
Uvularia 103
  U. grandiflora 103
    U.g. var. *pallida* 103

V
vegetable bulbs 11
Veltheimia 103
  V. bracteata 17, 103
  V. capensis 103
Veratrum 103
  V. album 103
  V. nigrum 103
  V. viride 103
vine weevils 72
viruses 72–3

W
wandflower *84*
water, growing bulbs in 65
watering 56–7
  containers 57
  indoor bulbs 65, 73
Watsonia 103

W. borbonica 103
   W.b. 'Arderne's White' 103
W. fourcadei 103
W. pillansii 17, 103
wet sites 106–7
white asphodel *78*
widow iris *88*
wild, bulbs in the 38, 45
wildflower meadows 24–5

windbreaks 110
windy sites 58, 110
winter 120
winter aconite *see Eranthis hyemalis*
winter protection 58
wood anemone *see Anemone nemorosa*
wood lily *see Trillium*

Y, Z

year-round displays 113
yellow asphodel *78*
Zantedeschia 21, 117, 119
   Z. aethiopica 103
      Z.a. 'Crowborough' 103
   Z. elliottiana 103
   Z. 'Odessa' 106

Z. rehmanii 103
Zephyr lily *103*
Zephyranthes 109
   Z. candida 103
   Z. citrina 103
   Z. grandiflora 103
   Z. rosea 103

Acknowledgements

BBC Books and OutHouse would like to thank the following for their assistance in preparing this book: Phil McCann for advice and guidance; Robin Whitecross for picture research; Lesley Riley for proofreading; Marie Lorimer for the index.

Picture credits

Key t = top, b = bottom, l = left, r = right, c = centre

PHOTOGRAPHS

All photographs by Jonathan Buckley except those listed below.

GAP Photos Maxine Adcock 109t; Lee Avison 83bc; BBC Magazines Ltd 109b; Pernilla Bergdahl 120tr; Dave Bevan 61(2), 93tc; Richard Bloom 17lt; Mark Bolton 25t, 29, 106bl; Elke Borkowski 36b; Lynne Brotchie 26(1); Nicola Browne 42; Simon Colmer 17lcb; Sarah Cuttle 65tl, 78tr, 108t; David Dixon 13t; Carole Drake 77tc; FhF Greenmedia 78br; John Glover 39, 40tr, 41b, 75br, 88tc, 91tl, 102tl, 108b; Anne Green-Armytage 38t; Jerry Harpur 15b, 26(2), 40l, 78tl, 84bc; Marcus Harpur 5r, 41tl, 77bl; Neil Holmes 83br; Michael Howes 78tc; Martin Hughes-Jones 20t, 33t, 75tr, 87br, 96tc, 101tr, 103tc, 104; Lynn Keddie 106tr; Geoff Kidd 97br; Michael King 21b; Fiona Lee 12t, 18t, 87bl; Jenny Lilly 90tc, 95br; Gerald Majumdar 73, 79bl, 88br, 101bl; Jonathan Need 81tl; Clive Nichols 9, 12b, 17rct, 107, 111b; Howard Rice 59b, 92l, 93br, 112; Rice/Buckland 45; S & O 23t, 85bl 91tc, 97bc; JS Sira 11, 61(1), 76bl, 79tr, 81bc, 91bc, 94tr, 98tc, 100bl, 101tl, 103bl; Friedrich Strauss 37ct, br, 111tr, 119tr; Graham Strong 78bc; Maddie Thornhill 110bl; Visions 79bc, 79br, 81tr, 93bl; Juliette Wade 35b; Mel Watson 37l; Jo Whitworth 27b, 99tc; Rob Whitworth 77bc; Dave Zubraski 30b, 91bl, 95tr

Andrew McIndoe 26(3), 55, 64t, 75bl, 76tc, 76bc, 82tr, 84tl, 84bl, 93bc, 95bc, 97bl, 98br, 101br, 103tr, 105t, 105tr

Garden Collection Andrew Lawson 89bl

Garden Picture Library Chris Burrows 88bl

GardenWorldImages.com Liz Cole 82tc, 98tl; Gilles Delacroix 80br; Adrian James 81bl; MAP/Arnaud Descat 83tr, 84tc; MAP/Nicole and Patrick Mioulane 79tc; Brian Mathew 90br; Trevor Sims 91br; Lee Thomas 96bc; Flora Toskana 84tr

Marianne Majerus Garden Images Andrew Lawson 22b, 52bl, 57; Marianne Majerus 2–3, 8, 14t, 14b, 19, 30t, 31, 33b, 37tr, 64b, 76tl, 96bl

Photolibrary/GPL Chris Burrows 88bl; Paroli Galperti 78bl, 89tl, 93tr, 95tl, 96br; Anne Green-Armytage 85br; Howard Rice 85tr; Frank Stober 98tr; Didier Willery 79tl; JS Sira 82tl, 100tc

Sue Gordon 46t

Terry Underhill 100tl

VisionsPictures.com Botanic Media Elburg 80tl

Robin Whitecross 27t, 87tc, 99bl

ILLUSTRATIONS

Julia Cady 22, 29, 32

Lizzie Harper 49, 51, 59, 69, 70b, 71tc & br, 72tl & tc

Susan Hillier 10, 11, 66, 68, 70t, 71tl, bl, bc & tr, 72bl, bc, tr & br, 73

Janet Tanner 47, 50, 54, 61, 63, 67, 69t

Thanks are also due to the following designers and owners, whose gardens appear in the book:

Marylyn Abbott, West Green House, Hampshire 105b; Beth Chatto Gardens, Essex 2–3, 5r, 21t, 30b, 31; Chiffchaffs, Dorset 33b; Will Giles, The Exotic Garden, Norwich 19; Green Island Gardens, Essex 76tl; Carol Klein, Glebe Cottage, Devon 114tr; House of Pitmuies, Angus 4; Christopher Lloyd, Great Dixter, East Sussex 14b, 23b, 24, 25b; Manor House Farm, Norfolk 64b; John Massey, Ashwood Nurseries, Staffordshire 21b, 28t; Merriments Gardens, East Sussex 12t; The Old Rectory, Haselbech, Northamptonshire 12b; The Old Vicarage, East Ruston, Norfolk 37tr; Pettifers Garden, Yorkshire 9; Sarah Raven, Perch Hill, East Sussex 15, 18b, 34t & b, 35t, 36t, 113; Rustling End 30t; Sleightholmedale Lodge, Yorkshire 8, 14t; Sue and Wol Staines, Glen Chantry, Essex 5l, 20b, 28b; RHS Garden Hyde Hall, Essex 26(2); RHS Garden Wisley, Surrey 17rct, 39, 41tl; Titsey Place 27b; Claudia de Yong 108t

While every effort has been made to trace and acknowledge all copyright holders, the publisher would like to apologize should there be any errors or omissions.